The *Other* Tudors

The *Other* Tudors

HENRY VIII'S MISTRESSES AND BASTARDS

PHILIPPA JONES

NEW HOLLAND

Published in 2010 by New Holland Publishers (UK) Ltd
London • Cape Town • Sydney • Auckland
www.newhollandpublishers.com
Garfield House, 86–88 Edgware Road, London W2 2EA, United Kingdom
80 McKenzie Street, Cape Town 8001, South Africa
Unit 1, 66 Gibbes Street, Chatswood, NSW 2067, Australia
218 Lake Road, Northcote, Auckland, New Zealand

10 9 8 7 6 5 4 3 2 1

A catalogue record for this book is available from the British Library

ISBN 978 1 84773 778 6

Publishing Director: Rosemary Wilkinson
Publisher: Aruna Vasudevan
Project Editor: Julia Shone
Editor: Sally MacEachern
Editorial Assistant: Cosima Hibbert
Inside design: Sarah Williams
Cover design: Phil Kay
Production: Melanie Dowland

Reproduction by Pica Digital Pte. Ltd., Singapore
Printed and bound in India by Replika Press

The paper used to produce this book is sourced from sustainable forests.

Contents

Chronology

―❦―

1485	August	22nd: Henry VII ascends to the throne
1486	January	18th: Henry VII marries Elizabeth of York
	September	Prince Arthur is born
1489		Princess Margaret is born
1491	June	28th, Prince Henry is born
1492		Princess Elizabeth is born (dies 1495 aged 3)
1496		Princess Mary is born
1499		Prince Edmund is born (dies in infancy); Mary Boleyn is born
1500		Elizabeth Denton becomes governess to the Princess Mary
1501	November	Prince Arthur marries Catherine of Aragon
1502	April	2nd: Prince Arthur dies
1503	February	11th: Princess Catherine is born(dies after three days);
		Elizabeth of York dies in childbirth
1505		(?) Margaret Shelton is born
1507		(?) Anne Boleyn is born
1509		Jane Seymour is born
	April	21st: Henry VII dies; Henry VIII ascends to the throne
	June	11th: Marriage to Catherine of Aragon; 29th: Margaret Beaufort dies
1510	May	Affair between Henry VIII and Anne Hastings
1511	January	1st: Prince Henry is born (dies in March)
1512		Catherine Parr is born
1513		Anne Boleyn joins the Court of Margaret of Austria
	September–October	Affair between Henry VIII and Etionette de la Baume
1514	January	Affair between Henry VIII and Elizabeth Blount begins (lasts to 1519)

		Louis XII of France marries Mary Tudor
	September	Affair between Henry VIII and Jane Popincourt begins (lasts to January 1515)
1516	February	18th: Mary I is born
1518		Last recorded pregnancy of Catherine of Aragon
1519	June	Henry Fitzroy, son of Henry VIII and Elizabeth Blount is born; Elizabeth Blount marries Gilbert Tailboys
1520		Affair between Henry VIII and Mary Boleyn begins; Katherine d'Eresby is born
	February	4th: Mary Boleyn marries William Carey
1521		Anne Boleyn returns to England from France; Anne Bassett is born
1522		(?) Catherine Howard is born
1523		Anne Boleyn is courted by Henry Percy, heir to the Earl of Northumberland
1524		Mary Boleyn gives birth to either Catherine or Henry Carey
1525		Henry Fitzroy is created Duke of Richmond and Somerset and Earl of Nottingham;
		Affair between Henry VIII and Mary Boleyn ends
1526	March	Mary Boleyn gives birth to either Catherine or Henry Carey; Affair between King Henry and Anne Boleyn begins
1527		Mary Perrot gives birth to John Perrot.
	July	First mention of Henry VIII 's divorce
1528		William Carey dies
1529		Catherine Parr marries Edward Borough
1530		(?) Thomas Stukeley is born
	November	Cardinal Thomas Wolsey dies
1532		Elizabeth Blount marries Edward Fiennes Clinton
	September	1st: Anne Boleyn is created Marquess of Pembroke
1533		Catherine Parr marries John Neville, Baron Latimer
	January	Anne Boleyn and Henry VIII marry
	April/May	Henry VIII divorces Catherine of Aragon

	September	7th: Elizabeth I is born
1534		Henry Fitzroy marries Mary Howard; Mary Boleyn marries Sir William Stafford
	September	7th: Katherine d'Eresby marries Charles Brandon, Duke of Suffolk;
		(?) Affair between Henry VIII and Joanna Dingley
1535		(?) Affair between Henry VIII and Margaret Shelton
	June	23rd: Etheldreda Malte is born (?)
1536	January	7th: Catherine of Aragon dies
	May	19th: Anne Boleyn is executed; 30th, Henry VIII marries Jane Seymour
	July	22nd: Henry Fitzroy, Duke of Richmond, dies
1537	October	Jane Grey, briefly Queen Jane I, is born
	September	Anne Bassett becomes a lady-in-waiting to Queen Jane
	October	12th: Edward VI is born; 24th, Jane Seymour dies in childbirth
1540		Elizabeth Blount dies
	January	6th: Henry VIII marries Anne of Cleves
	July	9th: Marriage to Anne of Cleves is annulled; 28th: Henry VIII marries Catherine Howard
1542	February	13th: Catherine Howard is executed
1543	July	12th: Henry VIII marries Catherine Parr; 19th: Mary Boleyn dies
1545	August	24th: Charles Brandon, Duke of Suffolk, dies
1547	January	28th: Henry VIII dies; Edward VI ascends to the throne
1548		Catherine Parr marries Thomas, Lord Seymour of Sudeley
	August	30th: Mary, daughter of Catherine Parr and Thomas Seymour is born
	September	7th: Catherine Parr dies
		Etheldreda Malte marries John Harrington
1549	March	20th: Thomas Seymour is executed
1550		Thomas Stukeley is the King's standard bearer in Boulogne
1552		Katherine d'Eresby marries Richard Bertie

1553	July	6th: Edward VI dies; 10th, Jane Grey is proclaimed Queen of England; 19th: Mary I ascends to the throne
1554		Anne Bassett marries Sir Walter Hungerford
	February	12th: Jane Grey is executed
1555		Thomas Stukeley marries Anne Curtis
	October–November	Etheldreda Malte dies
1557	July	16th: Anne of Cleves dies
	December	Mary Howard, Dowager Duchess of Richmond, dies
1558		(?) Anne Bassett dies
	November	17th: Mary I dies
		Elizabeth I ascends to the throne
1570	April	Thomas Stukeley retires to Spain
1571–3		Sir John Perrot is made president of Munster, in Ireland
1578	August	4th: Thomas Stukeley is killed at the Battle of Alcazar
1580	September	19th: Katherine d'Eresby dies
1582		John Harrington dies
1584–8		Sir John Perrot is made Lord Deputy of Ireland
1592	September	Sir John Perrot dies in the Tower accused of treason
1596	July	23rd: Henry Carey, 1st Baron Hunsdon, dies
1603	March	24th: Elizabeth I dies

10

Introduction

———

The life of Henry VIII (*see plate 1*) is probably the best defined of any king of England. Plays, films and television series have focused on Henry's life, particularly in relation to his six wives. Put simply, he loved his first wife, Catherine of Aragon (*see plate 4*), but divorced her because she failed to give him a son and grew old and unattractive. He married Anne Boleyn (*see plate 6*) for love and beheaded her when she, too, failed to give him an heir. Jane Seymour (*see plate 7*) was the quiet wife who died giving him that longed-for son. Anne of Cleves was the undesired one; Catherine Howard (*see plate 8*) the promiscuous one; and Catherine Parr the wife who survived Henry. However, this view portrays Henry as a two-dimensional, almost cartoon character, as epitomised by the Holbein painting (completed 1537) where he is dressed in red and gold, a massive figure standing, legs akimbo, seemingly the Lord of the World. In line with this image, he selects women to share his bed with a snap of his fingers and discards them just as easily when they cease to please him. All that matters to Henry is a male heir and nothing is allowed to stand in the way of his getting what he wants.

Of course, the real Henry Tudor is far more complicated. This book looks beyond Henry VIII's six wives, examining the women with whom the King had, or is believed to have had, affairs and the illegitimate children he is believed to have fathered. Beyond the limits of policy and diplomacy, it presents the King as a serial monogamist, a man who spent his life searching for the one, perfect woman he was destined never to find.

———

Henry was born a second son: he spent his childhood in the shadow of an elder brother who would one day be his king and master. In the space of less than a year, however, he had lost both his brother and his mother. He became the adored and vital eldest son, the Prince of Wales, the future king – and everyone around him suddenly treated him as such. He was expected to be stronger, wiser and more talented than anyone else. That Nature endowed Henry with a beautiful face, an admirable body and a quick and receptive mind led him eventually to believe all those who told him he was the best and worthy of the best.

While he did not lack male role models in his childhood and youth (his father; brother Arthur; great-uncle Jasper Tudor, who died when he was four; his mentor William Blount, Lord Mountjoy; companions such as Charles Brandon, John St John and Edward Neville), Henry lacked close female company. He had two sisters, but Margaret, two years older, was never a friend and Mary, five years younger, was too much the baby to be of interest. The most formidable lady in Henry's world was his grandmother, Margaret Beaufort, a woman devoted to the point of obsession to her only son, Henry VII (*see plate 3*). A woman of strong character, Margaret was already well past middle age, religious, a widow, obsessed with family, monarchy and wealth – Margaret, in fact, was the real power behind the throne. Elizabeth of York (*see plate 2*), Henry's mother, was not allowed to play a significant part in his life as his father and grandmother ruled his household. Mother and son only met on the occasions when Henry VII and Elizabeth visited the young Henry or he was brought to Court (in 1494, aged three, Henry came to London to be made a Knight of the Bath and Duke of York, for example). He also knew of Elizabeth from ballads sung about her:

In a glorius garden grene
Sawe I syttyng a comly queen
Among the flouris that fressh byn.
She gaderd a floure and set betweene;
The lyly-whighte rose methought I sawe ...[1]

12

Elizabeth of York embodied perfection to Henry, a view endorsed by everyone at Court. She was beautiful, elegant, serene, gentle, loyal, loving – everything that a wife and queen should be. Thus, Elizabeth became the ideal against which all the ladies in Henry's life were to be measured, and those that pleased him most invariably resembled her. Catherine of Aragon, his first wife and arguably Henry's true love, probably came closest. She was every inch a queen, Henry's intellectual equal, lover, friend, companion and counsellor. Catherine became to Henry what he perceived his mother had been to Henry VII.

There was a strong element of subservience in Elizabeth's relationship with Henry VII. Her motto was 'Humble and Reverence' and when Henry VII set Margaret Beaufort up as Elizabeth's superior in matters of state or, indeed, their personal life, Elizabeth appears to have said nothing. She bowed to her husband in every way, striving to serve him as the perfect wife and mother to his children. There is no record that she ever spoke out against him or contradicted him. Henry VIII similarly expected his ladies to treat him with humility and reverence. His favourites were those who followed his lead, made his opinion their own and sought to please him. Jane Seymour, first mistress and then queen, was a case in point; a large part of her charm was her total acquiescence to Henry's personality (this is discussed further in Chapter 10). Anne of Cleves, his wife, earned his friendship by giving in to him; on the other hand, Catherine of Aragon earned his enmity when she stood up against him. Anne Boleyn was beloved until she started arguing; and his last queen, Catherine Parr, almost lost everything when Henry believed that she was trying to influence him – to be the teacher in the relationship rather than the pupil (this is discussed further in Chapter 12). But where did this pattern begin?

The centre of attention from an early age, Henry became Prince of Wales at 11. By the time he was 14, he had started to take an interest in girls – to put it in context, the minimum age for marriage was 12 for a girl and 14 for a boy at the time. Life expectancy in the

16th century was about 35 and infant mortality was high and so it was not uncommon for a young couple to start their family in their mid to late teens. Henry was 19 when he came to the throne and he quickly married Catherine of Aragon, but it is highly unlikely that he was a virgin. Elizabeth Denton, a lovely lady and a servant of his family, was probably the first in what was a romantic, but stage-managed love affair organised by Henry VII and Margaret Beaufort (this is discussed in Chapter 2). However, when Henry became king, his only thought was to marry Catherine, his brother Arthur's widow, and set her on the throne at his side.

Perhaps one obstacle to Henry and Catherine enjoying a fairytale union was that they belonged to an age and to a social class that considered extramarital affairs for men as perfectly normal. The king was practically expected to take a mistress. Henry's grandfather, Edward IV, had been incredibly promiscuous; his great-grandfather, Owen Tudor, had a bastard son through a sexual liaison, as had his great-uncle Jasper Tudor. Henry VII, despite a reputation for fidelity, also had an illegitimate son, Sir Roland de Velville. It was, therefore, almost inevitable that Henry VIII would follow suit. He was, after all, extremely handsome and sexually desirable. The wealthiest and most powerful man in England, Henry was a leader of fashion and the focus of a Court that lived for pleasure. Women, often with the support of their families, quite simply threw themselves at him. Lord Herbert of Cherbury summed this up when he wrote, 'One of the liberties which our King took in his spare time was to love ... so it must seem less strange if amid many fair Ladies, which lived in his Court, He both gave and received temptation.'[2]

One of Henry's earliest mistresses, Anne Hastings, became the object of his attention while Catherine of Aragon was pregnant for the first time, and Henry was excluded from her bed. The affair was light-hearted, and would most probably have passed without incident but for the Duke of Buckingham, Anne's brother, who made the matter public and caused a scene. For a while after that, Henry returned to connubial bliss, although Catherine lost her baby, but when he took his armies to France in 1513, on his quest to conquer French territory, he fell in love with Etionette de la Baume, a lady of the Court of Margaret of Austria. Their affair was passionate, but brief – an amusing interlude on his part and a political manoeuvre on hers (this is discussed in Chapter 3). On Henry's return to England, with his wife pregnant again, Henry enjoyed another brief fling, this time with Jane Popincourt. These relationships were primarily harmless and fun.

If one looks at Henry's affairs of the heart, they can be divided quite neatly into those ladies who were important to him – and those who were not. His first wife, Catherine of Aragon, obviously was, but Anne Hastings, Etionette de la Baume and Jane Popincourt were not.

Henry's first big extramarital romance came in 1514 when he fell in love with Elizabeth (Bessie) Blount. She was his ideal woman: young, beautiful, intelligent, acquiescent, well raised, musical, an enthusiastic rider and a graceful dancer. While Catherine remained his wife and the future mother of his heir, Henry was no longer deeply in love with her. In a very short time, Bessie Blount came to mean everything to him and for five years they enjoyed each other, a physical relationship that only ended when Bessie informed the King that she was pregnant. A husband was quickly found for Bessie – a little late admittedly – but Henry publicly acknowledged their son, Henry Fitzroy (*see plate 10*), the future Duke of Richmond and Somerset – the only one of his illegitimate children that he did so with. The affair had been public, added to which the boy looked just like Henry and, perhaps more importantly, Bessie did not initially have a husband who could usefully take responsibility for the child. This affair and its outcome taught Henry a valuable lesson. From then on those 'light-hearted' mistresses had husbands that could 'hide' any child born to such a relationship.

Mary Boleyn (*see plate 5*), the first of the Boleyn women with whom Henry had sexual liaisons, was another such light-hearted lover. As soon as Henry declared his interest in her she was found a husband. Although some historians believe that Mary was a woman of loose morals – one who had been the mistress of Francis I of France – I do not believe that this is the case. Mary had sexual relations with only three men: Henry and her husbands, William Carey and William Stafford (discussed further in Chapter 5).

Henry's affair with Mary lasted until she had her first child, who arguably may have been Henry's. However, thanks to a compliant mistress and her even more compliant husband, no one needed to know. As the husbands of the King's ex-mistresses, Gilbert Tailboys (Bessie Blount's husband) and William Carey (Mary Boleyn's husband) never had reason to complain. They acquired charming, agreeable wives with equally acceptable dowries and also the sincere gratitude of their monarch.

Perhaps it seems strange that Henry's affairs with Bessie Blount and Mary Boleyn lasted for years and only ended when the ladies became pregnant. Was it that Henry could not accept a mistress who was also a mother? Did he feel that these children were, in some way, a kind of betrayal or danger? From personal experience Henry knew that bastards could potentially threaten a weak king or one without legitimate heirs. His own claim to the throne came from two bastard lines that had resulted in his father Henry VII, a man capable of toppling a dynasty.

Another way in which Henry could have felt betrayed is if he thought the pregnancies were deliberate. Both Bessie Blount and Mary Boleyn enjoyed five years of sexual intimacy with the King before they fell pregnant with their first children, suggesting that they were using some method of contraception. The experienced Catherine Howard is supposed to have commented, 'a woman might meddle with a man and yet conceive no child unless she would herself.'[3] Contraceptive methods existed, such as condoms, made of fine lambskin, known as 'Venus gloves'[4] but they were cumbersome to use and not always successful. The use of pepper as a spermicide was also unreliable. Anal sex was also recognised as an effective method of birth control. These methods, however, were considered immoral, if not illegal, between a man and woman as God had ordained sex as a means of procreation and to prevent it was contrary to the laws of God.

Although the pregnancies of Bessie Blount and Mary Boleyn may both have been accidents, the pregnancies of Henry's later liaisons with Jane Stukeley, Mary Perrot and Joanna Dingley may have been more the result of his carelessness. Perhaps he practised unprotected sex with them, not caring if he impregnated them or not? After all, Henry did not have to acknowledge any children or worry about them making any later claims to be his offspring. In an age without blood tests or DNA testing, claims concerning paternity were extremely difficult to prove or disprove. They relied on the characters of the parents, the physical appearance of the child and reports on the relationships of the wife. The wife of William Knollys, the grandson of Mary Boleyn and William Carey, finally had children after 20 years of childless marriage, when he was in his 80s. Suspiciously, his widow, Elizabeth, married Lord Vaux immediately after his death, but Knollys was no fool: his will did not acknowledge any children and he was officially recorded as having died without heirs. His 'son' was subsequently refused a place in the House of Lords on the grounds of 'adulterous bastardy'.[5]

By the time the King met Anne Boleyn, Henry had fallen out of love with Catherine of Aragon. They barely spent any time together and even the pregnancies that failed to go to term or ended in stillbirths had stopped. Henry was ripe for a real love – a deep, honest, true love that would replace what he had once had with Catherine. Anne Boleyn was the woman he chose, but it didn't stop Henry from continuing to enjoy other brief, light-hearted affairs. Jane Stukeley, Mary Perrot and Joanna Dingley, all of whom are discussed later in this book, belong to this group and it may be that there were others too. Each of these aforementioned ladies had a

17

child whom contemporary records claim was fathered by the King. The boys, Thomas Stukeley (*see plate 11*) and John Perrot (*see plate 12*), were said to resemble Henry VIII rather than the husbands of their mothers. All three ladies were considered to be 'safe' by Henry: Jane and Mary were married, while Joanna was a recent widow and would soon marry again. At a time (1526–33) when Henry VIII was being put through emotional turmoil by Anne Boleyn's refusal to become his lover and then by her increasing desire to become his wife, he must have found occasional passionate but meaningless episodes with beautiful, adoring, willing partners absolutely irresistible. None of these ladies would further complicate an already complicated situation by suggesting marriage.

Henry's wives, on the other hand, were part of an elaborate political network. When Henry married Anne Boleyn and their relationship became increasingly strained, Margaret Shelton, Anne's cousin, became his mistress for a short time. It may even be that Anne herself supported this move; if the King were to stray, much better that he do so with a member of the Boleyn–Howard faction (see page 102 – the Boleyn–Howard family tree) rather than with a lady belonging to some other great family reaching for power who would try and replace the Queen. When Anne finally fell from favour, it was Jane Seymour who used Anne's own strategy to get her way; she refused to surrender her virtue and held out for marriage. She was supported by a rival Seymour-based faction trying to oust the Howards from power.

When Jane Seymour died, after having given birth to Henry's son, the pattern changed. Having three illegitimate sons must have helped convince Henry to keep trying for a legitimate male heir with his wife, whoever she might be, and Edward's birth lifted the major pressure of securing the succession from Henry's life. Now his aims became different, as he looked beyond his own borders to select a queen for political gain. It was one of history's great ironies that, when faced with Spanish, French and Italian beauties, he ended up with Anne of Cleves, the plain daughter of a German duke. History usually has Henry turning straight from Anne to Catherine Howard, but, in fact, once Henry had decided that the Cleves marriage must be ended, he took a little time to find her successor. He had access to the Queen's ladies-in-waiting, the usual hunting ground for a king in search of female interest. He had met Bessie Blount when she was lady-in-waiting to Catherine of Aragon; Mary and Anne Boleyn both came to his attention through the same route, and Jane Seymour had been Anne Boleyn's lady. Now from amongst Jane Seymour's ladies, Henry showed interest in Anne Bassett, Elizabeth Brooke and Elizabeth Cobham, before finally settling on Catherine Howard, the most unsuitable lady of all. Catherine Howard had a loving nature and absolutely no self-control when it came to personable young gentlemen. She was devoid of any sense of self-preservation, actually bringing two ex-lovers into her household while she was Queen, one of whom she had previously acknowledged as her husband.

After Catherine Howard followed Anne Boleyn to the scaffold, Henry settled down to a quiet and contented old age with Catherine Parr, but old habits were hard to break. Whether he loved Catherine or not, it didn't take long for Henry to become irritated with her extreme Protestantism, and in the last months before his death, he was considering yet another change of wife. Katherine d'Eresby (*see plate 9*), widow of his best friend, Charles Brandon, was a good-looking lady and a renowned wit. She expressed her opinion freely without fear and was said to be deliciously malicious in her humour. Katherine's spice was attractive to the ageing Henry, but he never came to enjoy her charms and wit for himself. He died on the night spanning 27 and 28 January 1547.

Henry VIII enjoyed the reputation of a womaniser, but he was never in the league of other kings such as Charles II (1630–85; king of Great Britain and Ireland, 1660-85). He did not have a harem, although some historians suggest otherwise. He was a serial monogamist and was essentially a man who loved being in love. He was the king and a handsome, intelligent and charming man into

19

the bargain. He could have ordered any woman to his side, yet he set out to charm and to win; writing letters and poems, composing songs, sending gifts, arranging meetings, and behaving, in fact, like any lovelorn teenager. For Catherine of Aragon he arranged jousts and masques in the disguised character of Sir Loyal Heart. Mary Boleyn had a ship named after her. Anne Boleyn received love letters and jewels for years while she admitted her love for him, yet refused Henry a physical relationship. Jane Seymour was lodged in a house Henry could visit by secretly slipping away from Court. Anne Bassett was given a riding horse and saddle, and moved into the healing atmosphere of the country when she fell ill, and Catherine Howard was showered with clothes and jewels. Henry gave generously and expected complete adulation in return. He wanted to be forever that young man who had taken possession of a throne, the Great Lover, whom no woman could resist.

20

THE BOOK

This study examines all of the aforementioned women, as well as Henry's illegitimate children. Here you will find all the ladies who captured the heart of the King. Of the 'Great Loves', he was tiring of Catherine when he took up with Bessie Blount. Bessie had ceased to be his love when he adored Mary Boleyn. After Mary, he spent two years looking before he settled on her sister, Anne. Anne's loss of favour, opened the door for Jane Seymour; after Jane, Anne of Cleves came along. Anne vanished and Anne Bassett, Elizabeth Brooke and Elizabeth Cobham tussled for the position, only to be superseded by Catherine Howard. When Catherine could not hold Henry's affections, it was time for Catherine Parr, and finally Katherine d'Eresby, his last passion.

Of the 'Lighter Loves', Elizabeth Denton, Anne Hastings, Etionette de la Baume and Jane Popincourt belong to Henry's green youth, when he was trying his manhood, in love with life itself. Jane Stukeley, Mary Perrot, Joanna Dingley and Margaret Shelton are the result of Anne Boleyn keeping the King waiting and then, in his view, betraying him when it counted most; Henry, after all, was only human. These ladies gave him unconditional love and a hidden family of healthy, handsome, lively children, a source of secret pride.

Henry VIII's illegitimate children all played significant roles in the history of the period. His sons, Henry Carey (*see plate 13*), Thomas Stukeley and John Perrot and their half-sister Etheldreda Malte, all shared an ability to get away with almost anything. Henry Carey, nephew to Anne Boleyn and a Protestant, survived the reign of his half-sister, Mary I; and despite a rough manner, became one of Elizabeth I's most valued officers. Thomas Stukeley survived charges of piracy, spying and treason, and came away with nothing worse then a few weeks in prison. John Perrot, even when found guilty of defaming Elizabeth I, died of natural causes and not on the block.

As Henry VIII's bastard daughter, Etheldreda Malte grew up in the household of the country's most wealthy tailor. This glittering Tudor had the distinct auburn colouring and the sparkling wit. She married a ne'er-do-well, John Harrington, who faced death on several occasions under treason charges, but who survived to become rich and happy under Elizabeth I. Etheldreda protected her feckless husband and bore him a child, before dying quietly in their house near Bath. In 1554, she was one of the ladies who accompanied the future Elizabeth I, to the Tower where she was held by order of her sister Mary I; as their half-sister, both knew they could trust her loyalty and love (her mother's relationship with Mary I and Etheldreda's with Elizabeth I are explained in Chapter 9).

The lives of Etheldreda Malte, Henry Fitzroy, Henry Carey, John Perrot and Thomas Stukeley overlap and intertwine with each other and with those of their brother, cousin and sisters: Edward VI, Lady Jane Grey, Mary I and Elizabeth I. They burst like stars on to the scene, flame gloriously and are extinguished with a spark and then a whisper. Etheldreda had a daughter and Thomas Stukeley had at least one son, but their lines are lost. The family of Henry Carey flourished as did that of John Perrot – today one of the modern Perrots, of the bloodline of Henry VIII, is a dentist in Essex.

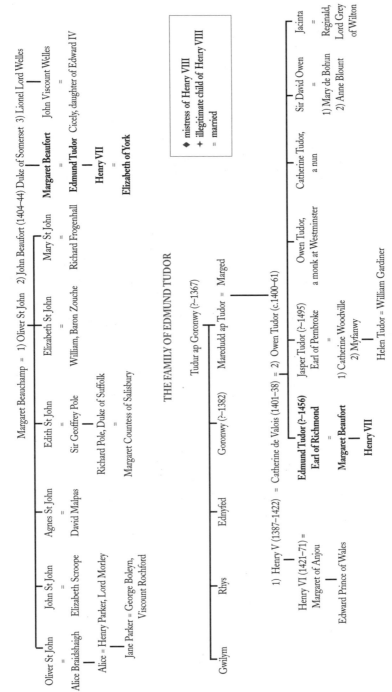

THE MATERNAL FAMILY OF MARGARET BEAUFORT

Margaret Beauchamp = 1) Oliver St John   2) John Beaufort (1404–44) Duke of Somerset   3) Lionel Lord Welles

Oliver St John   John St John   Agnes St John   Edith St John   Elizabeth St John   Mary St John   Margaret Beaufort   Edmund Tudor Cicely, daughter of Edward IV   John Viscount Welles

Alice Braidshaigh   Elizabeth Scroope   David Malpas   Sir Geoffrey Pole   William, Baron Zouche   Richard Frogenhall   =   =

Alice = Henry Parker, Lord Morley   Richard Pole, Duke of Suffolk   Henry VII

Jane Parker = George Boleyn,   Margaret Countess of Salisbury   Elizabeth of York
             Viscount Rochford

THE FAMILY OF EDMUND TUDOR

Tudur ap Goronwy (?–1367)

Maredudd ap Tudor = Marged

Gwilym   Rhys   Ednyfed   Goronwy (?–1382)

1) Henry V (1387–1422) = Catherine de Valois (1401–38) = 2) Owen Tudor (c.1400–61)

Henry VI (1421–71) =   Edmund Tudor (?–1456)   Jasper Tudor (?–1495)   Owen Tudor,   Catherine Tudor,   Sir David Owen   Jacinta
Margaret of Anjou   Earl of Richmond   Earl of Pembroke   a monk at Westminster a nun   =

Edward Prince of Wales   Margaret Beaufort   1) Catherine Woodville   1) Mary de Bohun   Reginald,
                              =   2) Myfanwy   2) Anne Blount   Lord Grey
                              Henry VII   of Wilton
                                                       Helen Tudor = William Gardiner

◆ mistress of Henry VIII
✝ illegitimate child of Henry VIII
= married

I

The Formative Childhood Years

—⁊∅⁊—

Henry VIII was very much a product of his family ambitions and their rise to power. His complex private life had its origins in his father's arguably weak claim to and lengthy fight for the throne, and the history of two families, the Houses of Lancaster and York. Descended through his mother, Margaret Beaufort, from John of Gaunt, Duke of Lancaster, the third surviving son of Edward III, and his mistress, Catherine Swynford, and through his father, Edmund Tudor, who was half-brother to Henry VI, Henry Tudor became the foremost Lancastrian claimant to the throne.

After the first usurpation of the throne of Henry VI by Edward, Duke of York, who became Edward IV, Henry Tudor, the 13-year-old Earl of Richmond, had no real protectors and disappeared into exile in the care of his uncle, Jasper Tudor. His grandmother was Catherine de Valois, sister of Charles VI of France, and exile across the Channel was a good deal safer than staying in England. Henry Tudor stayed in Brittany (a separate dukedom until 1488 when the heiress, Anne of Brittany, married Charles VIII of France) from 1471 to 1485 as the guest of Duke Francis II, the Marshall of Brittany. He ended up living in a chateau at Largöet, near Vannes, the home of the Marshall of Brittany, Jean de Rieux. As the years passed, increasing numbers of Lancastrians and Yorkist malcontents retreated to France and Henry Tudor was an acknowledged claimant to the English throne. The claim was deemed so serious that both Edward IV and Richard III went to some lengths to entice Henry Tudor back to England and to bribe or trick Louis XI of France and Francis II into sending him home. All attempts ended in failure and Henry's value as a rival to the

House of York increased. As a child, the future Henry VIII would have heard of his father's struggles as an exile in France. The lesson was twofold: firstly, that anyone who could not hold on to the throne faced exile and constant danger of assassination; secondly, that exiles were a menace, ready to return and seize the throne from the ruling king. This helped to make Henry VIII ruthless, more so once he had his son and heir. He would defend his throne for his dynasty, no matter how many lives were forfeit.

Henry Tudor spent 14 years in exile in Brittany, the formative years of his life, from the age of 13 to 27. He learned to speak and read French, and also took a French mistress with whom he had a son, Roland de Velville, born around 1474. The name is spelled in many ways, one of which is Vielleville, which indicates that the lady belonged to the de Vielleville family, Counts of Durtal. When Henry Tudor became king, Roland was knighted. He became a leading jouster for a period between 1494 and 1507 and was eventually made Constable of Beaumaris Castle. In his will, dated 1535, Sir Roland asked to be buried at Llanfaes Friary in Wales, where some of the earlier Tudors were buried. Part of his epitaph, written in Welsh, reads: '… a man of kingly line and of earl's blood …'[1] This statement was a discreet announcement of his paternity. Henry VII never formally acknowledged him, but everyone knew whose son Roland was. It could be said, therefore, that Henry VIII was following in the footsteps of his ancestors when he fathered bastard children, but with the knowledge that his own dynasty was founded on not one, but two bastard families, he perhaps did not feel confident enough to acknowledge his baseborn children.

Henry Tudor's triumph at the battle of Bosworth in 1485 was the culmination of years of plotting, abortive risings and failures. Richard III was dead, other claimants were too distant to the throne or too young and, as Henry stated in proclamations issued after Bosworth, he was king by right of descent and by possession. Henry VII further cemented his claim to the throne by marrying the rival family heiress, Elizabeth of York, eldest daughter of Edward IV.

Elizabeth grew up with the knowledge of her father's frequent and constant unfaithfulness to her mother, which was common gossip. Yet she saw that her father and mother still loved each other; she learned that a queen's duty was to produce heirs, smile and say nothing. Henry VIII would have observed that his mother, alluded to as the perfect king's wife, was always subservient to her husband, a mother to his children and a docile adornment to his Court. Here he found the template for his ideal queen.

Elizabeth fulfilled her destiny with calm good sense, her eldest child born eight months after her marriage. She bore her husband three sons – Arthur in 1486, Henry in 1491 and Edmund in 1499 – and four daughters – Margaret in 1489, Elizabeth in 1492, Mary in 1496 and Catherine in 1503 – losing one son and two daughters in childhood. She was idealised by many as the perfection of womanhood, yet her husband kept her powerless, giving authority and his affection and trust to his mother, Margaret. Elizabeth found herself playing second fiddle to her mother-in-law; at the Christmas festivities in 1487, Margaret wore the same costume, 'like mantell and surcott as the queen, with a rich corrownall on her hede.'[2] Margaret would accompany Elizabeth on state occasions, walking and standing directly behind her; she went on progresses with Henry and Elizabeth. At Woodstock and in the Tower apartments, Margaret's rooms adjoined the King's.

Margaret Beaufort was a wealthy woman in her own right; she managed her own affairs and kept tight hold on her wealth. She would demand her rights and pursue a debt to death and beyond. She taught her son the value of a well-filled treasury, but failed to make such an impression on her grandson, who may have been heartily tired of advice on the need for prudence. His father and grandmother both approved of his teenage years when he was kept on an allowance from his father without a privy purse of his own.

Henry VII had married a young, beautiful, virtuous, well born lady, but this had never stopped any of his predecessors or family members from engaging in extramarital liaisons. Taking a mistress and fathering children out of wedlock was commonplace. In a time when virtually all marriages were arranged for financial and family benefits, it was reasonable to seek love outside the marriage. Given that Henry VII was the king and a red-blooded male in a political marriage, it would have been amazing if he had not found affection with other ladies. The temptation was all around him: Elizabeth's ladies were chosen for their beauty and charm.

In the early years of his reign, Henry VII delighted in spending money on show and display. There were lavish building projects and splendid clothes for him, his family and courtiers, as well as extravagant pastimes. The King loved hunting and hawking, and when he rebuilt Sheen (after the palace on the bank of the Thames in Surrey burned down in 1497) he added 'houses of pleasure to disport in at chess, tables, dice, cards ...' and established a menagerie at the Tower, with 'lions, leopards, wild cats and rare birds ...'[3] He also enjoyed dancing and music. Two interesting references from his privy purse accounts may indicate that love and music can easily go together: 25 August 1493, payment 'to the young damsel that danceth' – £30; 13 January 1497, payment 'to a little maiden that danceth' – £12'.[4]

To offer these dancers the equivalent of the annual salary of a lady-in-waiting for one performance (or even several) seems a trifle excessive if dancing was all that was on offer. Henry VII was taking his pleasure in as safe a way as he could, in the company of young ladies whose social position meant that they could have no influence whatsoever. It was a lesson his son would have been wise to learn: taking mistresses who would not cause trouble. The difference was that whereas Henry VII wanted sex, Henry VIII wanted love.

PRINCE HENRY

Born on 28 June 1491 at Greenwich Palace, Henry was the second son of Henry VII and Elizabeth of York. Henry VII was 34 when his second son was born and had been king for six years. At the time of Henry's birth, Elizabeth was already recognised as a devoted wife and mother. The only surviving contemporary portrait of her shows a plump lady, pale skinned with fair, red-gold hair. Sources of the time give us further insight – the Spanish Ambassador wrote of Elizabeth that she was 'kept in subjection by the mother of the king', and was shown little love by either. Others described Elizabeth as beautiful, noble, beloved, great in 'charity and humanity.'[5]

Almost immediately, Henry was separated from his mother and given his own household at Eltham with his brother Arthur, the Prince of Wales, his sister Margaret and the children who followed. The Royal Court travelled a great deal, and it would have been almost impossible to take children with it as there were too many strangers, who might bring disease or attempt assassination. The King, however, needed to keep himself in the public eye, and the houses where he and his Court stayed needed to be cleaned, after only a few months, so the never-ending movement was a necessity for the King and Queen.

In June 1491 when Henry was born, Margaret Beaufort was in the midst of organising the royal nursery at Eltham; Elizabeth was hardly involved at all. Margaret would, therefore, be the person the young prince would come into contact with most frequently. Her religion now dominated her life. She had taken a vow of perpetual chastity and, despite being married, she dressed like a nun. Margaret's powerful, dominant role in Henry's life was to reinforce his distaste for strong-willed women and his liking for those who gave in to him rather than thwarted him.

By September 1494 the three-year-old Henry was already Constable of Dover Castle, Warden of the Cinque Ports, Earl Marshal of England and Lieutenant of Ireland. The Duke of York was added to his titles in answer to the claims of Perkin Warbeck (who claimed to be Richard, Duke of York, son of Edward IV, one of the lost Princes in the Tower who had disappeared whilst under the protection of their uncle, Richard III). Henry was first made a Knight of the Bath and, on 18 May 1495, Knight of the Order of the Garter. From the time he was first aware, Henry knew he was special, the centre of attention, as grown men – politicians and soldiers – bowed down to him.

Between late 1496 and early 1497 Arthur went to Ludlow, Shropshire, to set up a separate household as Prince of Wales. With Arthur gone, Eltham became the household of Henry, Duke of York. Even though his sister Margaret was older, as a son Henry took precedence. However, he would always stand second to Arthur, as the future king.

Some historians and novelists like to portray Henry as jealous, determined to outdo Arthur in everything to prove he was better. However, there is no evidence that Henry resented or was jealous of his brother, or that he failed to acknowledge that he would have to find his own place in the world, once Arthur became king.

During the Cornish 'rebellion' of 1497, the local people rose up against taxes forced on them by Henry VII to pay for opposing the pretender, Perkin Warbeck, in the north, far away from Cornwall, in southwest England. When it looked as if the Cornish rebels would reach London unopposed, Elizabeth of York and the young Henry sheltered at the Coldharbour, a house near the Tower of London, and then, on Monday 12 June, in the Tower itself.[6] Thus, Henry was finally able to spend time with his mother. They were together, without any other family members, and were in some danger. For a week they supported and encouraged each other.

Once the rebellion was crushed (with 2,000 dead at Blackheath in south London), the Cornish were allowed to return home, but were heavily fined. Later that same year some of the Cornish rebels joined forces with other West Country malcontents in support of Warbeck. Although the leaders were executed, the rest again received heavy fines. The result may well have been that six-year-old Prince Henry learned to distrust leniency. Two of his wives were to pay the price for this lesson. Other kings divorced unwanted wives and then imprisoned them or sent them to nunneries; Henry executed them.

Lord Herbert of Cherbury stated in *The Life and Raigne of Henry the Eighth*, published in 1649, that Prince Henry, as a younger son, was destined for the Church. There is no other evidence for this interesting claim. In fact, given the rate of infant mortality, Henry stood a good chance of becoming Prince of Wales and would have been educated accordingly. In his will, dated 14 October 1496, Jasper Tudor left his lands and wealth to Henry, to give some independence to the future king's younger brother; the will specifically mentions that if Henry became Prince of Wales, the estate was to go to Henry VII, Jasper's nephew, instead.

In 1494, John Skelton, an academic and poet, became tutor to Prince Arthur and later to Henry. Skelton was a notable Latin scholar, a skill much appreciated by Henry VII; he wanted the Prince to learn Latin as this was the language of kings, in which most communications were made. Henry VII himself had little Latin, and regretted it as this put him at a disadvantage in international circles.

By 1502, Skelton gave his services exclusively to Prince Henry. Delighted at the rank of his pupil, Skelton wrote in praise of his charge:

'There grows from the red-rose bush a fair-flowering shoot, a delightful small new Rose, worthy of its stock, a noble Henry born of famous line, a boy noble in the nobility of his father; and furthermore a brilliant pupil, worthy to be sung as such ...'[7]

Skelton taught Henry Latin grammar, rhetoric and logic; he further introduced arithmetic, geometry, astronomy, music and theology into the curriculum. Skelton wanted learning to be enjoyable, so he let Henry read the Latin poets and historians. Lessons were taught in English, rather than French or Latin, so that Henry would be fluent in his native language. Skelton may also have mentioned to Henry his own ideas about how abuses in the Church and the State needed to be removed, whilst the actual Church and State were protected.

Skelton was with Henry for a greater part of the day. Up for matins at 6 a.m., followed by breakfast, Henry would have had classes all morning and into the afternoon, breaking only to eat at 10 or 11 a.m. He then took part in sporting activities until evensong and his next meal at 4 p.m. After this would be entertainment until bed at 8 or 9 p.m.

Lord Mountjoy was taken into Henry's household as his companion, mentor and role model. Thirteen years older than Henry, Mountjoy's job was to teach him to behave like a gentleman. Mountjoy's grandmother was Anne Neville, sister of Cicely who married Richard, Duke of York in 1438, the parents of Edward IV. Mountjoy was an ideal role model in many ways – elegant, handsome, serious, sensible, beautifully mannered, intelligent and good at sports and games. He had studied at Queens' College, Cambridge and was a patron of the Dutch writer, philosopher and humanist, Desiderius Erasmus (1466?–1536). Mountjoy also liked women, marrying four times (the first time when Henry was six). Henry would have observed his mentor enter cheerfully into matrimony and would have learned a little about love and respect.

Skelton tried to teach Henry that his head should rule his heart and that he should not give way to passions, emotional or sexual. In 1501 Skelton wrote *Speculum Principis* (*A Mirror for Princes*), a textbook for young Henry with such aphorisms as, 'Choose a wife for yourself. Prize her always and uniquely.'[8] Skelton's writings may also have informed Henry's view that certain women were not to be respected – women who betrayed their husbands or lovers. In 'Womanhood, Wanton, Ye Want', comparing a woman's chastity to a locked door, Skelton wrote:

> *Your key is meet for every lock,*
> *Your key is common and hangeth out;*

Your key is ready, we need not knock,
Not stand long resting there about;
Of your doorgate we have no doubt ...[9]

This philosophy is reflected in Henry's attitude to several of his mistresses. They are the 'wantons' – ladies who betray their marriage vows, even with the King. They may be loved, but they can be left without feelings of guilt, as they are unworthy of his respect. The long-term mistresses may be found husbands, but they are faithful to the King; the husband is mere window dressing. They are worthy of respect as long as the King is their sole lover. Only when he was young and finding his feet did Henry take mistresses who had enjoyed previous relationships, Anne Hastings with Sir William Compton and Jane Popincourt with the duc de Longueville. In later years, Henry made a great fuss of demanding that his wives should be virgins when they came to the marriage bed.

The year before Henry's birth, Prince Arthur, then aged two, was betrothed to Catherine of Aragon, the daughter of Ferdinand of Aragon and Isabella of Castile, the rulers of Spain. The Spanish were constructing an alliance against the menace of France by marrying their children into the royal houses of England, Portugal and the Holy Roman Empire (based on Austria and the Netherlands). Ferdinand and Isabella, however, were unwilling to send their daughter to England while there were questions as to the strength of the Tudors' hold on the throne. In March 1500, after King Henry had executed a couple of Pretenders, along with the imprisoned, unfortunate Earl of Warwick who had a strong claim to the throne, the Spanish signed a treaty of alliance and said that Catherine would be in England in May (in fact she did not arrive until the following year). England was now safe. Even the young Prince could learn the lesson that a dead enemy is no threat.

When Catherine of Aragon arrived in October 1501, the Royal Family was at Richmond Palace. Henry VII waited until she was at

31

Dogmersfield, where he went to meet her. Prince Arthur came to meet them from Ludlow. The Princess was then taken to Lambeth Palace in London and Prince Arthur went to the King's Wardrobe, a royal residence near St Paul's Cathedral. It had been decided that the 10-year-old Henry would escort Catherine into the City of London two days before her wedding, so she could see the pageants and tableaux set up in honour of the marriage on her way to the Bishop's Palace, where she would stay until the wedding. All the displays praised Arthur's regal manliness and emphasised Catherine's role as the future mother of kings.

Henry also led the bride to church, and after the marriage returned Catherine to the Bishop's Palace for the banquet. After the feast, came the much disputed wedding night. Arthur contended that his marriage had been consummated. The morning after, he called ostentatiously for wine: He is reputed to have said, 'I have this night been in the midst of Spain, which is a hot region, and that journey maketh me so dry.'[10] This was later denied by Catherine. She maintained, when the question arose, that Arthur had wanted to appear more healthy and manly before his friends and servants. She said that she was sexually 'as intact as when I emerged from my mother's womb.'[11]

As regards Henry's marriage, there appears to have been one tentative suggestion that he might marry Eleanor, daughter of the Holy Roman Emperor, Maximilian, whose grandson Charles was promised to Henry's sister, Mary. Was this to reduce the number of heirs and claimants to the throne and to keep Henry from having a son for whom he might grow too ambitious? If Prince Henry did marry, it should certainly be to a lady who had no aspirations to the English throne through her own family or to a foreign princess who needed a resident prince consort to dwell abroad.

Shortly after Arthur and Catherine's wedding, Edmund de la Pole, Earl of Suffolk, the son of Edward IV's sister Elizabeth and a claimant to the throne, who had returned to England under the King's promise of safety, again fled to France, taking his brother

32

Richard with him. Driven by suspicion, Henry VII took immediate action against all those remaining who had any claim to the throne. In March 1502, William Courtenay (husband of Queen Elizabeth's sister Katherine), William de la Pole (brother of Edmund and Richard) and James Tyrrell (Governor of Guisnes, near Calais), who had received Edmund de la Pole when he fled in 1499, were all imprisoned in the Tower of London. William Courtenay was found guilty of treason and sentenced to death, but was merely imprisoned until Henry VII's death, when Henry VIII released him. William de la Pole stayed in prison for 38 years, and died there. JamesTyrrell was executed in May 1502, having supposedly confessed, almost 20 years after the event, that he had arranged the murders of Edward V and Richard, Duke of York, the Princes in the Tower, under orders from Richard III.

On a happier note, Henry VII and Elizabeth of York were delighted with their son's bride. Catherine of Aragon was pretty and mature beyond her years, only a year older than her husband. She had been brought up to play the part of the Princess of Wales and later Queen of England. She was plump and graceful, with small hands and feet, long chestnut-brown hair and a flawless, fair complexion. She was well read, regal, dignified and pious, although she lacked spontaneity or humour, and was incapable of subterfuge or compromise. Her husband was tall and fair, with the family good looks. The question of his health does not seem to have arisen. As it would have been of great interest to the other European rulers if Arthur had been sickly, it would have been avidly reported; it is therefore safe to say that he enjoyed reasonably robust good health. However, in view of what followed, Prince Arthur may already have been showing the first symptoms of the illness that killed him.

The couple set up their household and spent their brief married life at Ludlow Castle. On 2 April 1502, Prince Arthur died there, after only five months of marriage. For most of this time, he had been ill with 'consumption' and the longed-for second wedding

33

night never happened. The Prince's ailment is usually diagnosed as tuberculosis, but it may very well have been pneumonia. Catherine herself was extremely ill, so much so that she was unable to attend Arthur's funeral at Worcester Cathedral, and it was some months before she could be moved to London. Her mother-in-law, Elizabeth, sent a sombre, black-draped litter for Catherine to travel in slowly and safely to Durham House, on the Strand, where she set up her household and where Henry VII paid £100 a month to keep her in the style of Dowager Princess of Wales. Despite rumours to the contrary, Catherine showed no signs of being pregnant, wholly due, she would maintain, to nothing of a sexual nature having happened. She remained in England, waiting for her parents and father-in-law to decide what should become of her.

Henry VII decided that his second son, who was now Prince of Wales, should marry Catherine – chiefly so that he could maintain an alliance with Spain, and also, in no small part, so that he could keep her dowry. Henry VII's reputation for meanness was, it seems, well founded. Prince Henry does not appear to have been unwilling, as he seemed to admire his brother's bride and wished for the marriage.

The question of whether or not the first marriage had been consummated was ignored; a papal dispensation was issued that allowed Henry to have children with his brother's widow, regardless of her state of virginity. Strictly speaking, this second marriage was against church law if Arthur and Catherine had had sex, and Arthur's insistence that they had would later give Henry his grounds for divorce. The Catholic Church, basing its judgement on Holy Scripture, forbade a man to marry his brother's widow if they had had a sexual relationship. At the time, political expediency overrode Church law and the Pope absolved all parties from any sin.

Catherine maintained that she and Arthur had never consummated their marriage. Catherine was extremely pious and it is unlikely that she lied about something as serious as this, even with a papal dispensation. Had she not been a virgin when she married Henry she would, in her own eyes, have been guilty of a mortal sin. Catherine's later strength of conviction at the breakdown of her marriage to Henry VIII seems hard to imagine if she had known in her heart of hearts that her marriage to Arthur had been consummated. Catherine would not compromise as far as her religion was concerned and she would never tell a serious lie.

For the young Henry the change from Duke of York to Prince of Wales must have been an exciting one. He stepped into his brother's shoes, presumably with a mixture of sadness and delight. He took on many of his brother's officers of the Court. Skelton, however, lost his place as Henry's tutor. It may have been because his writing was getting more scurrilous (for example, the *Bouge of Court*, which painted the court as corrupt and self-seeking) and vulgar ('Womanhood, Wanton, Ye Want'), or because he had an arrogant, quarrelsome nature. In 1504, he was appointed rector of Diss, Norfolk, with a stipend and pension from the King. William Hone became Henry's new tutor. Unlike the colourful Skelton, little is known about the worthy, dull Hone.

Still ruled by his tutors, the young Prince slept, ate, studied, worshipped and played games; he signed documents, but never attended meetings. He also now learned Italian, Spanish, medicine, astronomy, geometry and arithmetic. When Lord Mountjoy was in England, they read history together and worked on Henry's Latin. Henry shared his lessons, in part, with his sisters, Margaret and Mary. He also shared lessons with the pages, who were his companions and personal servants. These included Charles Brandon, his best friend; John St John, his grandmother's great-nephew; Edward Neville (so physically like Henry that they were sometimes mistaken for each other); and Henry Courtenay, son of Elizabeth of York's sister.[12]

Just after Arthur's death, Henry suffered another bereavement. Elizabeth of York died on 11 February 1503, after giving birth to a baby daughter, Catherine, who also died a few days later. Elizabeth was just 38 years old. Shortly after her death, Elizabeth's children were taken to see her laid out in her robes of state. They knelt and prayed by her bed. Henry was just 12 years old, and was the King's only son and heir. What thoughts went through the boy's head as he gazed at the dead face of his beloved mother can only be imagined. To Henry, Elizabeth was a mixture of reality and myth – woman, queen and goddess – a child's ideal of female perfection. The impact of her loss and that last farewell in the darkened room with candles flickering made a lasting impression on the young Prince.

The Court became far more serious and much less fun with the deaths of Arthur and Elizabeth. It has been suggested that Prince Henry and Queen Elizabeth had been particularly close, forming an alliance as they were both 'powerless when compared with the King and Lady Margaret Beaufort.'[13] Henry had already suffered the loss of his siblings Elizabeth, Edmund and Arthur, and now he had also lost baby Catherine and his idolised mother. He grew to fear illness, and that those he loved could be taken from him without warning. He learned not to care too deeply for anyone, to avoid the hurt.

Over the years, Henry perfected an image of his dead mother that he used to measure other women against. Every wife and every mistress was assessed against this impossible yardstick.

Who was he to love now?

In August 1503, Henry escorted his 13-year-old sister, Princess Margaret, north on her way to marry the Scottish King, James IV. Margaret was a bossy, self-obsessed little madam, and it seems likely that Henry felt few qualms about losing her. His only female contacts now were his sweet little sister Mary and his elderly 58-year-old religious, dominant grandmother.

Henry VII, however, had already enjoyed one good and fruitful marriage – why not a second? He began looking for a new queen. Despite plans for Catherine to marry the new Prince of Wales, Henry VII tentatively suggested that he should marry the princess himself! Catherine's parents, Ferdinand of Aragon and Isabella of Castile vetoed the idea of this amended match. True, their daughter would be queen of England, but even if Henry VII gave her a son, the new baby would be unlikely to become king, with an existing and healthy Prince of Wales. Henry VII, at the age of 46, was already an old man by the standards of the day, and might die soon; Catherine would be a widow again, and this time would have no chance of marrying the next English king. Isabella described his suggestion as: '… an evil thing, the mere mention of which offends the ears, and we would not for anything in the world that it should take place.'[14] If it had been expedient, Ferdinand and Isabella would have agreed to the marriage in a second. However, they saw a better chance of a lasting alliance with Catherine married to the future King of England.

Instead, Isabella recommended Henry VII to consider marriage to Joan, the widowed Queen of Naples, the daughter of her husband Ferdinand's sister. She was 26 years old and 'particularly well-qualified to console him in his deep affliction.' However, she lacked a dowry, and she only held the throne of Naples for her own lifetime. Henry might like her 'comely neck' and 'womanly laughing cheer and good humour', but he wanted more material benefit from a bride.[15]

While negotiations continued, Isabella of Castile died, and the political climate changed dramatically. Ferdinand of Aragon married again, to Germaine de Foix of Navarre, and Henry VII may have briefly looked towards France for a wife. The Portuguese Ambassador, Thomas Lopez, wrote a letter dated 10 October 1505 to his master, Emanuel I of Portugal: 'Sire, the king of England is treating to get married in France to the daughter [sister – Margaret of Angoulême] of the Count of Angoulême, the Dauphin, or to his mother [Louise of Savoy] and he has sent thither for that purpose the Lord Somerset his ambassador.'[16] Possibly to spite Ferdinand, whom he suspected of duplicity in the marriage negotiations, Henry VII suggested that he might marry Margaret of Austria, sister of Philip the Handsome, the son of the Holy Roman Emperor. Philip had married Joanna, the eldest daughter of Ferdinand and Isabella; when Isabella died, it was Joanna, her eldest child, and not her

37

husband Ferdinand of Aragon, who inherited the throne of Castile. Ferdinand and Philip were at loggerheads over Joanna's inheritance and any suggestion that Henry VII was planning to ally himself to Philip would have annoyed Ferdinand greatly.

Margaret of Austria had first married John, Crown Prince of Spain, in 1497, but he died only a few months later. In 1501, Margaret married Philibert II, Duke of Savoy, who died in 1504. Now Henry VII put pressure on Philip the Handsome, pushing him to forward this marriage. A treaty of friendship was signed between Henry and Philip in London, on 20 March 1506, one element of which promised Henry VII the hand of Margaret, along with a dowry of 300,000 crowns and an annual income of 30,000. In addition, Prince Henry was to marry Eleanor, the daughter of Philip and Joanna, and Princess Mary was to marry their eldest son Charles, who was heir to Spain through his mother and to the Holy Roman Empire through his father.

Neither side seems to have pushed the marriage; Margaret herself was opposed to the union. Late in 1506, however, circumstances changed. Philip the Handsome died suddenly on 25 September, and Henry immediately approached Ferdinand, asking for the hand of his newly widowed daughter, Joanna; she had had six children with Philip – Charles, Ferdinand, Eleanor, Isabella, Mary and Katherine – which boded well for new princes and princesses of England.

On 15 January 1506, Philip the Handsome and Joanna had been stranded in England by a storm when their ship was damaged; Philip was on his way to Spain to attack Ferdinand, who was refusing to give up control of Castile to Joanna, as rightful heir. Prince Henry was sent to Winchester to meet Philip who had landed at Melcombe Regis, near Weymouth, Dorset. Joanna had stopped at Wolverton Manor, Dorset, as she was suffering from a bout of illness.

Philip and the young Henry took to each other immediately and were able to talk in French. Philip the Handsome was everything the Prince thought a king should be – handsome, religious, brave, aggressive in war, fond of wine, women (he enjoyed a string of casual sexual encounters) and song. Henry VII met the pair just outside Windsor the following day. During the month of the visit, Henry and Philip were constantly in one another's company. The King spent extravagantly to impress Philip and everything was sumptuous and exuberant. On 10 February Joanna joined the party at Windsor.

On leaving England Philip and Joanna went on to Spain. There they formulated a truce with Ferdinand who withdrew from Castile; however, when Philip died, on 25 September 1506, the cause was rumoured to be poison, administered on the orders of Ferdinand. Henry was devastated by the news of Philip's death. The loss of someone he admired raised an interesting mention of his mother's death and the effect that it had on the boy. He wrote to Erasmus on 17 January 1507:

'The news of the death of the King of Castile, my wholly and entirely and best-loved brother, I had reluctantly received very long before your letter ... For never, since the death of my dearest mother, hath there come to me more hateful intelligence ... because it seemed to tear open again the wound to which time had brought insensibility.'[17]

When Henry VII had met Joanna during this visit to England, albeit for a few days, he had expressed romantic feelings for her: 'If when she was in England I had acted as I secretly wished, I would by every means have prevented her leaving my court. But I was prevented by my Council.'[18] He told the Spanish Ambassador that he believed her to be unhappy rather than mad. He said Philip the Handsome's unfaithfulness obviously upset her. He, on the other hand, would love and cherish her.

Joanna appears to have suffered some kind of nervous debilitation. Her symptoms were depression (partly brought on by her husband's public infidelities) and a habit of forthright speech. The symptoms might indicate manic depression. Despite this, in England at least, the marriage was considered seriously. Dr Roderigo Gondesalvi de Puebla, the Spanish Ambassador in London from 1487, wrote to Ferdinand: '... the English seem little to mind her insanity, especially since I have assured them that the derangement of her mind would not prevent her from bearing children.'[19]

Ferdinand kept Henry VII dangling, right up until his death in 1509. In March 1507, Ferdinand wrote to his daughter Catherine, whom he was using as a go-between:

> 'She [Catherine] must tell the king that it is not yet known whether Queen Juana [Joanna] be inclined to marry again, but if the said Queen should marry again, it shall be with no other person than with the King of England ... But the affair must be kept most secret; for if Queen Juana should hear anything about it, she would most probably do something quite to the contrary.'

Catherine wrote to Joanna, despite his advice, in October 1507:

> '... the great affection he [Henry VII] had felt and still feels towards your Royal Highness from that time [the meeting in 1506] until now, is well known ... I do not doubt but that your Highness will become the most noble and the most powerful Queen in the world.'[20]

In reality, Ferdinand had no intention of letting the heiress of Castile out of his hands. He may very well have exaggerated Joanna's grief and depression on her husband's death, and had her confined as a madwoman. She was sent to the castle at Tordesillas, near Valladolid in Castile, the place where her grandmother was incarcerated after a metal breakdown. Poor Joanna finally died in 1555, having spent almost 50 years in confinement.

The 'Joanna Affair' led to the only recorded quarrel between Henry VII and his son. The King had received a letter telling him that Ferdinand's negotiations had been a sham and he was never to have Joanna. He called the Prince in to sympathise. Henry, with a lack of tact, was unenthusiastic and gave his opinion that Joanna was mad and the King was too old to be considering marriage. The King was extremely angry at such a blunt assessment of the situation and shouted at his son. One of the court ladies reported to the Spanish Ambassador, 'He scolded the prince as though he would kill him.'[21]

The Prince had another reason to throw cold water on the thought of his father remarrying. If there should be more princes, this could only be bad news for young Henry. He had the worrying example of his grandfather, Edward IV, before him; his brother George, Duke of Clarence, had tried to usurp his throne and his other brother, Richard, Duke of Gloucester, had actually deposed the rightful heir, Edward's son. All too often royal brothers had a habit of plotting to extend their own power and influence at the expense of the king and the kingdom.

However, as time passed, Henry remained the only son. As such, one of the first responsibilities of the new Prince of Wales was to contract an eligible marriage alliance. As early as June 1503, it was agreed that Henry and Catherine should marry the following year when he would be 14 and Catherine would be 19 years old.

A series of delays to Catherine and Henry's marriage followed, however. Isabella's death in November 1504, leaving her inheritance of Castile to Joanna, meant that Ferdinand of Aragon lost part of his enormous importance in European politics, as his area of direct influence was now in Aragon alone. Trade treaties drawn up under Isabella were cancelled, and it looked very much as if Ferdinand would be unable to pay the second half of Catherine's dowry of 100,000 crowns. In Prince Henry's name, the King arranged a formal protest by his son against the proposed marriage that had been made.

This left Henry VII in a strong position; he still had Catherine in England, complete with the papal dispensation for her marriage to her late husband's brother, and could resurrect the union at any time he wanted. He was also free to look elsewhere for a better match, or use the promise or threat of the marriage of the Prince of Wales in his continental diplomacy.

In 1504 Henry had expected to go to Ludlow, to enjoy at least limited power and freedom. Instead he was kept at Court under his father's watchful eye. He was the precious only son; if the King died, young Henry could be crowned and secure before any of the rival claimants even knew of the death. Henry VII and his mother, Margaret, wanted to keep both eyes on the Prince of Wales.

Everything we know about Henry indicates he hated this life. He was handsome and healthy; he was surrounded by servants and friends to whom his every word was law and he had witnessed Arthur's taste of independence. It is extremely unlikely that he found staying at home under the prying eyes of his father and grandmother at all to his liking.

In August 1504, the Spanish Ambassador to London, Hernan, duque de Estrada, wrote to Ferdinand and Isabella that Henry VII was devoted to his son: 'Certainly there could be no better school in the world than the society of such a father as Henry VII. He is so wise and attentive to everything; nothing escapes his attention.' He added that the King had told him, 'I keep the prince with me because I wish to improve him.'[22]

This attention must have stifled the young Prince Henry, however. The Spanish Envoy, Gutiérrez Gómez de Fuensalida, wrote in 1508 that Henry was kept under supervision as if he were a girl. He could only go out by one door into the park, and then only with companions selected by his father (young men such as Charles Brandon and Edward Neville). No one could approach or speak to him without permission. He slept in a room that connected only with his father's. He never spoke in public except to answer his father's questions; he never attended any council meetings or audiences with ambassadors or deputations. Fuensalida was supposed to talk to the Prince about his marriage to Catherine of Aragon, but he was not allowed to see him without his father being present, let alone talk to him in private. At Richmond, Henry spent most days in the tiltyard, sometimes watched by his father.

The Prince had his own suite of apartments in Westminster Palace, reached through those of the King. He had footmen, a gentleman usher, a groom of the privy chamber, tutors, minstrels and players. Here at least he might occasionally be alone with his friends. During the evening entertainments, lords and ladies gathered together to hear stories and sing songs about romance and courtly love, to flirt (and more). In courtly love, ideally one should be in love with someone unattainable, preferably above you socially. Henry had few places to turn for this kind of 'belle dame' – and so he focused his attention on Catherine.

In August 1504, the King went on progress with Prince Henry, Princess Mary and the Dowager Princess Catherine. Henry and Catherine spent time together riding, hunting and talking. It is impossible to know what they talked about, whether he felt sorry for her, alone in a strange country, unsure of her future, at the mercy of his father's whims. Perhaps they fell in love; perhaps they found company in a shared misery of powerless subjection. Catherine had a lot to be worried about. Her mother was dead, and there was now open conflict between her father and his son-in-law and daughter, Philip the Handsome and Joanna. Both parties sought to use Catherine to gain King Henry's support.

In October 1505, Henry sent a letter to Pope Julius II. The letter complained that Catherine had taken to fasting, prayer, abstinence and pilgrimage; and that this might affect her health and particularly her ability to have children later. The Pope wrote back, giving the Prince, as her betrothed husband, permission to order her to stop, 'We ... grant you permission to restrain the aforesaid Catherine, your wife, and to compel her not to observe

43

without your permission any vows or purposes of prayer, fasts, abstinences or pilgrimages ..."[23]

Poor Catherine began to look less and less like a future queen of England. Louis XII of France offered Margaret of Angoulême, the Dauphin's sister, as a future wife for the Prince. Philip the Handsome offered his daughter Eleanor but Henry VII held up the Prince's marriage for political reasons. This had a major effect on Henry – his later marriages, except one, were for personal desire rather than for political advantage. When Henry fell in love, he wished to form an immediate relationship; any suggestion that he couldn't or shouldn't took him back to the time of his subjection under the orders of his father and would be ruthlessly denied.

Henry VII set about cutting down the size of Catherine's establishment while she languished in political limbo. In December 1505 Catherine was invited to Court for Christmas. The King then closed her household at Durham House and told her that henceforward she would live at Westminster with a handful of servants (five ladies, a master of the hall, treasurer and physician), completely at his financial mercy. She was given a small suite of rooms as far away from Prince Henry as possible; he only saw her at church and when she was invited to join formal occasions. Her father, Ferdinand, sent her occasional gifts, but he expected her to use her tenuous position at court to work on his behalf.

It is sometimes amazing how badly parents can misjudge their children. The King had promised Henry that he would marry Catherine, then told him, no. Catherine was still there at Court; not only regal, young and lovely, but also living in fear and poverty because of his father. The situation could not fail to arouse in Prince Henry every emotion from sexual interest and a chivalric desire to rescue her, to an impotent pity that he could not do so, and a resultant despising of his father and hatred of his own powerless situation.

Despite his confined existence at his father's Court, Henry was developing into a remarkable young man. By the time he was 16,

Henry was described as extremely handsome, over six foot tall and well muscled. However, the King still treated his son and heir like a child, refusing him a separate household and doling out pocket money to him. These humiliations would never be forgotten; King Henry VIII would never allow anyone, by his estimation, to demean or belittle him in any way.

In 1508, aged 17, Henry began appearing in tourneys and jousts himself. He was magnificent and the people loved him, courtiers and commoners alike. He was not praised merely because he was the King's son; it would have been almost impossible for him to survive in the jousting field unscathed if he had not had the strength, skill and judgement to do well. He truly was a remarkable athlete.

There were no reported rumours about any sexual liaisons before Prince Henry's marriage; however, he was a healthy, handsome young man and Westminster was a big palace; Henry VII could not have watched his son all the time. When Henry VIII was married to Anne Boleyn, there was a vicious and certainly unfounded rumour that he had had affairs with Anne, her sister Mary, and their mother, Elizabeth Boleyn, who had been one of his own mother's ladies! Henry's response was, 'Never with the mother', although if she had been one of those ladies, young and lovely, it had at least been a viable possibility.[24]

In the last years of his reign Henry VII suffered from ill health, as did his aging mother. The Prince must have chafed under their control. In March 1508 the second half of Catherine's dowry arrived in England and there was no reason now why the marriage should not take place within a few months, as previously agreed. However, in 1509, as Henry became ill, plans for the Prince's marriage were proceeding, but with little mention of Catherine. The two foremost contenders were Margaret of Angoulême and Catherine's niece, Eleanor.

In April 1508 the King finally realised that Ferdinand had no intention of allowing him to marry Joanna and that the negotiations carried out through Catherine (all based on her father's lies) had been designed to gain advantage for her own marriage. Catherine suffered as a result; she was excluded from the May festivities in 1508. Her accommodation was moved at Easter to rooms over the stables. Her food was sometimes inedible and was enlivened only by occasional gifts from her friends. Her clothes were threadbare , her servants' worse, and she was forced to sell the plate and jewels that had originally formed part of her dowry as a means to survive.

This enabled Henry VII to now hold up the marriage on the grounds that Catherine's jewels and plate had been used or sold, and so their equivalent in coin must be provided to complete the dowry. He still thought he could force Ferdinand into letting him marry Joanna, and he wanted the marriage between Philip and Joanna's son, Charles, and his daughter, Mary, ratified; he was also enthusiastic about Henry marrying Charles's sister, Eleanor.

Despite all the talk of marriage, Henry VII ended his life without female company. His mother was a virtual recluse at the end, his eldest daughter was in Scotland, and his son's fiancée was living in poverty, ignored and shunned. Only his youngest daughter brought pleasure into his life – Princess Mary was a darling.

In 1509 Henry VII's health began to fail and he was too ill to attend the Easter services. Before his death, Henry VII's councillors, William Warham (Archbishop of Canterbury), John Fisher (Bishop of Rochester) and Richard Fox (Bishop of Winchester), asked him for his last wishes. They reported to Fuensalida that Henry VII had stated that he wanted his son to be free to choose a wife for himself. The Prince, however, said that his father told him to marry Catherine.

Henry VII died on Saturday, 21 April 1509 at Richmond. His mother was his chief executrix and the head of the council arranging his burial. After the King died, Margaret moved from Richmond to the Tower to be with her grandson before his coronation. At the funeral, on 11 May 1508, Margaret Beaufort was given precedence over her granddaughter, Princess Mary, and Catherine, the Dowager Princess of Wales and future Queen.

Within a week the new King's councillors were badgering Fuensalida to get the marriage with Catherine under way. Fox told him: 'You must remember now that the King is King and not Prince. One must speak in a different way in this matter than when he was Prince.'[25] The last money payment came remarkably quickly. Henry VIII wanted Catherine of Aragon, he wanted a Habsburg alliance against France, and he wanted a war.

On 11 June 1509 Henry VIII and Catherine of Aragon were finally married at Greenwich, to both personal and public rejoicing. On 23 June Margaret Beaufort watched the formal public marriage procession of Henry VIII and Catherine from a room in a house in Cheapside, hired for her by her grandson. Her granddaughter, Mary, kept her company. Margaret attended the celebrations, but soon became ill. She died on 29 June, in Cheyneygates, the abbot's lodging of Westminster Abbey. Her body was moved to the Abbey refectory on 3 July and finally buried in the Lady Chapel close to her beloved son.

Henry VIII was free at last.

THE HOUSES OF CASTILE AND ARAGON

The House of Castile

The House of Aragon

Henry III (1379–1406)
=
Catherine of Lancaster, daughter of John of Gaunt

Ferdinand I (1380 –1416), King of Aragon & Sicily
=
Eleanor of Albuquerque

John II (1405–54), King of Castile
=
Isabella daughter of John, Duke of Beja

John II (1397–1479), King of Aragon & Navarre
1) Blanche of Navarre 2) Joanna Henriquez

Isabella (1451–1504), Queen of Castile = Ferdinand II (1452–1516), King of Aragon

◆ mistress of Henry VIII
+ illegitimate child of Henry VIII
= married

Isabella (1470–98)
=
1) Alphonso, Prince of Portugal
2) Emanuel King of Portugal

Mary (1482–1518)
=
Emanuel, King of Portugal

John (1478–97)
=
Margaret of Austria

Joanna (1479–1555)
=
Philip the Handsome, Duke of Burgundy

Catherine (1485–1536)
=
Henry VIII, King of England

Mary I

Isabella of Portugal = Charles V (1500–58)

Eleanor (1498–1558)
=
1) Manuel I of Portugal
2) Francis I, King of France

Isabella (1501–26)
=
Christian II, King of Denmark

Ferdinand I (1503–34) Holy Roman Emperor
=
Anna of Bohemia & Hungary

Mary (1505–58)
=
Louis II, King of Hungary & Bohemia

Catherine (1507–78)
=
John III, King of Portugal

Mary
=
Maximilian II, Holy Roman Emperor

Joan
=
John, Crown Prince of Portugal

Philip II
=
Mary I, Queen of England

2

The First Encounter

—⟨⟨⟩⟩—

There is no concrete evidence of any sexual liaisons for Henry while he was Prince of Wales. However, he was a robust and lusty youth, surrounded by temptation in the form of sexually active friends and ladies of the Court who would have been only too pleased and proud to provide him with sexual amusement. An affair with a royal prince was not disgraceful, and could lead to prosperity for a noble family. The lady might expect to receive favours, both financial and in property, an arranged marriage with a substantial dowry if she was single, and there could be positions at Court for her family. If a royal mistress had a son, the child could expect an earldom and possibly a dukedom, with a chance that either he or his descendents would inherit the throne. There was an obvious historical precedent – Henry VIII himself was descended from John Beaufort, the bastard son of John of Gaunt by his mistress Catherine Swynford. Several powerful and wealthy noble families could trace their descent from the bastards of Henry I and his grandson Henry II.

Henry VII and Margaret Beaufort took care of every aspect of Prince Henry's life but however much a father may try to protect his son, love will always find a way. Henry was a tall, strong, handsome boy, and children were expected to mature at an earlier age at a time when the average life expectancy was only about 35. As an exceedingly good-looking young man and the future King of England, he would have been of considerable interest to the young ladies of the Court. It would have been sensible to allow him a mistress who would provide him with love and sex, but who could be guaranteed not to meddle in official Court business, demand unreasonable favours for herself and her family, or to entangle the emotions of the Prince too deeply. Elizabeth Denton, a lovely, experienced, loyal lady, was perfect.

Amongst the first business conducted early in Henry VIII's reign were items that strongly indicate this lady as his first love. Two entries in the Court records state:

'Elizabeth Denton, to have, for life, an annuity of £50, Greenwich, 21 June, [year] 1 Hen VIII';

'Elizabeth Denton, to be, for life, keeper of the King's place called Coldeharbrough, within the City of London, 3 July, [year] 1 Hen VIII'.[1]

Flemish artist Antonis van den Wyngaerde's view of London, the first panoramic map of mid-Tudor London dated 1540, shows the house known as 'Cold Harbour' to the left of London Bridge. The Tudor Coldharbour stood on the waterfront and a panorama dated c.1550 shows it in front of the tower of the Church of All Hallows the Great.[2] In 1483, Richard III granted Coldharbour to the Heralds and Pursuivants at Arms as its headquarters. Henry VII, however, took it back, and gave it to his mother for the duration of her lifetime. On Margaret's death in July 1509, Henry VIII gave the lease to the Bishop of Durham, Cuthbert Tunstal. Later Henry gave it to George Talbot, Earl of Shrewsbury.[3]

Margaret Beaufort spent most of her time at her house at Collyweston in Northamptonshire; however, she needed a London house and she kept Coldharbour. In 1501, Margaret received Catherine of Aragon there on her arrival from Spain for her marriage to Prince Arthur. Yet when Henry became King one of his first actions was to make a generous annuity to Elizabeth Denton, one of his servants, and, after his grandmother's death, to give a right of tenancy of her principal London residence to that same lady.

So who was Elizabeth Denton? She was one of Elizabeth of York's ladies at Court, listed on the payroll, and she also carried out at least one task for the Queen that entered the royal records in January 1503: 'Item to Mistress Denton for money by her paid to John Hayward skinner for furring of a gown of crimson velvet for the Queen of Scotts [Princess Margaret, Henry's sister] … 14s'.

The annual wage bill for Queen Elizabeth's ladies ran as follows: 'My Lady Katherine, hir pencon', for a year and a quarter £62 10s; 'My Lord Howard for the diettes of my Lady Anne' for a year £120; 'My Lady Bridget' £65 8d. Sisters of the Queen, Katherine was married to William Courtney, Earl of Devon; Anne had married Thomas Howard, Earl of Surrey (later 3rd Duke of Norfolk); and Bridget became a nun.

Apart from these three women, the highest reimbursement went to 'Lady Elizabeth Stafford', at £33 6s 8d. Next were 'Mistress Elizabeth Denton' and 'Lady Alyanor Verney', at £20 each. 'Mistress Anne Crowmer' and 'Mistress Mary Ratcliffe' received £10, as did 'Alice Massy the Queenes mydwif'. Seven ladies received £6 13s 4d, presumably the standard wage for a lady-in-waiting. William Denton, carver to the Queen, received a wage of £26 13s 4d.[4]

The one certain thing about Elizabeth Denton is that she was a beauty, as were all the ladies who waited upon the Queen, it seems. An ambassador, visiting Elizabeth of York, recorded that she was attended by 32 'companions of angelical appearance'.[5]

The Dentons appear to have had close connections with Margaret Beaufort. Elizabeth was not the only Denton serving in her household. Apart from William, the carver, James Denton, a lawyer was 'retained as "my lady's scholar at Orleans" by Lady Margaret in connection with her suit to recover money from the King of France in 1502.'[6] James was a graduate of the Universities of Valence and Cambridge. He became a royal chaplain before taking up a post as almoner (distributor of charitable alms) to Henry's sister, Princess Mary, when she went to France to marry Louis XII. In 1520, he was Canon at Windsor Castle and responsible for building works in the Lower Ward next

51

to St George's Chapel. By 1522, James had been elected Dean at Lichfield Cathedral, an unusual appointment as Denton was a lawyer and diplomat and neither a churchman nor theologian.[7]

Elizabeth Denton must have been a highly trusted servant. She replaced Elizabeth Darcy, Lady Mistress of the Royal Nursery under Edward IV and Henry VII, who, by 1497, had either retired or died.[8] By 1500, she was governess to the infant Princess Mary; later she was one of the entourage who went to Scotland with Princess Margaret in 1503 for her marriage (she received her wages in Scotland on 22 May 1505), and returned when James IV began reducing the number of English ladies in his new wife's household. It is obvious that the Tudors, especially Margaret Beaufort, placed enormous dependence on this lady and her family.

Elizabeth appears as a character in a novel by Michael Glenne, *King Harry's Sister*, which was published in 1952. A mixture of history and fantasy, he represents Elizabeth Denton as a malicious, scheming woman:

> 'Margaret's governess was a curious creature, ever derogating King James and his nobles and all things Scottish, eager to report fancied slights and discourtesies towards the Queen, partly to ingratiate herself more firmly with her mistress, and partly because her unwholesome spirit liked trouble-making for its own sake. Now she hurried up to Margaret licking her thin lips in anticipation of the reception her news would have, her black eyes gleaming balefully ...'

Sadly, Glenne gives no sources for his pen portrait of Elizabeth. It may be that he had some evidence for his version of her character, or it may be that he needed a meddling, spiteful character to support the plotline of Margaret as a spoiled brat, at odds with her doting husband, and chose Elizabeth because she was a real person who served in close proximity to the young

Queen. What he does is give us a physical picture of a lady with black hair, dark eyes, pale skin and thin lips. Had he at least seen a portrait of her?

Henry VIII's rewards to Elizabeth Denton were made within weeks of his ascending the throne. While he would want to reward loyal family servants, there must have been many people who had served his family and who deserved to be rewarded. One conclusion could be that Elizabeth had provided a service to Henry that was not set down in the Court records. Given that she had been a loyal servant to Margaret Beaufort, it might make sense that, to make sure that there were no unwanted complications, Henry's grandmother selected the lady for his first lovemaking experience.

Whether she was Henry's choice or chosen by those who had his best interests at heart, whoever made the decision had the good sense to choose a married lady as his first sexual conquest, one who was experienced and discreet.

In the Blackfriars church of St Anne on Lombard Street, a lady named Elizabeth Denton is buried. Her will, dated 26 April 1518, leaves a generous bequest: '... To the intent that the same Prior, &c. shall pray for the Soul of my late Husband, my Soul, and all Christen Souls ...'[9] The church was eminently suitable for the final resting place of a high-ranking court lady. Several minor members of the Royal Family were buried at St Anne's, as well as a number of people from notable noble families.

THE HOUSE OF STAFFORD, DUKES OF BUCKINGHAM

Edward Stafford (1378–1403), Earl of Stafford = Anne of Gloucester, daughter of Thomas of Woodstock, son of Edward III

Anne Stafford (1408–32)
=
1) Edmund Mortimer, Earl of March 2) John Holland, Duke of Exeter

Humphrey Stafford (1402–60), Duke of Buckingham
=
Anne, daughter of Ralph Neville, Earl of Westmorland & Joan Beaufort

Humphrey Stafford (?–1455)
Earl of Stafford
=
Margaret, daughter of Edmund Beaufort,
Duke of Somerset & Eleanor Beauchamp

Henry

Edward

George

William
Earl of Wiltshire
=
Constance Green

John,
=
John Talbot,
Earl of Shrewsbury

Catherine
=
1) William Beaumont
2) William Knyvett

Joan
=
1) Aubrey de Vere
2) Thomas Brooke,
Baron Cobham

Anne
=
Robert Dunham

Margaret

Henry Stafford (1455–83), 2nd Duke of Buckingham
=
Catherine Woodville

Edward (1478–1521) Duke of Buckingham
=
Alianore Percy

Elizabeth
=
Robert Radcliffe, Earl of Sussex

Henry (1479–1523),
Earl of Wiltshire

◆ Anne Hastings
=
1) Sir Walter Herbert 2) George Hastings, Earl of Huntingdon

Henry Strafford (1501–63)
=
Ursula, daughter of Margaret Pole,
Countess of Salisbury

Elizabeth (1494–1558)
=
Thomas Howard, Duke of Norfolk

Catherine
=
Ralph Neville, Earl of Westmorland

Mary
=
George Neville, Baron Bergavenny

◆ mistress of Henry VIII
+ illegitimate child of Henry VIII
= married

3

The Longed-for Wife
and the Maids of Dishonour

—◈◈◈—

I t was not until the death of Henry VII in 1509 that Henry VIII was able to marry. Just why Henry chose to marry Catherine of Aragon is open to much speculation. Years later, Edward Hall (c.1498–1547), historian and lawyer, explaining why Henry had married his first wife, wrote: 'The king was moved by some of his Council that it should be honourable and profitable to his realm to take to wife the lady Katherine [sic], late wife to Prince Arthur his brother deceased, lest she, having so great a dowry, might marry out of the realm, which would be unprofitable to him …'[1]

Finances had little or nothing to do with it, however. Henry was simply in love with Catherine. She was, by all accounts, a most lovable person, and he had had time to get to know her and appreciate her finer points. They had also both suffered emotionally because of Henry VII, and this forged yet another link between them. Some scholars suggest other reasons for the marriage which include Henry's jealousy of Arthur, and a desire to prove he was better in everything; the idea that Henry VIII wanted what his father had told him he could not have (Henry even went as far as to say that his marriage was in response to a deathbed request by his father, which was almost certainly untrue); and that marriage with Catherine gave Henry a Spanish alliance against France, the traditional enemy of England.

On his ascension, Henry VIII quickly seized the reigns of power, ordering the arrest of his father's unpopular ministers, Sir Richard Empson and Sir Edmund Dudley (who had advised the late King on ways of increasing taxation), and set about spending the contents of the carefully guarded royal treasury. Marriage to Catherine demonstrated to everyone that Henry was his own man, and not bound by the decisions of his predecessor. It also placed him at the centre of European politics, allied by marriage to Spain and the Holy Roman Empire, both allies against Henry's chosen enemy, France.

When Henry VIII came to the throne, he had a stable kingdom, a considerable personal fortune, a significant place in European politics and such personal qualities as youth, health and beauty in his favour. Pietro Pasqualigo, the Venetian Ambassador, wrote in 1510:

> 'His Majesty is the handsomest potentate I ever set eyes on; above the usual height, with an extremely fine calf to his leg, his complexion fair and bright, with auburn hair combed straight and short in the French fashion, and a round face so very beautiful that it would become a pretty woman, his throat being rather long and thick. He plays well on the lute and harpsichord, sings from book at sight, draws the bow with greater strength than any man in England and jousts marvellously.'[2]

On 11 June 1509, the royal marriage between Henry and Catherine was solemnised with church services at Greenwich (south London), and a series of jousts and pageants, the nature of which had not been seen before. Catherine was the Queen of Love, and Henry, her devoted knight. Embroidered and appliquéd Hs and Ks (for 'Katheryn'), and the emblems of Henry's Tudor rose and Catherine's personal symbol, the pomegranate, were hung around Greenwich. Other Court decorations included castles for Castile, and bundles of arrows for Aragon.

Despite Catherine being a virgin (according to her testimony), they seem to have found considerable physical pleasure in each other from the outset. The choosing of a royal wife was often seen as a diplomatic, logical matter of choosing a woman of royal blood, who came from a prolific family, and whose marriage alliance would be of the greatest good for the country. However, both Henry VII and Henry VIII demanded more than an historic bloodline and broad hips in their queens.

Henry had no fear that Catherine would not please him. She was pretty, intelligent and elegant – every inch a queen. She was Henry's match intellectually and shared his interests, was delighted to ride with her husband and also go hawking. They could talk about politics, literature, religion, and the joys and stresses of royalty. She enjoyed the lavish shows that Henry put on. She was his lover, friend and councillor. He could place complete faith in her. Indeed, while Henry was campaigning in France in 1513, Catherine acted as Regent in England, and ordered the campaign that repulsed an attack by the Scots on the northern border. Catherine's only real fault as queen was her inability to give birth to a healthy prince, and in the end that was enough to lose her the faithfulness of the King.

Henry himself, was much admired and continued to receive plaudits. In 1519, Sebastian Giustinian, the Venetian Ambassador, wrote of Henry:

> 'He is much handsomer than any other sovereign in Christendom, a great deal handsomer than the King of France; very fair and his whole frame admirably proportioned ... He is very accomplished, a good musician, composes well, is a most capital horseman, a fine jouster, speaks good French, Latin and Spanish, is very religious ...'[3]

Henry was very attractive to women and he soon succumbed to temptation.

ANNE HASTINGS

Henry's first mistress after he became king, Anne Hastings, might have been a passing fancy but she was a member of a most noble family, the Staffords, with connections to the new Queen.

Edward Stafford, Duke of Buckingham, had been a friend to Catherine of Aragon from the time of her arrival in England and had sent her fruit and game during her widowhood when Henry VII had kept her short of money. He was favoured by Charles V, the Holy Roman Emperor, Catherine's nephew. Buckingham was one of the country's leading nobles, and a possible candidate for the throne (should Henry die childless) through his legitimate Plantagenet connections. Buckingham had royal blood – perhaps more than Henry Tudor. Buckingham's grandfather, Humphrey, the 1st Duke, was the son of Anne, daughter of Thomas of Woodstock, youngest son of Edward III, all by direct lawful descent.

Buckingham was a contemporary of Arthur rather than Henry, as he was 13 years old when Henry was born, and the two never really became friends. Buckingham became Lord High Steward for Henry VIII's coronation, then Lord High Constable and a Privy Councillor. In 1513 he was with Henry's army in France, and on 13 August 1514 he was one of the nobles who attended Henry VIII and Princess Mary at her marriage with Louis XII of France. Much of this, however, was expected of a nobleman of his rank and he was not a member of Henry's inner circle.

Buckingham's relationship with the King was also strained by his marriage to Alianore, daughter of Henry Percy, 4th Earl of Northumberland, who also had royal connections. Their son, Henry Stafford, married the daughter of Margaret Pole, Countess of Salisbury, the King's cousin. It must have seemed to Henry VIII that the Staffords were allying themselves with other powerful noble families who could also potentially make a claim on the throne.

To make matters worse, Buckingham was an arrogant and quarrelsome man, convinced of his own superiority. His power lay in his wealth, inherited position and his presence at Court. He used the law, his wealth and position to achieve his ends and to do whatever he wanted. Buckingham made it very clear that he resented the number of lesser-born councillors who were close to the King. He disliked Thomas Wolsey particularly, but was not clever enough to mask his dislike. It was reported that Buckingham spoke out against both Wolsey and the King himself.

He is supposed to have said that Henry 'would give his fees, offices and rewards, rather to boys than to noblemen.'[4] This was a sly, derogatory reference to the number of relatively humble young men who were close to the King, such as Charles Brandon and Sir William Compton, someone who Buckingham particularly loathed. Henry tended to listen to and take advice from whoever was closest to him at the time, rather than listening to several opinions and making a reasoned decision. He also liked advisers who shared his enthusiasms – if they could joust, hunt, write music and poetry, play or sing, dance, dispute philosophy or theology, they were more likely to be close enough to make their views known and to influence Henry. Once Henry had made his mind up, right or wrong, he rarely changed it.

Henry's brief affair with Anne Hastings, one of the Duke's married sisters, while Catherine was pregnant with her 'honeymoon' baby (a premature, stillborn girl) gave Buckingham another reason to be angry with the King. Catherine's pregnancy was a cause for rejoicing, but it also meant that Henry was excluded from Catherine's bed. Henry's eye started to roam, and where better to find some female company than amongst his wife's ladies? It was a pattern that was to be repeated throughout Henry's life. He rarely had to go looking for female companionship when such a number of agreeable, beautiful and talented women were so close at hand.

Catherine had a large household, but her ladies-in-waiting only numbered eight. They formed the most important group, closest to the Queen. At the start of Catherine's reign, these ladies included:

Elizabeth Stafford, sister of the Duke of Buckingham, recently married to Robert Radcliffe, Lord Fitzwalter (later Earl of Sussex);

Anne Stafford, sister of the Duke of Buckingham, a widow, recently married to Sir George Hastings, heir to the Earl of Huntingdon;

Margaret Scrope, wife of Edmund de la Pole, Earl of Suffolk, in the Tower since 1506 because of his Yorkist connection (the Earl of Suffolk was executed 1513);

Elizabeth Scrope, second wife of John de Vere, Earl of Oxford, Lord Admiral*;

Agnes Tilney, Countess of Surrey, married to Thomas Howard, Earl of Surrey (later Duke of Norfolk), Treasurer*;

Anne Hastings, daughter of Sir William Hastings, married to George Talbot, Earl of Shrewsbury, Lord Steward*;

Mary Say, Lady Essex, married to Henry Bourchier, Earl of Essex, Captain of the Gentlemen Pensioners*;

Anne, sister of Sir George Hastings, married to Thomas Stanley, Earl of Derby.

*Senior Court Officials

The next rank of ladies were the maids of honour, chief amongst whom was Dona Maria de Salinas, one of Catherine's Spanish ladies. It was said that Catherine loved her 'more than any other mortal.'[5] This lady married a widower, William, Lord Willoughby d'Eresby, Master of the Royal Hart Hounds, in June 1516. She remained loyal to Catherine throughout her painful widowhood, and was with her at Kimbolton Castle, in Huntingdon, when she died. Lady Elizabeth Boleyn was another maid of honour; the daughter of the Earl of Surrey (later Duke of Norfolk), Elizabeth was married to Sir Thomas Boleyn of Hever. She was the mother of a son and two daughters, George, Mary and Anne. These ladies formed the immediate household of the Queen. Their charms and talents showed off the Court to advantage and one of their main roles was to entertain the Queen in the performing arts and with conversation, amusing her and enlivening her day.

As the Queen's lady-in-waiting, Anne (Stafford) Hastings, a noble, young and beautiful matron, formed a part of the King's immediate circle. She was already engaged in an affair with Sir William Compton (the King's friend and Groom of the Stole or Stool) when Henry, having been largely kept away from sexual temptation by his father, sought her affections. If the gossip at the time was correct, Anne transferred her affections from Compton to the King.

Things became more complicated, however, when gossip began to spread about Anne Hastings, Sir William Compton and Henry. The banker Francesco Grimaldi related the story to the Spanish Ambassador, Luiz Caroz, who promptly reported it to Catherine's father, Ferdinand of Aragon. He said that Henry's 'butler, Conton' (Compton) acted as a go-between for the King and his mistress.

Anne Hastings allegedly told her sister Elizabeth about her affair with Compton – and then with Henry. Elizabeth, in turn, told her own husband, Anne's husband and her brother. Buckingham, not unsurprisingly, saw this as a blow to the honour of the noble Staffords. He was also enraged by the fact that the affair was common knowledge: Luiz Caroz didn't just keep this gossip for the diplomatic channels; he wrote to the Duke of Almazan in Spain on 28 May 1510, and gave him all the salacious details. His primary source was Grimaldi, whose own informant was Francesca de Carceres, a former lady-in-waiting. Tired of attending a dowager princess who seemed to be doomed to live in poverty for years, and denied a chance to return to Spain and marry, Francesca accepted the hand of the elderly but wealthy Grimaldi. Francesca, despite leaving her mistress, remained in contact with the Court so her news was at least credible.

According to Caroz, Buckingham confronted Compton when he found him with Anne in her room. He is reported to have shouted, 'Women of the Stafford family are no game for Comptons, no, nor for Tudors neither.'[6] On hearing this, Henry summoned the Duke, presumably to reprimand him for making such a public outcry. Buckingham and the King had an angry exchange, and Buckingham left the Palace in a temper, refusing to return for several days.[7] The whole affair ended with the disappearance of Anne Hastings from Court, sent by her husband to a convent to reflect on her behaviour.

Henry, in his anger, ordered Catherine to dismiss Elizabeth Stafford from her household, and banished her and her husband, Sir Robert Radcliffe, from Court. Grimaldi reported that the King said that if he had his way, he would banish all gossiping women. The whole affair upset Catherine, and not just because of her husband's infidelity. Elizabeth Stafford was a close friend and she had been sent away for exposing the King's affair. In one blow, Catherine had lost a friend, two ladies-in-waiting – and respect for her husband. Henry and Catherine had their first serious fight as a result. She let the King see how angry and hurt she was, making a bad situation worse – Henry could never bear to be told that he was in the wrong.

Buckingham should have been more careful. He had made an enemy in the King, which would later prove to be his undoing. In 1520, Wolsey claimed that he had received an anonymous letter accusing Buckingham of treason. In 1521, after an investigation, he was arrested and sent to the Tower. The charges were quite frivolous; they included the testimony that Buckingham had openly said that he would kill the King. Buckingham was not allowed to question witnesses, and it became obvious that the King wanted a guilty verdict, with the sentence of death. Buckingham's crime was, in part, that he had a dynastic claim to the throne at a time when the King was still without a legitimate male heir and the fate of Richard III at the hands of a usurper, Henry VII, was still fresh in everybody's minds. On 17 May 1521, Edward Stafford, 3rd Duke of Buckingham, was executed on Tower Hill.

—⟨∿∿⟩—

On 1 January 1511, a son was born to Henry and Catherine – Henry, Prince of Wales, Duke of Richmond and Somerset. The

19-year-old father was thrilled with his son and heir, and took him to Walsingham, in East Anglia, to give thanks to the Virgin Mary for so great a gift. The baby was immediately given a household of 40 persons, and Henry made gifts to those who had already or in the future would serve his son most closely – £10 to the midwife who attended the Queen, and £30 to his nurse, Elizabeth Poyntz, sister of Henry's great friend, Edward Poyntz. Louis XII of France, and Margaret, Duchess of Savoy were invited to be the baby Henry's godparents.[8]

To celebrate Catherine becoming the mother of the future king of England, a great tournament was held in her honour, and 'The Knights of the Savage Forest' jousted for her pleasure. Sir Valiant Desire, Sir Good Valour and Sir Joyous Thought were joined by a tall and skilful knight who took the title Sir Loyal Heart (*Coeur Loyale*) – none other than Henry himself. Sir Loyal Heart was, of course, victorious, not just because he was the King, but because he was a superb jouster, with excellent skill. According to the 1511 Tournament Roll, held by the College of Arms, the knights were King Henry: *Coeur Loyal* (Sir Loyal Heart); William, Earl of Devonshire: *Bon Vouloir* (Sir Good Valour); Sir Edward Neville: *Vaillant Desyr* (Sir Valiant Desire) and Sir Thomas Knevett: *Bon Espoir/Joyeule Penser* (Sir Joyous Thought).[9]

On one evening of the celebrations a masque was held during which Henry appeared as one of six knights, incognito: they were named Good Courage, Good Hope, Valiant Desire, Good Faith, Loyal Love and, of course, Loyal Heart. They were all dressed in purple, their clothes stiff with gold embroidery, featuring appliqués of the linked initials H and K in solid gold. When the dancing had finished, Henry tried to give the gold initials on his doublet to his fellow dancers. The guests, seeing him apparently giving away these valuable trinkets, fell on the King and his friends tearing their rich clothes off them, stripping them to their shirts and stockings. The King chose to take it as a great joke (thereby earning his nickname of Bluff [jovial] King Hal); when the ladies were

63

threatened with a similar fate, he took Catherine's hand and they adjourned to a happy and noisy party in his private chambers. They must have appeared to be the most fortunate couple in the world.

Sadly, the baby prince, so much desired, lived only a few months, dying in March. Catherine had a further stillborn boy; then in 1513 a living son was born, although he died within a few days. However, Henry and Catherine were young. Infant mortality was very high in Tudor England, but Catherine was fertile and, God willing, she would soon give birth to a healthy son.

ETIONETTE DE LA BAUME

In 1512, Henry organised his first campaign in France, a disastrous invasion of Gascony that ended in retreat. Henry had entered the war in support of his Spanish father-in-law, Ferdinand, supposedly to seize Aquitaine for England (this had been an English province during the time of the early Plantagenets). In fact, Ferdinand only wished to invade Navarre on his own behalf and in the name of his wife; when he had taken Navarre, he pulled out of the campaign. This left Thomas Grey, Marquis of Dorset, to make his best way home, with a sick and resentful English army.

In 1513, however, Henry himself led his army on his first campaign abroad, with slightly more success. Henry invaded France, this time with papal approval. Pope Julius II had been opposed to France since Louis XII had ordered a General Council of the Church in 1511 in direct opposition to the Pope, and now he denied Louis XII's papal title of Most Christian King. The Pope agreed to bestow the title on Henry, if he conquered France. Julius II also gave papal blessing to Henry becoming king of France, providing his army could achieve this.

On 30 June 1513, Henry arrived in Calais to lead an army of 40,000 men. He learned that part of the army was already moving on Thérouanne, in northern France, under the command of the Earl of Shrewsbury. Henry's army spent three days at Arques and on 1 August they marched to Thérouanne. The army moved slowly since Henry had gone to war accompanied by a village of tents, including one made of cloth of gold, a portable wooden palace in easily assembled sections and almost 1,000 personal servants.[10]

After the ill-fated attempt by the French to resupply the besieged Thérouanne on 16 August, known as the Battle of the Spurs (said to have been given this name by the French because the turning point was their numerically superior cavalry turning tail and fleeing, spurring their horses to greater speed), the town capitulated on 23 August.

All of the high-ranking prisoners belonged to the King. Two of the most distinguished captives were the chevalier de Bayard and Louis d'Orléans, duc de Longueville. Bayard, a soldier famous for his skill and his adherence to a knightly code of honour, was sent to visit a number of Flanders towns (to keep him out of the war) for six weeks. The duc de Longueville, on the other hand, was sent to England where he stayed, as a guest of the Court, until the war was over. He lodged for a time in the Tower, chiefly because Catherine of Aragon, who had been told to entertain him, was concentrating on the threat of a Scottish invasion of England, but Longueville was no common prisoner. During his time in England, Louis XII used him as an informal ambassador. It was Longueville who did most of the negotiating, on the King's behalf, for the hand of Princess Mary, Henry's sister. When Longueville eventually returned to France, he wrote a charming letter to Catherine asking to be remembered 'to all his fellows, both men and women.'[11]

After Thérouanne, Emperor Maximilian persuaded Henry to go on to Tournai, a city which lay close to the Low Countries (which he ruled), and which he wanted to add to his territories. Maximilian's daughter, Margaret of Austria, Duchess of Savoy, was Regent of the Low Countries (the Netherlands) for his young grandson, Charles. The Council of Tournai were in a quandary; on one hand, Louis XII was insisting that they held the city for France (even though they had few soldiers and their defences were quite ruined), and on the other hand, Maximilian and Henry were threatening to attack if they did not immediately agree to place themselves under Imperial rule. They tried appealing to Margaret of Austria to act as mediator, but she had no influence with Louis XII, and little, if any, on her father and Henry (who wanted to win a glorious campaign).

On 10 September Maximilian sent in an ambassador – either the city proclaimed for him and became his vassal or it refused, which would be an admission of support for France, and Henry would attack and destroy it as an enemy. Henry and Maximilian stayed with Margaret at Lille, and she joined their conferences, trying to win some kind of compromise for Tournai. However, the negotiations dragged on, and Henry spent his time being entertained by Margaret and her ladies.

Henry was given a magnificent suite of four rooms and on the first night Margaret and her companions joined Henry and his gentlemen for dinner. Afterwards, Henry stripped to his shirt, and he and Margaret danced for hours. The next day he gave her a large and very valuable diamond. Late on the 13th September, Henry finally left to go back to his camp, although he and his followers made a gift of a mass of jewels and jewellery for Margaret and her ladies, in admiration of their entertainment ('banquets, plays, comedies, masques, and other pastimes'[12]).

On 16 September, despite the advice of the richer men of Tournai, the majority decided to declare for France; they displayed the Tournai banner and the fleur-de-lis, and manned the walls. Throughout the 16th and 17th, Henry's guns pounded the virtually defenceless town. On 23 September, after a long bombardment and several days of negotiations, Tournai surrendered to Henry – as King of France!

On 25 September Henry rode into Tournai, heard mass at the cathedral, accepted the allegiance of the defeated people and returned to his camp. On 8 October he held a tournament at which Margaret was the chief guest. After jousting in the pouring rain, a banquet was held and then there was dancing into the night. The Ambassador from Milan tried to talk business with Henry, who fobbed him off, telling him to talk to the Bishop of Winchester instead, 'And so I left his majesty talking with the damsels.'[13]

On 13 October, Henry and the bulk of the army left Tournai; Sir Edward Poynings and 5,000 troops remained behind to garrison the town. The war with France was short-lived, partly because Pope Julius II died in June 1513 and Leo X became Pope. He at once set about making peace with Louis XII, and the papal justification for Henry's presence in France was overturned. In early 1514, Ferdinand of Aragon, then Maximilian, and finally Henry himself, all signed peace treaties with France. As part of the English agreement, Henry got to keep Tournai (which he eventually sold back to the French) and Louis XII married Henry's sister, Mary.

There were rumours that Henry VIII had taken a Flemish mistress while he was campaigning abroad. The time he spent with Margaret and her ladies could mean that one lady in particular became the King's 'companion'. Whereas this might feasibly have been a real love affair, it also kept Henry occupied while Maximilian negotiated for Tournai's surrender. The Milanese Ambassador wrote reports from Lille stating that he had a problem arranging a formal meeting with Henry, 'as he was then in a hurry to go and dine and dance afterwards.' Although the King left to continue the war, he seems to have been reluctant to leave Lille; five days later: '… the King of England came here … and so last night the King was here, passing almost the whole night in dancing with the damsels.'[14] The one firm piece of evidence for an affair is a letter, dated 17 August 1514. It is written in French, and starts with the information that the lady concerned sends a bird and some roots 'of considerable value' to Henry. The reference to roots might seem a trifle odd for a lady to send a king, but Henry had an interest in medicinal plants. The letter then reads on:

'When Madame [Margaret of Austria] went to see the Emperor her father and you at Lille, you named me your

page, and you called me by no other name and you told me many beautiful things ... about marriage and other things, and when we parted at Tournay you told me, when I married, to let you know and it should be worth to me 10,000 crowns, or rather angels. As it has now pleased my father to have me married, I send the bearer, an old servant of my grandfather, to remind you. In your house at Marnoy, near to Besenson [Besançon, eastern France].
Your most very humble servant, G (?) La Baume'.

The French historian, Père Anselme, suggested that the 'G' of the signature could be an 'E'. He linked this to Etionette de la Baume, who married Ferdinand de Neufchatel, seigneur de Marnay, on 18 October 1514.[15]

Etionette was the daughter of Marc de la Baume, seigneur de Chateauvillain and comte de Montrevel. Her husband, Ferdinand, was born somewhere around 1452, so he would have been about 60 at the time of their marriage. He had had two previous wives, Magdalena von Vinstingen (married in 1468) and Claude de Vergy (married in 1497). Although Ferdinand had no son, he did have six daughters born between 1469 and 1500. Each of his first two wives gave him three daughters; Etionette, despite eight years of marriage, did not have any children, so there can be no suggestion that Henry VIII had a child by Mlle de la Baume.[16]

If Etionette caught Henry's fancy, she would have been young, probably in her mid-teens, fair haired, extremely pretty and lively. She would have been an excellent dancer, played a musical instrument, sung like a bird, been well read and a good rider. The fact that she had been the mistress, however briefly, to a king would not have harmed her marriage prospects. As well as her connections to the Imperial Court, she came from a noble family and she also had Henry's monetary wedding gift. Ferdinand de Neufchatel would have found her as charming as the English king had done.

JANE POPINCOURT

Etionette de la Baume is referred to as the King's Flemish Mistress (since Henry met her in Flanders). A second lady, Jane Popincourt, is also given this title, possibly as her family had connections with the Flanders region that covered southern Holland, Belgium and northern France at this time. The title 'Flemish' is a misnomer as, in fact, both were French.

The earliest reference to Jane comes from the Privy Purse Expenses of Elizabeth of York in 1498. At the time of the death of Prince Edmund in 1500, all the courtiers at Eltham, home to the royal children, were provided with black cloth for mourning garments, including Jane Popincourt. In June 1502, Robert Ragdale was hired to make and repair clothes for Elizabeth of York, her daughters Margaret ('the Queen of Scots') and Mary. The sum of 7d was spent on 'mending of two gowns for Johanne Popyncote.'[17] She must have started in the household of Elizabeth of York, but she was attached to the staff of the Princess Mary almost from the time of the Princess's birth in 1496. Jane's main responsibility was to teach her French. In 1509 Jane was still with Mary. Amongst court expenses are 50s paid to 'Jane Popyncote.'[18]

At the Christmas festivities of 1514, a masque was held in which four ladies danced in the character of Ladies of Savoy and four gentlemen as Portuguese. The ladies were Lady Margaret Guildford, Lady Elizabeth Carew, Lady Fellinger and Bessie Blount; the gentlemen included the King, the Earl of Suffolk, Sir Nicholas Carew and Lord Fellinger, who was part of the Imperial diplomatic mission. At this time Bessie Blount became Henry's mistress. She did not appear at the next performance on Twelfth Night, when the dancers represented Dutch citizens. The gentlemen were the same, but the ladies (Guildford, Carew and Fellinger) were joined by Jane Popincourt, who must have been an excellent dancer.[19]

At this point Jane Popincourt was already the mistress of the duc de Longueville. By September 1513, Henry had won the

69

cities of Thérouanne and Tournai and his most prestigious captive, the duc de Longueville, had been brought back to England until a ransom could be negotiated and paid. Longueville was truly a noble captive; his great-grandfather, Jean du Dunois, known as the 'Bastard of Orleans', was the illegitimate half-brother of Charles, duc d'Orléans, the father of Louis XII. Both Charles and Jean were also the grandsons of Charles V of France.

While at the English Court, Longueville took Jane Popincourt as his mistress. His rank, good looks and charm endeared him to the English Court, even to the Spanish Catherine, and his presence in England became particularly useful when Louis XII and Henry VIII decided to cement their alliance through the marriage of Louis to Henry's sister Mary.

This offer of marriage came at an opportune moment. In 1505, 11-year-old Mary had been betrothed to five-year-old Charles, Catherine's nephew, then King of Castile and heir to the throne of Aragon and the Holy Roman Empire. Her marriage had been part of Henry VII's political plan to form an alliance with the Spanish–Imperial faction. Henry VIII maintained this alliance, marrying Catherine and enjoying Imperial support in his French War. As the victory of Thérouanne was celebrated, it was agreed that Charles and Mary should be married by May 1514; by late 1513 Mary was ordering fabric to make gowns for herself and her ladies for their meeting with her promised husband at Calais early the following year. A list of Mary's household officers was drawn up, furniture and plate assembled, and a magnificent wedding outfit ordered.

Politics, however, is an unstable basis for planning such an event. Ferdinand of Aragon suddenly made peace with Louis XII, and then Emperor Ferdinand did the same. Henry was left alone to face France. The new Pope, Leo X, requested that Henry make peace with Louis; grudgingly Henry finally agreed. It seemed that the political scene was also to have an effect on Mary and Charles's marriage; May came and went, and then the wedding was postponed to June due, it was reported, to Charles being ill. It became clear that some of Charles's advisers no longer favoured the English marriage, as Henry and Ferdinand were no longer friends and allies. ('The Council of Flanders answered that they would not receive her [Mary] that year, with many subtle arguments by reason whereof the perfect love between England and the Low Countries was much slaked.')[20] As a result of this cooling in English–Imperial relations, Henry offered Princess Mary's hand in marriage as part of his settlement with Louis XII, who leapt at the offer. Instead of demanding lands and one and a half million gold crowns for ending the war, Henry was prepared to sanction the wedding and settle for a payment of only 100,000 crowns.

In July 1514 at Wanstead, Mary publicly repudiated her marriage with Charles, adding that it was of her own free will. Mary and Charles had been betrothed for six years and the agreed date for the wedding in May had been ignored by this time. Within a month she was promised to Louis and a letter had been sent to the Pope, indicating that all this was the Emperor's fault.

Longueville acted as the French King's representative in the exceptionally swift negotiations. The 52-year-old Louis XII was gaining a young lady of 19 as his wife, one who was generally accepted to be the most beautiful princess in Europe. When the marriage took place on 13 August 1514, Longueville was the proxy for Louis XII. The Archbishop of Canterbury carried out the service and Longueville placed a ring on Mary's finger, after which the party proceeded to High Mass. The religious ceremony complete, there was feasting and dancing before Mary, dressed in her nightgown, was put into bed and Longueville, removing his stocking, laid his naked leg in bed with her, touching hers, thereby symbolically allowing the royal couple to be legally bedded and formalising the marriage.[21]

Longueville's affair with Jane Popincourt lasted until it was time for him to return to France with the bridal party; his ransom had been paid so that he was now free to leave. Jane and Longueville had been giving conversational French lessons to Mary to help her with life at the French Court and Jane would undoubtedly prove immensely useful to the English princess. No one could have foreseen any difficulty with the Princess's servant going with her to France.

The only person who could have put a stop to this plan was the King of France himself. A list of the servants that Mary intended to bring with her was presented to Louis XII for his approval. However, the English Ambassador, the Earl of Worcester, is said to have informed Louis about Jane's reputation and the nature of her relationship with Longueville. Louis XII vetoed Jane coming to France and she was forced to remain in England. Considering the number of noble French families who were founded by royal bastards (including Orléans–Longueville), it might seem unlikely that Louis refused Jane's entry on moral grounds. However, Longueville was his second cousin, and Longueville's wife, Jeanne de Hochberg, mother of his four children (Claude, Louis, Francois and Charlotte) was also a royal kinswoman, the granddaughter of Yolande de Valois, sister of King Louis XI. One suggestion is that the French King was fond of Jeanne and wanted to spare her the anguish of seeing her husband openly living with another woman. It may simply have been that Louis saw the relationship as an insult to the royal family as a whole.

Yet another reason for his decision may be more political. The most notable Popincourts in France were the family of Jean de Popincourt, Premier Président of the Parlement de Paris in 1400 until his death in 1403. Popincourt was a knight, a chevalier, seigneur de Noisy-le-Sec, Liancourt and Sarcelles. His son, Jean II, followed his father to become a magistrate, and his son, Jean III, was an MP in 1455, Procureur General in 1456, Président de Comptes in 1459, Président of the Parlement under Louis XI, and Ambassador to England. He had one daughter, Claudine, who married Jean du Plessis, seigneur de Perrigny in 1463.[22]

As Jane was related to the Ambassador this would have enabled her family to send her to England with his party and for the pretty, lively, charming child to have made an impact on the English Court and been invited to stay as one of the Queen's ladies. In France, however, the family's strong political position meant that it was felt safer to keep her away from the centre of political life in the Royal Court at the Louvre. This fear was probably unfounded as everything suggests that Jane was an uncomplicated young woman, more interested in romances, fashion and shopping than politics. It is far more likely that Louis XII simply disapproved of his cousin's open flaunting of the marriage vows, with a woman whom he felt was unsuitable. Louis XII is reported to have referred to Jane as an immoral woman and to have stated that he would see her burned alive before he would have her anywhere near his new wife, Mary.

Jane, forced to remain in London, put herself under Henry's protection and became, for a brief time, his mistress. The affair was short-lived and probably light-hearted, without deep passion on either side. What is certain is that when Louis XII died on 1 January 1515, Jane made plans to join Longueville immediately and Henry very generously made her a gift of £100. The Court of Louis's successor, Francis I, was altogether more welcoming to Jane and she travelled to Paris with all haste. Once in France, Longueville and Jane resumed their relationship, and she lived with him at the Louvre. She wrote a series of letters to her friend, Princess Mary, full of chat about French fashion, but with nothing about politics. It was a short-lived pleasure: Longueville, died in 1516.

———∽∿∽———

In 1514, Catherine of Aragon had another baby boy, who lived for only a few hours, and later in the same year she suffered a stillbirth of yet another son.

Apart from the dalliances with the Flemish ladies and Anne Hastings, Henry appears to have been faithful to his wife during the first years of their marriage. Catherine was physically attractive, they were both young, and she had given firm evidence of being fertile. Henry himself had been one of seven children, of whom four had survived, and Catherine was one of five children who grew to maturity. They might look forward to a large and healthy family in time.

However, in 1514 the first proper crack appeared in their marriage. Cardinal Wolsey was negotiating the Treaty with France, and one of his ploys was that Henry would divorce his Spanish Queen. This negotiation tactic would not have been taken very seriously, partly because Catherine was pregnant at the time. Still, the suggestion had been voiced and Henry's advisers could see marriage as a possible future bargaining tool in European diplomacy.

In that same year Princess Mary married Louis XII, but after 11 weeks the bridegroom was dead. Remembering her brother's promise that if she married Louis, she would be free to choose her next husband, Mary acted on it before Henry could change his mind. Unwisely, as it turned out, Henry sent his friend Charles Brandon to collect Mary from France. Brandon was Mary's choice as a second husband and they married in France, throwing themselves on Henry's mercy when they got back to England.

Francis I, the new king of France, had actively supported Mary and Brandon in their marriage. Mary had earned his animosity when she had refused his sexual advances, and Francis used the occasion to take revenge. Not only did he encourage Mary, a Princess and Dowager Queen, to marry the son of a poor knight, but he also ensured that Henry VIII had the humiliation of having a commoner for a brother-in-law and lost the power that his sister's marriage prospects would give him in European politics. At least one part of the plan failed; Brandon was Henry VIII's closest friend and while he may not have been happy about the marriage, in time Henry forgave his favourite sister and his dearest friend.

Charles Brandon's love life turned out to be quite as complicated as his friend Henry's would become. As a young man

Brandon had been betrothed to Anne, daughter of Sir Anthony Browne, and before being formally married they had a daughter. However, Brandon then revoked his promise of marriage with Anne and married her aunt, Margaret Mortymer, daughter of the Earl of Northumberland and a wealthy widow. Things did not go as well as hoped and Brandon divorced Margaret after a year, or at least he meant to. He married Anne and had a second daughter. On Anne's death he took up the wardship of Elizabeth Grey and betrothed himself to the little girl; when she grew old enough, however, Elizabeth repudiated the betrothal. This left Brandon free to accept when Princess Mary asked him to marry her. A papal bull was required to sort out the mess of the betrothals and marriages (it turned out the divorce had not been legally completed) to Anne Browne and Margaret Mortymer.

Henry's cronies were a dissolute crowd. Wolsey fathered at least two bastard children. The Duke of Norfolk had a long-term affair with Elizabeth Holland, daughter of his steward. Henry Norris, George Boleyn and others were reputed to be equally lax in their morals. As far as mistresses went, Henry had behaved with considerable restraint and modesty until this point.

THE FAMILY OF ELIZABETH BLOUNT

Sir John Blount of Sodington (?–1423) = Juliana Foulhurst

Sir John Blount of Kinlet = Alice, daughter of Kynard Delabere

Humphrey Blount of Kinlet (?–1477) = Elizabeth, daughter of Robert Winnington

Sir Thomas Blount of Kinlet (c.1456–1525) = Anne, daughter of Sir Richard Croft

Sir John Blount (1484–?) = Katherine, daughter of Sir Hugh Perzhall

Key

◆ mistress of Henry VIII
+ illegitimate child of Henry VIII
= married

Sir George Blount
=
Constance Talbot

Henry Blount
=
Joanna Somerville

◆ **Elizabeth (Bessie) Blount** =
1) Gilbert Lord Tailboys
2) Edward Fiennes, Lord Clinton

Issue

George, Baron Tailboys
=
Margaret Skipwith

Elizabeth Tailboys
=
Thomas Whimbish

Robert, Baron Tailboys

+ **Henry Fitzroy, Duke of Richmond** (1519–36)
=
Mary Howard

Bridget Fiennes
=
Robert Dymoke

Catherine Fiennes
=
William, Lord Burgh

Margaret Fiennes
=
Charles Willoughby

4

The Worldly Jewel and the Plotting Widow

——⟡——

The Court of Henry VIII was graced by two descendents of Robert le Blount, a Norman knight who came over with William the Conqueror: William Blount, 4th Lord Mountjoy, Prince Henry's childhood mentor, and Elizabeth (Bessie) Blount, Henry's mistress and mother of his son. Their common ancestor, Sir John Blount of Sodington (c.1298–1358), was born during the reign of Edward I. He had five sons: William was descended from the second son, Sir John Blount of Sodington, and Bessie from the fourth son, Sir Walter Blount of Barton and Belton.

Bessie Blount's family was socially of modest stock. Her mother was Katherine, daughter and coheiress of Sir Hugh Pershall of Knightly, Staffordshire, who had held a place at Court briefly in 1502 as lady-in-waiting to Catherine of Aragon when she was at Ludlow. Amongst the spouses of Bessie's siblings there were no great titles.

William Blount, Lord Mountjoy, however, came from a family that played a prominent role at Court. After his time as tutor and mentor to the young Prince Henry, Mountjoy was given the post of Catherine of Aragon's Chamberlain and his wife was one of her ladies. It was probably through family influence that Bessie, a distant cousin of Blount, found her place beside them as a lady-in-waiting. She was just the kind of young woman to catch Henry's attention: blonde, beautiful and vivacious. She was a very good singer and dancer and wrote her own music – valuable assets in the service of a musically inclined young king who enjoyed the spectacle of masques in which he and his friends took part. In 1513, when she came to Court, Bessie received a year's wages as a lady-in-waiting of 100s (£5).

Bessie made such an impact on her arrival that the King fell deeply in love with her. Lord Herbert of Cherbury wrote of Bessie that she 'was thought for her rare ornaments of nature and education to be the beauty and mistress-piece of her time.'[1] Henry and Bessie were reported to have fallen in love, or at least declared their affair, at a New Year Party in 1514; certainly her name is on the list of those who took part in the celebrations.

From 1514, Bessie became the King's mistress for about five years. In 1518, her talents were demonstrated when Cardinal Wolsey hosted a banquet in honour of the betrothal of Henry's infant daughter, Princess Mary, to the dauphin of France. One of the performers was Bessie Blount, singing a song she had written, with music by William Cornish, Master of the King's Chapel.

Edward Hall wrote of Henry and Bessie: 'The king in his fresh youth was in the chains of love with a fair damsel, called Elizabeth Blount, daughter of Sir John Blount, knight … she won the king's heart, and she again showed such favour that by him she bore a goodly man-child, of beauty like to the father and mother. This child was well brought up, like a Prince's child.'[2] – the child in question was Henry Fitzroy (the surname means 'son of a king' in French). Bessie gave birth in 1519. Henry and Catherine's daughter, Princess Mary, was three at the time. Bessie went to have her child at a house, given to her by the King, at Blackmore, near Chelmsford in Essex. After Bessie gave birth, Catherine of Aragon visited her to congratulate her whilst Wolsey set about finding her a husband.

According to Philip Morant's *The History and Antiquities of the County of Essex* (1768), Blackmore was reported to have been one of 'Henry VIII's Houses of Pleasure and disguised under the name of Jericho, so that when this lascivious Prince had a mind to be lost in the embraces of his courtesans, the cant word amongst the courtiers was, that he was gone to Jericho.'[3] Morant's conclusions are inaccurate. Henry never kept a brothel and rarely enjoyed more than one physical relationship at a time. In fact, the house in question was Bessie's home. The name of Jericho applied primarily to one hall or building ('a tenement called Jericho'), a relic of the time when Blackmore belonged to a monastery.[4]

Bessie was henceforward known as the 'Mother of the King's Son'. She married Gilbert Tailboys some time around 1519, just after the birth of her son. From then on Bessie and her son were shown considerable respect around the Court, almost as if he were legitimate. After all, a bastard son might just inherit where a legitimate daughter might not.

The marriage between Bessie and Gilbert benefited both parties and they seem to have cohabited quite happily. Gilbert was the son of Sir George Tailboys. In 1509, at the time of the accession of Henry VIII, Sir George was Keeper of Harbottle Castle, and in 1513 he was in France with the King's army. However, in March 1517, Sir George was declared insane, and his person, heir and estates were placed under the guardianship of Cardinal Wolsey. In 1531, Sir George passed into the care of the Duke of Norfolk, and finally died on 21 September 1538.

His son and heir, the young Gilbert, had been taken into the household of Wolsey, and when he agreed to marry Bessie Blount he was given the manor of Rokeby in Warwickshire and land in Yorkshire the following year, as his bride's dowry. He also gained the favour of the King and the Chancellor, as well as a beautiful, agreeable and fertile wife. In March 1527, Gilbert was one of the gentlemen of the King's chamber, and in November 1529 he was given the title of Baron Tailboys of Kyme.

Bessie went on to have three children with Gilbert. Their eldest son, George, became Baron Tailboys on his father's death, but died without an heir in September 1539. The second son, Robert, had predeceased him, also without heirs, and the title now fell to the third child, a daughter, Elizabeth. She took the title of Baroness

Tailboys, with the proviso that the title should pass to her husband as soon as they had produced a child. As it turned out, she married twice, to Thomas Wymbish and later to Ambrose Dudley, Earl of Warwick, but neither marriage produced a child and with her death in 1560, the title of Baron Tailboys became extinct.

—◆◆◆—

Not everyone approved of Wolsey's role in the affair. One of the charges brought against him later, indicating his unfitness to be a Minister of the Crown or a churchman, was, 'We have begun to encourage the young gentlewomen of the realm to be our concubines by the well marrying of Bessie Blount; whom we would yet by sleight, have married much better than she is; and for that purpose changed her name.'[5] At the time, however, Wolsey had pleased the only person who mattered. In June 1525, the Cardinal wrote to Henry, and asked after 'your entirely biloved sonne, the Lord Henry Fitzroy.'[6] The two men, King and Cardinal, could correspond about a base-born son with ease. Wolsey also had a bastard son, Thomas Wynter. The boy was made Dean of Wells, and later Provost of Beverly, Archdeacon of York and Richmond, and Chancellor of Salisbury – all while he was still at school and despite the fact that plurality (the holding of more than one church post) was illegal. It was said that the boy's income was £27,000 a year.

In 1525, when he was six, Fitzroy was awarded his own household at Durham House, in the Strand, London. According to Hall, Wolsey was given the task of setting it up. This year was to become crucial in Fitzroy's life and he now had a London house. Later he was given Baynard's Castle, near St Paul's, possibly one of the greatest houses in London. A prominent member of the household was the boy's nurse, Agnes Partridge, who received 50s a quarter. Fitzroy was that most remarkable of boys, an acknowledged royal bastard. He lived in considerable state, as if he were a prince of the blood. His furniture included a throne and canopy of estate, made of cloth of gold fringed with red silk.

In 1525, Fitzroy was also made Lord Lieutenant of Ireland and Warden of the Cinque Ports, became a Knight of the Garter, and was given the titles of Earl of Nottingham (held by Richard, Duke of York, younger son of Edward IV), Duke of Richmond (held by Henry VII before he became king) and Duke of Somerset (held by the King's great-grandfather). He was thereafter known by his title the Duke of Richmond.

The reason for the sudden influx of titles was political. In this crucial year there was a breakdown in diplomatic relations with Charles V, King of Spain. He had been betrothed to Henry VIII's daughter, Princess Mary, for several years and now he needed a wife and a lot of money quickly. His ministers believed the marriage with Mary would not be finalised for some time and so turned to a more immediate and wealthy bride, Isabella of Portugal. After such a loss of diplomatic face, Henry sought to strike back at Charles through his aunt, Catherine of Aragon.

Richmond had been living quietly, and was now six years old, a fine, sturdy, little Tudor. Within days of the news from Charles, Richmond was brought into the limelight, given significant posts and made an earl and a duke (the highest level of nobility). The titles alone were not enough; Richmond needed estates to support his new position. Later that year Letters Patent, dated 11 August 1525, were issued that awarded Richmond lands and money that had belonged to Edmund Tudor, John Beaufort, Duke of Somerset, and Margaret Beaufort. Most of his holdings were in Lincoln, Somerset and Devon. He was given Colyweston (Margaret Beaufort's house) and Corfe Castle.[7] At this time Richmond was also made Lord Admiral, Keeper of the City and Castle of Carlisle and first Peer in England.

Of course, Catherine complained – through his actions, Henry was as good as nominating Richmond as his successor, passing over their legitimate daughter. In retaliation, Wolsey reorganised her household and dismissed her Spanish women (at least those who were not his spies). When she went to Henry, Wolsey had already told him that these women were the ones who had persuaded her to complain about Richmond in the first place. Henry was adamant that the ladies should return to Spain. He then sent Princess Mary to Ludlow, in the Welsh Marches, ostensibly to begin her duties as Princess of Wales, but in fact to separate mother and daughter, knowing how much it would hurt Catherine. However, some consolation was that the Princess's governess was the Countess of Salisbury, Catherine's old and trusted friend.

Richmond now outranked everyone at court, even Princess Mary. Henry's intention was obvious: to set his bastard son up to succeed him should he fail to have a living male heir.

In time, however, Henry got over his pique and he resumed a life of sorts with Catherine. They read and hunted together, although their sex life had virtually ended. Catherine's last pregnancy had been in 1518 and it was now clear that there would be no others.

It was now decided that Richmond should set up a court of his own. Princess Mary was at Ludlow, so it seemed a logical step to send Richmond north to the border counties. He set out in the early summer and by 26 July 1525 he had reached Stoke Newington, Middlesex, home of William Jekylle. He moved on to stay with Catherine Parr's mother, at Hoddesdon (her brother-in-law was in Richmond's household), then to Buntingford, then Shengay, Cambridgeshire. Richmond reached York on 18 August and, on the 28th, he went on to Sheriff Hutton, Yorkshire, once a principal residence of Richard III. At York, he was joined by his recently appointed secretary, John Uvedale. Richmond stayed mostly at Sheriff Hutton, and sometimes at Pontefract.

When the young Duke travelled, he was attended like a prince. Richmond had his own household officers at Sheriff Hutton; these included Brian Higdon, Dean of York, as his chancellor; Sir William Bulmer as Steward of the Household; Sir Godfrey Engleham, treasurer, and a number of councillors including John Palsgrave, 'schoolmaster'; and Walter Luke, 'general attorney'. Also attending was Sir William Buttes, Henry VIII's personal physician, present to look after Richmond.

The Duke had his servants, and these servants also had servants. From chaplains, ushers, grooms and footmen to carvers and servers; from cooks, bakers, brewers, stablemen and yeomen to an apothecary and the keeper of the garde-robe, the household numbered several hundred people. With such a formidable array of service, the wage bill for the year 1525 came to an astonishing £3,105 9s 8d, including food, clothing, etc. Clothes for the Duke alone cost £88, while £4 10s went on hounds, £3 18s 8d on players and minstrels, and £11 17s 10d for alms to the poor and needy.[8] An inventory of Richmond's wardrobe included: gowns of crimson damask [patterned silk], embroidered all over with gold; black velvet embroidered with a border of Venice gold [real gold thread]; purple satin tinsel [a fabric woven of silk and metallic thread] and a mantle of the garter of purple velvet and the garter wrought with Venice gold.

On 10 October (after reaching Sheriff Hutton), William Frankelyn, the Chancellor of Durham, wrote to Cardinal Wolsey, updating him on the journey:

> 'I assure your Grace my lord of Richmond is a child of excellent wisdom and towardness, and for all his good and quick capacity, retentive memory, virtuous inclinations to all honour, humanity and goodness, I think hard it would be to find any creature living of twice his age able or worthy to be compared to him ... with what gravity and good manner he desired to be recommended unto the King's Highness, the Queen, and your Grace, I doubt not but the said Mr. Almoner [Edward Lee] will advertise your grace at his coming.'[9]

Richmond's tutors were John Palsgrave and Dr Richard Croke, a Greek scholar who taught him Greek and Latin. Thanks to

Croke, Richmond wrote 'in a clear Italian hand', which appears in letters to his father. Croke was also proud of the fact that, at eight, Richmond was translating Caesar's texts unaided. Apparently Henry had promised his son that, as soon as he was able to translate Caesar's *Commentaries*, he should have his first suit of armour.

Bessie also kept in touch with her son. Palsgrave wrote to her that he was 'inclined to all manner of virtuous and honourable inclinations as any babe living.'[10] He went on to report, '... the King's Grace said unto me in the presence of Master Parr [Sir William Parr, Chamberlain] and Master Page [Sir Richard Page, Vice-Chamberlain], "I deliver," quoth he, "Unto you three my worldly jewel ...".'[11]

As Richmond's aunt, Margaret, Queen of Scotland, took a natural interest in the Duke, particularly as he might one day be king of England. A letter from the Queen to Sir Thomas Magnus (surveyor and general receiver of Richmond's estates), dated 25 November 1525, mentions: '... our good nephew the duke of Richmond and Somerset ... We desire you affectionately to have us recommended unto him, as we that shall entertain our dutiful kindness, as natural affection aright towards him, as we that is right glad of his good prosperity, praying the same to continue.'[12] Queen Margaret was determined to put herself and her son, the future James V of Scotland, in Richmond's good graces and, by doing so, to gain her brother Henry's approval as well.

In 1525, the question of a marriage for Henry's only surviving lawful daughter was raised again. Since the Spanish were now no longer Henry's preferred allies, he was looking to France for a new alliance. As part of negotiations, the question of the marriage of Princess Mary was raised. This time, she was to marry Henri, second son of Francis I, and Richmond was to marry one of his daughters. Thus, eventually one of the French King's children would share the English throne, thereby creating an alliance between France and England against Spain. As it was, nothing came of the plan as events were developing in another direction.

Two weeks after the formal betrothal of Princess Mary to Prince Henri, a church court was assembled in London to discuss the question of Henry VIII's divorce from Catherine of Aragon.

In 1526, as the French marriage for Richmond had come to nothing, the situation in Italy caught English attention. On 11 February 1527, Wolsey received a letter from Sir John Russell in Rome, concerning Pope Clement VII's niece, Catherine de Medici. This extremely wealthy heiress had attracted the attention of Monsieur de Vaudemont (the future Duke of Lorraine), who wanted to marry her, as did James V of Scotland and the Duke of Ferrare. '... then I showed Sir Gregory [Casale, Ambassador to Spain] that I thought she should be a mete marriage for my lord of Richmond.' Russell reported that he had not pressed the matter and would not do so without Wolsey's agreement. It was not forthcoming and Russell allowed the matter to drop.[13]

Speculation was rife as to who would be chosen as Richmond's bride. Spain was once more a potential ally, and Sir Richard Lee approached Charles V about his female relatives. The daughters of the Queen of Denmark (Charles's sister), Dorothea and Christina, were mentioned. Princess Maria, the daughter of the Queen of Portugal (another sister) was already promised in marriage, although Wolsey suggested Richmond should marry her and that the couple should be given the Duchy of Milan. Once again, the marriage plans came to nothing. Foreign kings were reluctant to marry their sisters and daughters to a royal bastard while there was still a chance that Henry would have a legitimate son.

In May 1528 the sweating sickness had reached Pontefract. The Council moved Richmond to Ledestone, a priory house near Castleford, with just five servants to reduce the risk of infection, and asked for a physician, just in case. Having received remedies concocted by the King, Richmond wrote to Henry: '... thanks be to God and to your said highness, I have passed this last Summer without any peril or danger of the ragious sweat that has reigned in these parts and other, and much the better I trust with the help of such preservatives as your highness did sent unto me, whereof most humble and most lowly I thank the same.'

On 9 August 1529, aged just 10, Richmond was summoned to attend Parliament as one of the House of Lords. From then on, he would live in London, closer to his father, with a suite of rooms at Windsor usually assigned to the Prince of Wales (Princess Mary was given rooms of lesser magnificence). On 2 December, the new Duke of Northumberland replaced Richmond as Warden of the Northern Marches. However, Richmond did not remain without a major role in government for long. On 22 June 1530 Richmond was made Lord Lieutenant of Ireland, with Sir William Skeffington as his Deputy. It was a courtesy title only; Richmond never visited Ireland.

⟞~ノ/ノ/~⟝

In April 1530, Gilbert Tailboys, Richmond's stepfather, died and was buried at Kyme. In 1532, the widowed Lady Tailboys was approached by Lord Leonard Grey, brother of the Earl of Dorset and later Lord Deputy of Ireland. He wrote to Cromwell: 'Written at Kayme, my lad Taylbusshe house, the 24 day of May, at 12 of the clock at noon … so it is I have been hunting in Lincolnshire, and so came by my lady Taylbusshe homewards, and have had communication with her in the way of marriage, and so I have had very good cheer with her ladyship, ensuring you that I could be better contented to marry with her (God and the king pleased) than with any other lady or gentlewomen living.'[14]

Whereas Lord Leonard Grey was enthusiastic for the match, Lady Tailboys was less so. She may have had her eye on a greater prize. Now Henry VIII was talking about a divorce, why shouldn't he marry his old mistress and legitimise their son? Unfortunately for Bessie, Henry had already fallen in love with Anne Boleyn. Two years later, she married again, to the young and handsome Edward Fiennes Clinton. One of the King's attendants, Clinton was the son of Thomas, Lord Clinton and Saye, and had been made a royal ward when his father died during his minority.

According to the *Dictionary of National Biography*, 'she [Bessie] was old enough to be her boy-husband's mother.' Actually Bessie was in her mid-thirties and her husband Clinton (born in 1512) was 22, hardly a 'boy-husband'. She was already the mother of four children, and with Clinton, Bessie had three daughters: Bridget, who married Robert Dymoke (a cousin of Lord Tailboys); Katherine, who married William, Lord Burgh; and Margaret, who married Charles, Lord Willoughby of Parham.

Clinton went on to forge a formidable career. A charming and talented young man, in 1540 he started in the service of Lord Lisle, the Lord High Admiral, and in 1544 led the fleet supporting an attack on Edinburgh. For his services, he was knighted by Edward Seymour, Earl of Hertford and Duke of Somerset (Jane Seymour's brother and Lord Protector under Edward VI). Between 1547 and 1550, Clinton was governor of Boulogne and in May 1550 he was appointed Lord High Admiral. A year later he became a Knight of the Garter. His skills were recognised so that, although he was deprived of his post during the early years of Queen Mary's reign, he was reappointed and carried on as Lord High Admiral under both Mary I and Elizabeth I.

—◦◦◦—

Henry VIII kept a firm eye on his beloved son, Richmond, moving him between royal palaces so as to always have him near. Between 1530 and 1532 he principally lived at Richmond Palace. His life at Court is beautifully described in a poem written by his dearest friend and brother-in-law, Henry Howard, Earl of Surrey:

> *... As proud Windsor, where I, in lust and joy,*
> *With a king's son my childish years did pass ...*
> *The large green courts, where we were wont to hove,*
> *With eyes cast up unto the maidens' tower,*
> *And easy sighs, such as folk draw in love.*
> *The stately sales; the ladies bright of hue;*

The dances short; long tales of great delight;
With words and looks that tigers could but rue,
Where each of us did plead the other's right ...
The gravelled ground, with sleeves tied on the helm,
On foaming horse, with swords and friendly hearts ...
In active games of nimbleness and strength
Where we did strain, trailed by swarms of youth,
Our tender limbs, that yet shot up in length ...
The wild forest, the clothed holts with green,
With reins availed and swift ybreathed horse,
With cry of hounds and merry blast between,
Where we did chase the fearful hart a force ...[15]

Eustace Chapuys, the Imperial Ambassador (1529–45), wrote that when travelling in the company of the Duke of Norfolk, he had been told that the King himself had selected Surrey as Richmond's 'preceptor and tutor ... so that a friendship thus cemented promises to be very strong and fair.'[16] Thus, Surrey was to be Richmond's mentor as Mountjoy had been the King's. The young men hunted deer and played tennis, but mostly turned their attentions to the young ladies of the Court. In the evenings there was dancing and the young men pleaded each other's case to the giggling girls. Marriages would be arranged, but it was no sin for a young lady of the gentry or the minor nobility to become the mistress of a Royal Duke, like Richmond, or the heir to the country's premier dukedom, like Surrey. If Richmond should become king, and Surrey, then Duke of Norfolk, should be his closest friend and adviser, a mistress of either might expect to do very well out of any liaison. It was common for members of the nobility to break the rules and indulge in love affairs outside matrimony.

One fascinating reference is to the tennis matches: it was the fashion for the ladies to watch from an upper gallery when observing a game of tennis. However, a young lady could slip downstairs and hide behind the barriers that lined the court. Thus the young man would 'lose' his ball and be obliged to go and look for it behind those selfsame barriers.

Henry VIII had chosen well for his son's mentor. The King had an affection for the young Earl of Surrey who was seen as an ornament to the Court, growing into a soldier and poet. Surrey and Richmond lived together at the palace as closest friends. After Richmond's death Surrey was arrested for striking a man in Hampton Park who had cast doubts on Surrey's loyalty. However, the King reduced his sentence to a period of confinement at Windsor during which he wrote a number of poems including one as a testament to his love for his friend.

In autumn 1532, Henry went over to France to meet with Francis I, accompanied by a vast retinue, including Richmond. The *Chronicles of Calais* recorded the event: 'The 11 day of October, Henry the Eighth, king of England, landed at Calais, with the Duke of Richmond, his bastard son ...'[17] Richmond remained there and by 25 October Henry VIII and Francis I were returning from their meeting at Boulogne, when 'without the town [Calais] about the distance of two miles, the Duke of Richmond, the king's base son, with a great company of noblemen which had not been at Boulogne, met them, and saluting the French king, embraced him in a most honourable and courteous manner.'[18]

Henry had brought Anne Boleyn with him as his consort on this state visit, not Catherine of Aragon. As a result, neither Francis I's wife, Eleanore, nor his sister, Marguerite, attended. Francis's hostess on this occasion was his mistress, Anne de Pisseleu d'Heilly, duchess d'Étampes. It was an odd royal visit for the King of England, to bring his mistress and bastard child, and leave his wife and daughter at home.

When Henry VIII and his retinue returned to England, Richmond and Surrey stayed on in France. The French King was pleased to entertain such a promising youth, and Richmond and his followers were proud and pleased to be feted by the French Court. Richmond enjoyed the company of the dauphin Francois and his brother, Henri d'Orléans, as well as their sisters. They hunted, played tennis, gambled and, if rumour is to be believed, behaved like teenage hooligans, riding the streets at night, beating people up and raising riot.

Everyone seemed keen to praise the Duke. There is, however, one dissenting voice that shows Richmond in a different light. A poem–history of the life of Sir Nicholas Throckmorton (a younger son with no hope of inheritance), included the following description of his life as a page to a temperamental young man, during his time at the French Court:

> *A brother, fourth, and far from hope of land,*
> *By parents' hest, I served as a page*
> *To Richmond's duke, and waited still at hand,*
> *For fear of blows that happen'd in his rage.*
> *In France with him I lived most carelessly,*
> *And learned the tongue, though nothing readily* ...[19]

On 26 November 1533 a papal dispensation was sought in order that Richmond might marry 'Lady Mary.' It has been suggested that this dispensation had been requested so that Richmond could marry his half-sister, Princess Mary, daughter of Catherine of Aragon. In fact, it refers to his proposed marriage to Mary Howard, daughter of the Duke of Norfolk. A dispensation was necessary because Henry VIII had married Norfolk's niece, Anne Boleyn, which meant that Mary Howard and Richmond were now more closely related.[20]

Richmond began to participate more in Court life. On 20 January 1534, he attended a Chapter of the Garter to elect James V of Scotland to a vacant place and in May he represented his father at the head of the Garter procession. Between 15 January and 30 March, Richmond attended Parliament on 32 of the 45 days that it was in session. However, between 12 June and 18 July 1536, he was absent, most probably ill.

Richmond was also interesting himself in his estates with increasing confidence. He wrote to Cromwell on 13 June 1535, a petition carried by William Byttilcome: '… being burgesse of the parliament of my said town … I and Sir Giles Strangeways with other of my council have seen and viewed a certain breech above my town of Poole called Northavyn point, and so perceive by the same that by reason of the sea it will be not in process of time greatly prejudice and hindrance to the king's highness in his customs there, but also ensure and be to the great annoyance and decay of my said town by reason of the same.'[21] Richmond had descended on Poole with his entourage of around 600 on something akin to a royal progress. He was met with cheering crowds, listened to loyal addresses and accepted gifts. He now clearly saw himself as a royal prince, a possible future king, and was acting accordingly.

A letter from Richmond at Sheffield to Cromwell, 4 July 1534, advising him 'here in the country where I lie, I have no park nor game to show sport or pleasure to my friends when they shall resort unto me', indicates that Richmond was now hoping for more than a suit of armour from his doting father. He sent a list of the royal parks in the area, and hinted rather heavily that he hoped the King would help him remedy the matter of his having nowhere to hunt with his friends. Richmond had a passion for hunting and was not above removing woodland to enlarge his deer parks or riding down crops during the chase. This was an attitude typical of the nobility of the day, considering no one's rights or welfare but their own.[22]

His official duties increased in line with his new status. In November 1534, Richmond, as England's Admiral, was called on to entertain the French Admiral of the Fleet. After New Year at Collyweston, Richmond was back in London adding his presence to the entertainments for Chapuys, the Imperial Ambassador, who had come to make sure the Princess Mary was well. She had earned Henry VIII's displeasure through her refusal to sign his Act of Succession which would make her a bastard: she had lost her governess, the Countess of Salisbury (replaced by Lady Shelton), and had been so ill that it was feared she might die.

In 1535, Henry seems to have decided that Richmond should have a taste of responsibility. It was planned that he should lead an army to pacify Ireland and could then be officially titled King of Ireland. An army was assembled; the Duke of Norfolk, an experienced campaigner, joined Richmond, but they never sailed. At Christmas 1535, Richmond was with his father at Windsor.

Richmond had always enjoyed a tolerable relationship with Anne Boleyn, but all this was to change. With the arrest of Anne, rumours began to fly around Court, one of which was that she had practised witchcraft to ensnare the King. The rumours also stated that Anne had poisoned Catherine of Aragon, and that she had planned to do the same to Princess Mary and Richmond, in order to clear the path to the throne for her own child. Chapuys wrote to Charles V:

'The very evening the concubine [Anne Boleyn] was brought to the Tower of London, when the Duke of Richmond went to say goodnight to his father, and ask his blessing after the English custom, the King began to weep, saying he and his sister, meaning the Princess [Mary], were greatly bound to God for having escaped the hands of that accursed and poisoning whore, who had determined to poison them.'[23]

The evidence for poisoning seems to have been supported by Jane Parker, George Boleyn's wife, who claimed that while Richmond and Surrey were in France, in July 1533, they both became ill after sharing a cup of wine. George Boleyn had been at the French Court with the Duke of Norfolk at that time and George had abandoned his belongings and headed for England as soon as the young men fell ill. The implied conclusion was that he had attempted to poison the chief rival to his sister's children.

Richmond attended Anne Boleyn's execution in 1536. He was accompanied, amongst others, by Surrey, Thomas Audley, the Lord Chancellor, Charles Brandon and Thomas Cromwell, Henry VIII's minister and the author of the whole fiasco. The Lord Mayor and aldermen also attended, as did ordinary members of the public. Richmond was 17 years old, and was probably already ill with the disease that killed him. He did, however, inherit some of Anne's lands and those of her fellow victims, including property that Anne had snatched from the estate of the dead Catherine of Aragon. When George Boleyn was executed, his posts of Constable of Dover Castle and Warden of the Cinque Ports went to Richmond.[24]

Through Henry's marriage to Jane Seymour in 1536, all three children (Richmond, Mary and Elizabeth) were now equally illegitimate. A new Act was therefore passed: should Jane Seymour fail to produce a legitimate heir, the King was to nominate his successor from amongst his bastards. He would then be able to lawfully choose Richmond. This meant that the young Duke took on a higher profile; as Robert Radcliffe, Earl of Sussex, remarked, 'If all the children were bastards, it was advisable to prefer the male to the female for the succession to the crown.'[25]

When Parliament opened in June, Richmond was part of the procession, walking in front of the King carrying the Cap of Maintenance, made of crimson velvet lined with ermine, traditionally carried by the senior member of the House of Lords. Richmond had largely kept out of serious politics up until that point; he had the rank, the money, the education, but not the power. Now he was married to the daughter of the Duke of Norfolk, England's premier duke, and was being groomed for future kingship.

Despite his father's deep affection, Richmond was still vulnerable to Henry's current wave of paranoia. He had not gone to Ireland, yet his army still existed. Cromwell, who had engineered the downfall of Anne Boleyn, seems to have started to undermine

Richmond as well, telling Henry that the young man was, 'very likely to fall into inobedience and rebellion.'[26] Actually, Cromwell was almost certainly trying to discredit the powerful Duke of Norfolk, Anne Boleyn's uncle and Richmond's father-in-law, so as to totally destroy his influence at Court. Discrediting Richmond was merely a means to this end.

Meanwhile, Richmond and his bride set up home at the newly renovated St James's Palace, and things would have gone well if he had not developed a serious cough with chest pains. By the summer, Richmond was seriously ill, and unable to attend the closing of Parliament on 18 July. His physician, Dr William Buttes, was called in almost immediately, but too late. On 22 July 1536 Richmond died in great secrecy. So sudden was the event at St James's Palace that some of his belongings, including his chapel furniture, were still at Tonge, a manor house near Sittingbourn, Kent, where it had been sent in anticipation of Richmond's arrival.

When the King was told his son was dead, he was at Sittingbourn, daily expecting Richmond. What happened next is almost inexplicable. There was no autopsy, no public mourning or state funeral. Henry's response to the death of his 'worldly jewel' was to take Jane Seymour to London and to call on his daughter, Mary, advising her that she might now move into Richmond's apartment as 'Second Lady of the Kingdom'. Norfolk was told to take care of Richmond's remains. Mary Howard took as much of her gold and silver plate as she could carry (her only asset), returned to her father's house and enquired after her widow's pension. She was told there would not be one.

Rumour said that at first Richmond's body was hastily buried at Thetford, in a stable yard, and moved later. Another version, probably correct, said his body was placed in a sealed coffin and transported in a cart covered with straw to rest in Thetford Priory, where others of the Howard family were buried. Here it lay for two years; when the Priory was dismantled during the Reformation, Richmond's remains were moved and he lies in St Michael's

Church, in Framlingham, with his duchess, under a once-splendid monument, amongst his wife's Howard relations.

Richmond is believed to have died of tuberculosis, although the secrecy and speed of his burial might be due to the fact that he died, or was suspected of having died of pneumonic plague. The main symptoms of this are fever, headache, weakness and rapidly developing pneumonia with shortness of breath, chest pain and coughing, all symptoms that Richmond showed before his death. The pneumonia progresses for two to four days with death from respiratory failure and shock. Richmond was only 17, 'having pined inwardly in his body long before he died.'[27] If the illness had been developing for some time, it was probably not plague, but his quick death may have convinced his attendants that it was.

When it came to the treatment of his corpse, the speed of his sickness and death may simply have overwhelmed the King. The death of his beloved son may have devastated his father. He had lost his only son who had died without heirs. Henry's instructions to Norfolk may have been misinterpreted or confused by the chain of instruction, so that the body was roughly coffined and transported by Norfolk's servants.

But why did his father ignore him so completely? This might support the theory that Henry believed that Richmond was part of a planned revolt against the Crown, rising from his powerbase in Lincolnshire. It would not be the first time an heir decided not to wait for his inheritance, and the affair could have been triggered by Jane Seymour's pregnancy. A living, lawful male child would have put Richmond firmly out of contention for the throne. In fact, there was an uprising in Lincolnshire in September and October 1536, not long after Richmond's death. Would he have supported this action, had he been alive? Did Henry believe his son had been actively involved in this disturbance? Certainly supporters of the revolt came from South Kyme, Tailboys lands, and the leaders included Bessie Blount's son-in-law, Robert Dymoke, and Richmond's servants, Sir John Russell and Sir William Parr.

95

Yet, when things calmed down, the King berated Norfolk for the nature of his son's burial. Henry's usual response to loss was to run from it and act as if he wasn't involved. His defence mechanism had been activated and he thought he could trust Norfolk to do the right thing for his own son-in-law. As they had not communicated face-to-face, the King and Norfolk had each misinterpreted what was to be done. The King wanted the whole painful matter to be over quickly; Norfolk mistook speed for privacy and secrecy.

On 24 December 1540, Sir John Wallop wrote to King Henry. He had been at a banquet with the dauphin and the duc d'Orléans, King Henry's godson. The dauphin Francois 'began to speak of my lord of Richmond, lamenting his death greatly, and so did Monsieur d'Orléans likewise ...'[28] The French princes could still remember Richmond fondly, and Sir John was confident enough of the King's feelings to pass the comment on to him. This tends to support the notion that it was sudden, overwhelming grief that kept Henry from mourning his son at the time, not fear of his betrayal. He could still listen, as a proud father, to compliments about his lost son.

———

In 1540, Bessie Blount died. Her husband, Lord Clinton, married again a year later, to Ursula, daughter of William, Lord Stourton, and they had two more daughters and three sons. Ursula died in 1551 and the following year Clinton married for the last time, to Elizabeth Fitzgerald, the daughter of the Earl of Kildare and widow of Sir Anthony Browne. Like Bessie Blount, Elizabeth was a renowned court beauty, and was the inspiration for the Earl of Surrey's poetry, featuring as 'fair Geraldine'. The couple had no more children, and Clinton died in 1585.

———

Richmond's widow, Mary Howard, was approached two years after his death with an offer of marriage. A letter from Sir Rafe Sadyler to Cromwell, dated July 1538, puts the case for Jane Seymour's brother, Thomas. This turned out to be part of an elaborate plot by Jane's brother, and to a lesser extent, her father, to regain influence over the King.

The family to which Mary Howard belonged had aspirations to greatness, but were latecomers to the nobility, despite their title. The first Earls of Norfolk had been the Bigods, under the Norman William I. When the family line died out, Edward I resurrected the title, raised to a dukedom, for his youngest son, Thomas of Brotherton. In 1397 the dukedom passed through marriage to the Mowbrays until James, the 5th Duke, died in 1476. This last male Mowbray left an infant heiress who was married to Richard, Duke of York, the younger of Edward IV's sons. Little Anne Mowbray died before her husband met his mysterious end in the Tower of London with his older brother, Edward V. The Mowbray title fell into abeyance, although the Mowbray name and bloodline survived through female lines. One of these was through little Anne's great-aunt, Margaret de Mowbray, who had married Sir Robert Howard.

On little Anne Mowbray's death, Richard III formally gave the title of Duke of Norfolk to Sir John Howard of Stoke Neyland. Besides being the son of Margaret de Mowbray, sister of the 2nd Duke, he was a renowned warrior and supporter of Richard and his party, who later became Constable of the Tower of London. Being Richard's man, however, meant that the title was lost when Sir John Howard died at Bosworth fighting for the King; it took his son 20 years to get his title back from Henry VIII. Sir John's grandson, Thomas, Duke of Norfolk, was the father of Mary, Dowager Duchess of Richmond, and Henry, Earl of Surrey.

For a time, back in 1536, it looked as if the Howard star was in the ascendant. So popular with the King was Surrey that Anne Boleyn even suggested that he should marry the 'bastard' Princess Mary. There was every chance that Richmond would become King and Mary Howard would be Queen. As Richmond's closest friend, Surrey could expect to play a major role in government. It may also have entered his mind that if Richmond should die without heirs, why should he not nominate his brother-in-law or nephew as his successor? However, with the death of Richmond and the birth of Prince Edward to Jane Seymour, everything changed. Power now lay with the Seymours.

In 1543, after Anne Boleyn's execution, Norfolk decided that his family should regain their influence by allying with the Seymours, brothers to Queen Jane and uncles to the future King Edward. To this end, he suggested to his widowed daughter that she entertain the offer of marriage from Thomas, the younger of the brothers. Although Surrey was, in general, violently opposed to the men about the King, as typified by the Seymours who came from the lesser nobility, he foresaw a way of gaining control of the throne, using his sister, and was apparently in favour of this particular match.

The whole plan was laid bare when the Duke of Norfolk and the Earl of Surrey were suddenly arrested on charges of treason. Sir Richard Southwell (one of the accusers), John Gates and Wymond Carew went immediately to Kenninghall to question Mary Howard and Elizabeth Holland, the Duke's mistress. They arrived at the house so unexpectedly that Mary had just risen, and was dressed in a loose robe, a type of housecoat. According to these gentlemen, she was 'sore perplexed, trembling and like to fall down' when she realised that her father and brother were accused of treason. She fell to her knees and protested their innocence, although she qualified her support of her brother by saying of him 'she noteth [him] to be a rash man.' The three gentlemen searched the house; they found nothing in Mary's rooms, since she had sold most of her property to pay her debts when her husband died.[29]

However, they found a quantity of jewels in Elizabeth Holland's rooms. This lady, the daughter of the Duke's steward, had been the Duke's mistress for some years. The Duchess of Norfolk lived separately from her husband, partly because of this scandal. Elizabeth's jewels and property were officially confiscated, the house was inventoried and locked up, and the ladies were escorted to London for further questioning. Once there, under further interrogation, Mary admitted the plan by her family to marry her to Seymour, 'while her brother also desired, wishing her withal to endear herself so into the King's favour, as she might the better rule here as others had done and that she refused.' Surrey's plan had been that she should pretend to agree to marry Seymour, but that she should, in fact, attempt to entrap the King into a romantic liaison, so that her brother could control the King through her.

Sir Gawen Carew gave evidence of a conversation he had had with Mary some time previously about her brother. She told Carew about the offer from Seymour, and Surrey's advice that: '... she should in no wise utterly make refusal of him [Seymour], but that she should leave the matter so diffusely that the King's Majesty should take occasion to speak with her again; and thus by length of time it is possible that the king should take such a fantasy to you that ye shall be able to govern like unto Madame de'Éstampes.' This lady was the powerful mistress of Francis I, far more influential than his queen. Mary Howard then told Carew how she felt, 'whereupon she defied her brother and said that all they should perish and she would cut her own throat rather than she would consent to such a villainy.'[30]

In her testimony, Mary repeated remarks by both her father and brother criticising the number of commoners now gathered around the King. Elizabeth Holland, desperate to cooperate and get her jewels back, supported Mary Howard's testimony. She agreed about Surrey, but added that the Duke had not approved of Surrey changing his coat of arms to include the royal arms of Brotherton, and had forbidden her to embroider it on any of the household linens or otherwise display it.

Henry VIII was bedridden during one of his periods of ill health, but daily reports of the trial of Norfolk and Surrey were sent to him. Copies survive with the King's notes on the points being made, which were sent back to the judges. One reads, 'If a man compassing himself to govern the realm do actually go about to rule the king and should for that purpose advise his daughter or sister to become his harlot … what this importeth?'[31]

In the event, Norfolk and Surrey were both convicted and sentenced to death; Norfolk was sent to the Tower to await his execution, but Surrey's death warrant was signed immediately. He was beheaded on 19 January 1547. He left behind him a wife (Frances Vere, the daughter of the Earl of Oxford) and five children – Jane, Thomas (now Earl of Surrey), Katherine, Henry and Margaret. The children were removed from their mother's care and housed with their aunt, Mary Howard, living first at Mountjoy House, in Knight Rider Street, her London residence since her husband's death. At Christmas 1551, Mary received an annuity of £100 towards their household expenses, and the same amount the following year. The Duke, still in the Tower, was allowed £80 a year for his keep; his gaoler was Sir John Markham.

The children were soon moved to Reigate Castle, where they continued their education. Unlike her brother and father who were Catholic, the Dowager was a Protestant, and she hired John Foxe, a Protestant cleric, as the children's tutor. Foxe was a fine scholar. Whilst acting as their teacher, he wrote his *Tables of Grammar*, published in 1552. He is, of course, better known for another of his works, *The Book of Martyrs*.

The fortunes of the children changed radically when Mary Tudor became Queen. During the reign of Edward VI, Norfolk remained in the Tower while Mary Tudor stayed at Kenninghall, the Norfolk family house. When Edward VI died and Princess Mary was summoned to London in a plot by Northumberland, Duke of Somerset, to prevent her taking the throne, it may have been the Norfolk servants at Kenninghall who helped to persuade her to go to Framlingham instead. It was from there that she mounted her successful campaign to secure the throne as Mary I.

As she rode on London, Queen Mary was joined by Anne, Duchess of Norfolk, and one of her first actions was to order the release of the Duke. He was Earl Marshall at her coronation, and Lord High Steward at the coronation banquet. The Dowager Countess of Surrey and her children were summoned to rejoin the family at Mountjoy Place in London. The Duke now took responsibility for his grandchildren, and one of his first moves was to hire a Catholic priest, John White, to be their new tutor and to re-educate them as Catholics. Foxe had wisely already left the household at Reigate and gone abroad to Flanders.

The Duke was not angry with his daughter. He left her the sum of £500 in his will, in acknowledgement of her care for the children during his imprisonment. He died on 25 August 1554, aged 80, and was succeeded by his grandson Thomas. This young man had learned nothing by the experiences of his father and grandfather. He was heavily involved in a plot whereby he was to marry Mary, Queen of Scots, and gain the throne by murdering Elizabeth I. He was arrested for treason and died, like his father, on the scaffold.

Mary Howard died in December 1557, and was buried at Norwich Cathedral with all the pomp due to her station. The mourning procession included the Dean and Canons of the Cathedral, the Mayor and Aldermen, the chief officers of the Duke's household with white staves, the Garter King at Arms and heralds following the Howard banners. The chief mourner was her sister-in-law, the Dowager Countess of Surrey, now remarried to Thomas Steynings.

101

THE MATERNAL FAMILY TREE OF ANNE BOLEYN

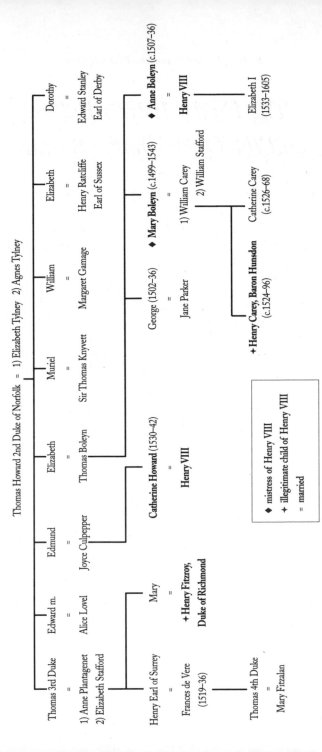

Thomas Howard 2nd Duke of Norfolk = 1) Elizabeth Tylney 2) Agnes Tylney

◆ mistress of Henry VIII
+ illegitimate child of Henry VIII
= married

The First Mistress Boleyn
and the Questionable Bastard

―――⋙⋘―――

In 1516, Catherine of Aragon had a daughter, Mary, who lived and thrived. The Queen was delighted with her new baby and now knew she was capable of bearing a living child. The King, happy in the knowledge that he had a daughter as well as a thriving bastard son, could look forward to the birth of a lawful heir with renewed confidence.

However, in 1518, a new plan was hatched, since Catherine had failed to have a living son. The Princess was betrothed to the dauphin of France; and one of the clauses in the marriage contract allowed that if Henry VIII had no son, Mary and the dauphin would rule England. The French came to London in September, and the English went over to Paris in December, for signature of the contract. Catherine, in the meantime, had given birth to an eight-month, stillborn daughter. The Venetian Ambassador, Giustinian wrote that it was 'the sole fear of the kingdom that it may pass through this marriage into the power of France.'[1]

The Ambassador to France was Sir Thomas Boleyn, an experienced European diplomat. He had sprung from humble beginnings (his grandfather had been a merchant), but marriages into various noble families by his grandfather, father and himself had moved the Boleyns to a higher social position. Sir Thomas was the kind of man to appeal to the King; he was a keen sportsman, a skilled jouster and an excellent diplomat, and his marriage to Elizabeth, the daughter of the Duke of Norfolk gave him the entrée to the King's immediate circle.

It was at this time that Cardinal Wolsey set in motion a piece of diplomacy that became known as the Treaty of London. An agreement was drawn up whereby more than 20 European states, including England, France and the Holy Roman Empire, agreed to a universal peace. As part of this, Henry VIII held a meeting with Charles V of Spain who had also just been elected Holy Roman Emperor (his maternal grandparents were Ferdinand and Isabella, rulers of Castile and Aragon; his paternal grandfather was Maximilian, the last Emperor). Despite the Treaty of London two years previously, in May 1520 Charles visited England to formulate a tentative alliance against France. Despite the previous promise of marriage to the French dauphin, discussions now included a suggestion that Charles should marry the four-year-old Princess Mary.

However, Henry had not completely abandoned the idea of a French alliance. In celebration of the peace, in 1519, he had agreed to a meeting with Francis I on French soil which eventually took place on 7 June 1520 at the site that became known as the Field of the Cloth of Gold.

Early in that same year, Henry is believed to have fallen in love with Mary, the eldest daughter of Thomas Boleyn. Mary was born in c.1499, George in c.1504 and Anne in c.1507, although there is considerable debate about the dates and the order of the births of the daughters. Given the number of children who failed to survive infancy, it was not considered that important to record the dates of the births of children, especially those of daughters.

Thanks to her father's friendship with Henry VIII, and her mother's family connections and previous post as one of the ladies to both Elizabeth of York and Catherine of Aragon, Mary soon gained her place at Court as a lady-in-waiting to Catherine. Mary Boleyn had been one of the ladies who accompanied Henry's sister, Mary, to France when she married Louis XII in August 1514. When the party arrived, Louis sent many of Princess Mary's English ladies back to England, although Mary Boleyn was one of those who stayed behind. After the wedding Louis sent still more of the older, more opinionated ladies back to England, but again 'Madmoyselle Boleyne' stayed with Mary. The Princess said of the young ladies who remained that they were, 'such as never had experience nor knowledge how to advertise or give me counsel in any time of need.'[2]

Had Mary Boleyn been born around 1499, as is believed, she would have been in her mid-teens when she joined the French Court. One reason for her staying, when so many senior ladies were repatriated, may have been her lack of experience in guiding the Queen, but it may also be due to the fact that the heir to the throne, the dauphin Francis, wanted her to become his mistress. Over 20 years after the event, when he was king, Francis wrote that Mary Boleyn was *'per una grandissima ribalda et infame sopre tutte'* ('a very great slut with a most infamous reputation').[3] It is comments like this that have led to the suggestion that Mary was a wanton, with a string of lovers. There is, however, no evidence other than the malicious and spiteful remarks of a probable rejected lover, Francis I, who has seen the object of his affection take up with someone he envied and disliked, Henry VIII.

Francis also lashed out at another lady who had repulsed his advances. The young Mary Tudor had married Louis XII, his predecessor, and when he died Francis had tried to seduce her, only to be repulsed. Some years later Francis scribbled graffiti on a portrait of Mary, *'plus sale que royne'* ('more dirty than queenly').

Some credence has been given to the idea that Mary Boleyn was the mistress of the dauphin, given the lax morals of Francis I's court. Sieur de Brantôme wrote that: 'Rarely did any maid or wife leave that court chaste.'[4] However, the comment by Francis I is the only evidence for Mary Boleyn's supposedly loose behaviour, so it is more likely that she remained chaste and Francis remained a frustrated would-be lover.

Another supposed piece of evidence supporting Mary Boleyn's lax behaviour comes from Lord Herbert of Cherbury's *Life and*

105

Raigne of King Henry the Eighth, published in 1649. He quotes William Rastall, a judge and author of a life of Sir Thomas More, saying that a youthful Henry VIII had had an affair with Elizabeth Boleyn while her husband was in France as part of an embassy, and that Anne was the King's daughter. It is just conceivable that this might be true if Anne was born in 1507, as Henry would have been about 15 years old when she was conceived. Rastall also claimed that when Anne was 15, she had some kind of illicit relationship with a household servant, and was sent to France in disgrace. Here, according to Rastall, it was Anne rather than Mary, who 'behaved herself so licentious, that she was vulgarly called the Hackney of England [a hackney was a horse hired out and ridden by anyone who could afford the hire charge], till being adopted to that King's [Francis's] familiarity, she was termed his Mule.'[5] Since these comments are obviously not applicable to Anne, who was only a child under her father's care during her time in France, it has been assumed that they must apply to Mary when, in truth, they were written to discredit Anne and are largely based on vulgar invention, aimed simply at damaging her reputation.

If Mary had had a reputation for loose behaviour, she would never have been permitted to go to France with Princess Mary in the first place. Certainly there is no evidence to suggest that she was sexually active or had any other lovers. If she had behaved in a disgraceful manner whilst in France, there seems to have been no retribution on her return to England as she retained her place at Court.

In April 1515, Mary Boleyn returned to England with Mary Tudor and her new husband, Charles Brandon. The Boleyn daughter who stayed in France was Anne. By 1520, Henry and Mary Boleyn were lovers. Since, besides being king, Henry was a handsome young man, and Mary was a lovely young woman, this may have been a genuine love affair. Again, if Mary had been truly promiscuous, particularly with Francis I, it is extremely unlikely that Henry would have had anything to do with her. Although

Henry had an affair with Jane Popincourt after she had been the mistress of Longueville, it was only a light-hearted romance of short duration, and Henry liked Longueville. He would not have taken a mistress who had once been intimate with Francis I whom he disliked intensely.

Once the affair was in physical progress (or about to take that final step), Mary was married to William Carey of Aldenham, Hertfordshire, one of the gentlemen in the household of Cardinal Wolsey. Henry would never again make the mistake of risking a pregnancy in an unmarried lady. For a second time, when a mistress needed a 'diplomatic' husband, Wolsey could be relied upon to produce a well born young man from his household. Carey was directly descended from King Edward III; his mother, Margaret Spencer, was a cousin of Margaret Beaufort's. The wedding took place on 4 February 1520; Henry VIII was one of the guests and, according to the King's Book of Payments, made a wedding gift of 6s 8d, a modest sum.

Bessie Blount had her son in 1519. Mary Boleyn was married in February 1520 to William Carey and the affair probably began shortly after. By 1523 Mary was Henry's acknowledged mistress as in that year he named one of his ships the *Mary Boleyn*. Mary finally became pregnant in June 1525. Carey received royal grants in 1522, 1523, 1524 and 1525, which seems to indicate the duration of the affair.[6] If Henry's passion was running true to form, once Mary became pregnant (either by Henry or her husband), the King's interest would cease.

Anne Boleyn's first recorded appearance at Court was with her sister in a masque held in March 1522 in honour of an Imperial delegation to arrange the marriage between Charles V and Princess Mary. There was a Château Vert (a wood and plaster life-size model of a Castle painted green and decorated with leaves and flowers) defended by eight ladies representing the female virtues, each accompanied by a boy chorister of the Chapel Royal as a female vice, and attacked by eight men as the male virtues: the

107

ladies wore white satin with the name of their character embroidered in yellow satin 24 times on the dress, a caul (hair net) of Venetian gold with a Milan bonnet (cap). The 'Vices' were dressed as Indian women, and the missiles were dates, oranges, fruits and sweetmeats.

The Virtue of 'Beauty' was danced by Mary Tudor, Duchess of Suffolk; 'Honour' was the Countess of Devonshire; Mary Boleyn was 'Kindness', her sister Anne was 'Perseverance' and their sister-in-law, Jane Parker, was 'Constancy'. The other ladies were 'Bounty', 'Mercy' and 'Pity'. Mary's 'Vice' was 'Unkindness' and her 'Male Virtue' was 'Attendance'. Anne's were 'Jealousy' and 'Youth'. Eventually, the ardour of the men overcame the disdain of the ladies, and they were led out of their green-painted 'castle' to dance.[7]

It is a strange irony that the King's mistress, Mary, played the role of 'Kindness', while her sister Anne seemed to look to her future courtship in the role of 'Perseverance'. Jane Parker, who would become their sister-in-law, embodied 'Constancy' only in her constant appearances in the tragedies that followed the Boleyns, contributing by her testimony to the deaths of her husband, George Boleyn, Anne Boleyn and their cousin Catherine Howard.

Both Mary Boleyn's children were born after her marriage, and there is no serious contemporary suggestion that either was the child of the King. There is some dispute as to whether Catherine or Henry was born first, one in 1524, while the affair was in progress, and the other in 1526, after the affair is supposed to have ended. Baby Henry was said by some to bear a resemblance to Henry VIII (like the King's other male bastards), but portraits of the period make it difficult for modern researchers to be sure of any resemblance. The male fashion in the first half of the 16th century was for heavy facial hair.

However, there were obviously rumours about Henry Carey's parentage. John Hale, a Cambridge fellow and vicar of Isleworth, was executed for treason in May 1535 (with the Blessed Richard

Reynolds and four Carthusian monks). Amongst the evidence against him was a statement that: 'John Hale, vicar of Iselworth, said that a Brigettine of Sion [a monk from Sion abbey] once showed him "young master Carey", saying he was Henry's bastard.'[8]

Henry Carey received an education suitable to his rank as the son of William Carey and Mary Boleyn. Nicholas Bourbon became a tutor to the sons of nobles, including Thomas (son of Sir Nicholas Harvey), Henry Norris's son and Henry Carey. Bourbon wrote the *Nargarum* (literally, a book of stuff and nonsense); printed in 1538, it is dedicated to the kings, Francis I and Henry VIII. He wrote in Latin:

You, oh queen [Anne Boleyn], gave me the boys to educate.
I try to keep each one faithful to his duty.
May Christ grant that I may be equal to the task.[9]

It is often said that Thomas Boleyn owed his dramatic career rise to first one, then the other of his daughters becoming the King's mistress. Thomas Boleyn, however, was already an up-and-coming politician before 1520. In 1511 he was Governor of Norwich Castle; in 1512 he was Ambassador to the Low Countries. By 1514 he was Ambassador to France, and in 1516, Ambassador to the Imperial Court. In 1518 he was back in France, and in 1521 he was with Wolsey at the Congress of Calais. In 1525 he became a baron and in 1529 he was made Lord Privy Seal. Part of his rise may have been due to his daughters; part may have been because of his friendship with the King; most was certainly due to his own talents.

The affair between Henry and Mary Boleyn ended some time in 1525. It was not until 1528 that Mary's sister, Anne, is mentioned as having taken the King's fancy. He did not abandon one sister for the other.

In 1525 Catherine of Aragon was now 40 and unlikely to have any more children. In July, Cuthbert Tunstal, Bishop of Durham, wrote from the Imperial Court that he had advised Charles V that Henry had given up hope having another child with Catherine, 'seeing the Queen's Grace hath long been without children.'[10] It may have been this final realisation that made Henry start to consider divorce. Mary Boleyn was out of the picture, married to William Carey. Henry was now looking less for sexual gratification, and more for another queen and mother of the future Prince of Wales.

On 4 May 1527, a masque was held to celebrate England's peace with France and Princess Mary's betrothal to a French prince. The King and Queen were there, as was Margaret of Scotland, Henry's widowed elder sister. Princess Mary was dressed in her finest, and Spinelli, the Venetian Ambassador, wrote, 'her beauty produced such an effect ... that all other sights ... were forgotten and they gave themselves up solely to the contemplation of so fair an angel.'[11] Just two weeks after the betrothal of Mary to the French prince, a church court was assembled to discuss the King's divorce.

Mary Boleyn might no longer be the King's mistress, but her husband remained a member of his immediate circle. William Carey shared the King's appreciation of art, assembling his own collection. He introduced Dutch artist, Lucas van Horenbolte, to the English Court around 1525. One of Horenbolte's first commissions was to produce a portrait of the King; he painted the first true English miniature of Henry (now in the Fitzwilliam Museum, Cambridge, England) and is known to have created similar portraits of both Catherine of Aragon and Catherine Parr (also possibly Anne Boleyn and Jane Seymour, although the provenance for these pictures is less certain). His sister, Susannah, and father, Gerard, joined him in England: Susannah was an illustrator of manuscripts, but Lucas is listed in court records as a 'pictor maker', a formal court painter. On his arrival in England, Hans Holbein was a student of Horenbolte for a while; it was from Horenbolte that he developed some of his skill at miniature portrait painting.

William Carey was a gentleman of the privy chamber and one of Henry's close attendants, and Anne Boleyn was at some pains to acknowledge his support. Carey was at Greenwich when the plague broke out. The King quickly moved the healthy elements of his Court to Waltham, and sent Anne Boleyn to Hever Castle, where she and her brother George both fell ill, but subsequently recovered. William Carey also fell sick, as did two of Henry's close friends, Sir William Compton and Sir Edward Poyntz. All three died.

A penniless widow with two children, Mary Boleyn fell on hard times. Her father refused to help her, and Mary was reduced to asking Anne to intercede on her behalf. Henry wrote to Anne:

'As touching your sister's matter, I have caused Walter Walshe to write to [Sir Thomas Boleyn] my mind therein ... for surely what soever is said, it cannot so stand with his honour, but that he must needs take her his natural daughter, now in her extreme necessity.'[12]

111

Thomas Boleyn, once the King had spoken on the matter, arranged for a small annuity to be paid to his eldest daughter and her family. Henry VIII awarded the wardship of Henry Carey to Anne Boleyn, presumably so that she could protect her sister's son who might also, just possibly, be his own. There was no great estate that could be dipped into for a substantial revenue, and no inheritance for which to arrange a suitable marriage; the guardian of little Henry could only look after his interests.

In 1532, when Henry went on a royal visit to France, one of those attending Anne was her sister. A meeting with Francis I led to his making those unpleasant remarks about Mary's virtue. Once back in England, with Anne firmly established as Queen, Mary became one of her ladies-in-waiting.

In 1534, Mary Boleyn remarried to William Stafford, one of the King's Gentleman Ushers, and a soldier from the Calais garrison. Mary described him as being 'poor, but of good family.' The marriage was made in secret, as Mary seems to have fallen into disfavour with her family. As the Queen's sister, she would be expected to make a far better marriage to one of the Queen's supporters, someone with sufficient fortune to take care of her and her children and to enhance her sister's Court.

After her marriage, Mary wrote to Cromwell, then the King's first minister:

> 'It is not unknown to you the high displeasure that both he [Sir William] and I have, both of the King's Highness and the Queen's Grace by the reason of our marriage, without their knowledge ... Consider, that he was young, and love overcame reason ... I saw all the world set so little by me, and he so much ... I dare not write to them [her family], they are so cruel against us.'[13]

The King wrote to George Boleyn asking him to contact his father about helping Mary. The couple were given the manor of Rochford, in Essex, a Boleyn family holding, to add to Stafford's land at Grafton and Chebsey, Staffordshire. Mary Boleyn retired there and seems to have stayed quietly out of the way.

Despite the sisters being at odds, the closeness of the Boleyn family was noted and utilised. When Anne miscarried in January 1536, Francis I was told the story, also reported by Chapuys to Charles V, that Anne was not really pregnant at all. She and her sister Mary had invented the story between them to keep Henry believing that Anne could give him the son he wanted.[14]

From her marriage in 1534 until her death on 19 July 1543, Mary Boleyn lived on the estate at Rochford. She bore William Stafford two more children, a boy and a girl; the boy's name has not survived and he died before he reached the age of 10, while the girl, whose name was Anne, probably died in infancy. Mary found a place at Court for her daughter, Catherine Carey, as one of the maids of Anne of Cleves. Catherine caught the attention of Sir Francis Knollys, one of the King's gentlemen, who married her around 1540.

After Mary's death William Stafford married Dorothy Stafford, a cousin, daughter of Sir Henry, Baron Stafford, and granddaughter of the last Duke of Buckingham. They had two sons, Sir Edward and William. Dorothy Stafford was Mistress of the Robes to Queen Elizabeth, and a good friend. William Stafford and Dorothy were obliged to spend some time abroad during Queen Mary's reign, and a third son, John, was born at Geneva in 1556; John Calvin was his godfather. William Stafford died in Geneva, and Dorothy argued with Calvin, moved to Basle, and then to England where her son John had to be naturalised.

—◦◊◦—

Despite his mother's unfortunate second marriage, Henry Carey remained in the wardship of his aunt, educated by Nicholas Bourbon. After Anne's fall from grace and death in 1536, he may have stayed at Court in the care of another guardian or returned to his mother.

113

Safely married and within his majority, Henry Carey began his career in 1547 when he was returned as the MP for Buckingham. Two years later Edward VI granted him manors at Little Brickhill and Burton, Buckinghamshire. However, he lived quietly under Mary I, which was a wise idea for anyone who could claim a blood relationship with Anne Boleyn.

Elizabeth I was very fond of her Carey cousins and showed it almost as soon as she ascended to the throne. On her accession, Henry was knighted and in January 1559 was created Baron Hunsdon with a pension of £400 p.a. and the manors of Hunsdon and Eastwick in Hertfordshire and land in Kent. In October 1560 he was appointed Master of the Queen's Hawks (his office was responsible for the purchase, breeding, housing and training of hunting birds for the Queen and her Favourites) and in May 1561 Hunsdon was made a Knight of the Garter. He was later appointed to the post of Captain of the Gentlemen Pensioners, her personal bodyguard, in 1564, a post he held until 1568.

Much of his life was spent on the northern borders, protecting England from marauding Scots. In August 1568 Hunsdon took up his post as Governor of Berwick-upon-Tweed, Northumberland, and Lord Warden of the Eastern Marches. He was a good soldier, popular with the troops, but was less polished as a courtier. He was, however, totally trustworthy and loyal to the Queen, so much so that she chose him to be one of the commissioners at the trial of Mary, Queen of Scots. In 1569 he was instrumental in putting down a rebellion against Elizabeth in the north, organised by the Duke of Norfolk and the Earls of Westmorland and Northumberland. In one engagement, Hunsdon, with about 1,500 troops, defeated an army of around 3,000 rebels.

In 1577, his loyalty and honesty were rewarded when he was elected a Privy Councillor. In 1581 he was appointed Captain General of the forces controlling the English borders and in 1587 he became Lord Warden General of the Northern Marches. The following year, when England was threatened by the Spanish Armada, he came south to command the Queen's Bodyguard of 36,000 troops based at Tilbury, as Principal Captain and Governor of the Army, 'for the defence and surety of our own Royal Person,'[15] as the Queen wrote to him. In 1590, he became joint Earl Marshall of England with Lord Burghley and Lord Howard of Effingham. Hunsdon was Chief Justice of the Royal Forces from December 1591 until his death in 1596. By a remarkable coincidence, he was also one of the commissioners at the trial of John Perrot, another one of Henry VIII's illegitimate sons, in March 1592.

In July 1585 Hunsdon was given the post of Lord Chamberlain of the Household. One of his duties was to organise the royal entertainments, including masques and plays. Probably the best of the Elizabethan theatre companies was the Lord Chamberlain's Men, with Hunsdon (followed by his son George) as their patron. The company included William Kemp, Philip Burbage and William Shakespeare. Between 1594, when the company came under Hunsdon's wing, and 1603 when Elizabeth died, the Lord

Chamberlain's Men produced *Titus Andronicus, The Taming of the Shrew, Love's Labours Lost, Romeo and Juliet, Two Gentlemen of Verona, The Merchant of Venice, Richard II, Henry IV, Henry V, Hamlet, A Comedy of Errors, A Midsummer's Night Dream* and *Twelfth Night.* In 1599 Burbage, Shakespeare and others of their company built the Globe Theatre on Bankside, Southwark in south London, as a permanent home for their troupe. Their success meant that they could now cease the tours that were essential to lesser companies and which the Lord Chamberlain's Men had done for years before.[16]

Hunsdon had another theatrical connection. In 1592, he took as his mistress a lady called Emilia Bassano, a member of the famous Italian family of musicians. She wrote a book of largely religious poetry and was particularly skilled in playing the virginals. When Bassano found herself pregnant, she married another Italian musician, Alphonse Lanier. Her son by Hunsdon, christened Henry, was born in early 1593 and took the surname of Lanier; Henry Lanier would later become a court musician to Charles I. Emilia went on to have several more children by her husband. She is one of the ladies tentatively identified as being Shakespeare's Dark Lady of the Sonnets and it is believed that she had an affair with the playwright.

Hunsdon died on 23 July 1596 at Somerset House in London. He had married Anne, daughter of Sir Thomas Morgan of Athelstone, Herefordshire, and had a family of seven sons and three daughters. Elizabeth I tried to give him one last gift as he lay dying; she had never given him a noble title above baron, and now she offered to resurrect the title of Earl of Wiltshire, once held by his grandfather. Hunsdon refused, blunt as always. 'Madam', he is reported to have said, 'As you did not count me worthy of this honour in life, then I shall account myself not worthy of it in death.'[17]

Despite this last refusal, as a token of her love, Elizabeth paid for his monument set up in Westminster Abbey. It is truly

115

magnificent: 36 feet high, made of marble and alabaster, bearing the Carey arms, argent, on a bend sable three roses of the field (a silver background with a thick black bar diagonally with three silver roses on it). The inscription reads:

> 'Consecrated for the burial of the Hunsdon family. Here sleeps in the Lord Henry Carey, Baron Hunsdon, one-time Governor of the town of Berwick, Warden of the east marches towards Scotland, Captain of the gentleman-pensioners, Chief Justice of the Forests south of the Trent, Knight of the Order of the Garter, Lord Chamberlain of the Lady Queen Elizabeth, sworn of the Privy Council, and first cousin to the aforesaid Queen. Together with him is buried Anne, his dearest wife, daughter of Thomas Morgan, knight, who bore him many children, of whom there survive George, John, Edmund and Robert, knights, Catherine, Countess of Nottingham, Philadelphia, Baroness Scrope, and Margaret, Lady Hoby. He died 23 July 1596 aged 71. His son, George Carey, Baron Hunsdon, member of the Order of the Garter, Captain-General of the Isle of Wight, Chamberlain of the household to Queen Elizabeth, Privy Councillor, and his wife Anne, placed this monument to the best of fathers and dearest of husbands, in his honour and memory, and being mindful of their own and their family's mortality.'[18]

Hunsdon's sister, Catherine, became a gentlewoman of the privy chamber; her husband, Sir Francis Knollys, was made Vice-Chamberlain of the Household. Catherine married Sir Francis in April 1540, bearing their first child a year later. If she had been born after her brother in 1526, she would have been 14 when she married and 15 when she had her first child. However, had she been born in 1524, she would have been 16 when she married and 17 when she had their first son. In her research, writer and historian Sally Varlow points out that a year before Catherine married she was chosen as one of the maids of honour to Anne of Cleves; maids were generally at least 16 years old, and in 1539 Catherine would have been only 13 if she had been born after Henry, but almost 16 if she had been born first in 1524.

One other piece of evidence is a portrait, 'Probably Catherine, Lady Knollys', which carries the inscription, *'Aetatis suae 38 An Dom 1562.'* The lady in the portrait was 38 years old in 1562; if the sitter is Catherine Carey, this puts her birth date firmly in 1524 and makes her Henry VIII's child rather than her younger brother. The problem is that the identity of the lady in the portrait is by no means certain. There are no incontrovertible portraits of Catherine Carey that it could be compared to as a means of confirming the identification.[19]

Catherine Carey was a close friend to Elizabeth I until she died in 1569. Elizabeth gave her an affectionate nickname, her dear 'Crow'. The Queen was devastated by her death and spent the lavish sum of £640 2s 11d on a magnificent funeral and tomb for her in Westminster Abbey in London. Sir Francis was away from home, attending Mary, Queen of Scots, at Bolton and Tutbury, when Catherine became seriously ill and died. Elizabeth blamed the Scottish queen for causing Sir Francis to be away from home; believing that his absence added to his wife's unhappiness and hastened her death.

THE FAMILY OF THOMAS STUKELEY

Sir Lewis Pollard = 1) Agnes Hext 2) Jane Pruett

◆ Jane Pollard
=
Sir Hugh Stukeley
(c.1496–1559) of Affeton

Hugh Pollard

Richard Pollard

John Pollard

Robert Pollard
=
Agnes, daughter
of Richard Chichester

Anthony Pollard

Grace

Elizabeth
=
Sir John Crocker

Agnes
=
Humphrey Moore

Thomasin
=
Vice Admiral Sir George Carew

Philippa
=
Sir Hugh Paulet

Lewis Stukeley
=
1) Anne Hill
2) Janet Powlett

Issue

Anne
=
William Bellew

Mary
=
1) Tristram Larder
2) John Prideaux

Issue

Elizabeth
=
John Wadham

Issue

Agnes
=
John Giles

Katherine
=
John Carew

Awdrie
=
1) William Yeo
2) Roger Gifford

George

+ Thomas Stukeley
=
1) Anne Curtis
2) Elizabeth Peppard

William Stukeley

Hugh Stukeley
=
Amias Stukeley

Frances Pollard

◆ mistress of Henry VIII

+ illegitimate child of Henry VIII

= married

6

The Wool Merchant's Wife and the Amazing Mercenary

———

Thomas Stukeley was born some time between 1523 and 1530, the third of five sons and six daughters of Sir Hugh Stukeley (or Stuckley) of Affeton, near Ilfracombe in Devon, and Jane, daughter of Sir Lewis Pollard, who married in 1520. The family lived in some splendour, according to the Devonshire Directory of 1850: 'In the farmhouse called Affton Barton are some remains of the ancient castellated mansion, which was the seat of the Affeton family in the 13th and 14th centuries ... This was one of the most splendid seats in the county, and had an extensive park ...'¹ Sir Hugh died in 1560 and was succeeded to the Affeton estate by his eldest son, Lewis, who married twice. He had at least three children by his first wife, Anne Hill, and two by his second, Janet Powlett.

Thomas was commonly believed to be the bastard son of Henry VIII and, like the King's other sons, looked a good deal like him. The behaviour of Edward VI, Mary I and Elizabeth I towards Thomas indicates that they also believed that he was the King's son, especially since he created havoc and escaped without punishment: a spy, a double agent, a pirate, a bankrupt, a forger, a liar, a fraudster and, finally, a traitor, Thomas suffered no more than a few months in prison as a result. He lied to, and manipulated, all three sovereigns, yet his charm and their belief that he was Henry's son arguably saved him from punishment again and again.

In 1547, Thomas was the King's standard bearer in Boulogne; he would have had to be in his mid-to-late teens to hold such a post. This means his birth came about at some point during the period when the King was losing interest in Catherine of Aragon and pursuing Anne Boleyn; this was also the period when Henry had his affair with Mary Berkeley, the wife of Sir Thomas Perrot.

Sir Hugh Stukeley was a major figure in local politics and occasionally had the opportunity to entertain the King at his Devonshire home. He was also a wealthy man, related by marriage to most of the prominent West Country families. His father, Sir Thomas Stukeley, had been a body servant to the King in 1516, and Sir Hugh had contacts with the Court and King. Therefore, the relationship between his wife, Jane, and Henry VIII may have taken place at Affeton.

So notorious was Thomas's life that it gave rise to a play, *The Battell of Alcazar, fought in Barbarie, between Sebastian King of Portugal, Abdelmelec King of Morocco, with the death of Captain Stukeley*, written by George Peele and published in 1594. It was later performed under the title *The Famous History of the Life and Death of Captain Thomas Stukeley*. The play may have been written to entertain, but it was about someone who had died in living memory. It may be that some of the incidents portrayed were based on known facts. From the play come the following lines, recited by Thomas as he lies dying in the closing moments:

> *Harke friendes, and with the story of my life*
> *Let me beguile the torment of my death.*
> *In Englands London, Lordings, was I borne,*
> *On that brave Bridge, the barre that thwarts the Thames …'*

If Sir Hugh was in London on business or attending the Court or Parliament, Lady Jane may have accompanied him, and thus Thomas could also have been conceived and born in the city.

James Fitzgerald, an Irish exile, met Thomas in Rome and seemed unable to decide his antecedents. He wrote of the man:

'… who by some was said to be an illegitimate son of Henry VIII, King of England; by others, son of an English knight and an Irish lady; by others, Irish by both parents, who either from anger at the English, or from religious motives, or desiring war and revolution in hopes of gain, or aspiring to reign, being perhaps a man of royal blood, was supplicating in the name of the Irish for succour against the English.'[2]

Thomas, following the custom of the day, would have left home at an early age to enter another household where he would be taught polite behaviour and given a good start in life. The Archbishop of Cashel reported that Thomas had served Charles Brandon, Duke of Suffolk, Henry VIII's brother-in-law, until the Duke's death in 1545. Thomas had two relatives in the Suffolk household – Sir Hugh Paulet and Sir George Pollard (both of whom were related to the Stukeleys through marriage) – who would have been instrumental in gaining a place in the household for their nephew. If Thomas was believed to be the son of Henry VIII, the household of the King's brother-in-law would be admirably suitable for the young Thomas. For a brief time, between 1545 and 1547 when he held his first recorded post, Thomas may also have been in the household of John Vesey, the Bishop of Exeter. The Bishop was a valued adviser to the King and spent most of his time either in London or at his home, Moor Hall, in Sutton Coldfield in Birmingham.[3]

121

Thomas's first noted appearance was in the company of Edward Seymour, Earl of Hertford and Duke of Somerset, acting as the King's standard bearer at Boulogne in 1550 and paid 6s 8d a day. When Boulogne was returned to the French, Edward Seymour came back to England with Thomas as part of his household. Thomas seems to have landed up in the service of one of the country's most prominent nobles, the brother of Jane Seymour and uncle to the reigning Edward VI.

In April 1551, Thomas was at the French Court of Henri II. One of the Embassy to the Court, Sir John Mason, wrote from Amboise to the Council on 22 April 1551 concerning the presence of several of his party including 'Mr Stucley' who 'had been made very much of' at the Court. Thomas came back to England, but when Edward Seymour lost power in October, he returned to Henri II. He seems to have made his mark as a soldier and was believed to have entered the French King's service. When Thomas returned to England in September 1552, a letter was sent to Edward VI, apparently from Henri II:

> 'Most high and mighty prince, we most affectionately and heartily recommend to you our dear and good friend, Thomas Stucley, an English gentleman, who during these wars has ever behaved himself well and valiantly in our service. He has given us to understand that he had a very great mind and desire to return into England. But since he fears that he is in some fault for having heretofore departed out of your Realm without asking your leave, we beseech you... for our love and at our prayer to forgive him this fault, and to take him back to your good favour and service, assuring you that so employing him you shall find that you are well served.'[4]

Thomas's return to London was not without incident. Edward VI's journal recorded that Thomas, 'declared how the French King, being wholly persuaded that he [Thomas] could not return again into England, because he came away without leave upon the apprehension of the Duke of Somerset his old master, declared to him his intent.' Once Henri had made peace with Spain, this 'intent' was a plan to take Calais back, invade England somewhere near Falmouth on the south west coast, and support a Scottish invasion from the north, under the leadership of Francis, duc de Guise.[5] According to Thomas, he had agreed to become a spy and had been encouraged to return to England to gather intelligence for the French.

So serious were the implications, the Head of the King's Council, Sir John Dudley, Duke of Northumberland, now took an interest. He wrote to his secretary, William Cecil (later Lord Burghley under Elizabeth I), ordering him to Court with all haste. On 19 September, Cecil took Thomas's deposition, in which he claimed that he had returned from France to bring information about Henri II's plot against England. The plan that Thomas reported was that, 'First the Scots were to enter Northumberland in force. Then the Duke of Guise with one army would land at Dartmouth ... while Henri himself with another army would land at Hellforth, so as to take Falmouth on the weak side, by land, not by water.'[6] According to Stukeley, once there, Henri II planned to take Dartmouth and Falmouth as French territory and restore Catholicism in these provinces.

To Northumberland and Cecil, all this may have seemed too good to be true. It was. Thomas offered to return to France to carry on his intelligence work, claiming to have close contact with Henri II and with Anne, duc de Montmorency, Constable of France. While Cecil was keen that Thomas should return, Northumberland wrote to Sir William Pickering, the English Ambassador in Paris, telling him to ask the King if these stories of invasion were true. He added that this was 'only to try Stucley's truth.'

Pickering's reply was as expected. He stated that Thomas had never mentioned any of this to him. For good measure, he added that Thomas had not had any contact with Henri II and had only once acted as an interpreter for Montmorency when he wished to question some English captives. Someone was telling lies.

Thomas was arrested and sent to the Tower. The French were told that it was for uttering slanders about the French King, 'as other runagates [illegal exiles] do,' hoping this would 'make him [Henri II] suspect the English runagates that be there.' Henri II certainly responded with caution, insisting he was innocent of any plot against England and his dear brother, Edward VI, and trusting that Thomas would be duly punished for his evil words. In the climate of the time, although it looked as if Thomas had fabricated his story, Northumberland still retained some uneasiness about the

123

'plot'. Thomas, as becomes clear, could talk his way out of anything. If Edward VI believed Thomas was his half-brother, this would go some way to explaining why he was not immediately executed for his activities. In fact, in 1553, once the furore died down, Thomas was released. In debt, he went this time to Emmanuel Philibert, Duke of Savoy, with a letter of recommendation from Mary I. In October 1553, he went with the Duke to the Emperor's Court in Brussels, attached to the English Embassy of Sir William Drury. In February 1554 Thomas wrote to Mary I himself:

> 'I do most humbly submit myself unto your clemency and beseech you to employ me at any time ... so now, having obtained the copy of an important letter from the French king to his ambassador in England, I send it by a gentleman of my band, who, I beseech you to tender being a gentleman of such honesty, wit, and experience, as ought to be commended to your Majesty ...'[7]

Once again, Thomas had assumed the role of acting as an agent for the English Crown, authorised or not. The letter in question from Henri II, giving his opinion that Mary I should never marry Philip II of Spain, stated that there would be war between France and England by the end of the year. The letter went on to ask for information about the English ships that were to go to Spain to fetch Philip to his wedding so that they could be intercepted. Henri II finished by saying that he would offer support to any Englishmen who rose in revolt against the Spanish marriage. There was, indeed, a rebellion led by Sir Thomas Wyatt in 1554, which failed for general lack of support. Fortunately, Thomas Stukeley was abroad when it happened, although some of his cousins were involved.

In October 1554, Thomas wrote to Mary I again, from the Emperor's camp at Hesdin. The letter was a masterpiece of persuasion. Thomas praised the Queen and her generosity. He claimed that her brother had agreed to pay his debts and that part of his trouble stemmed from his ill treatment at the hands of Northumberland, who Mary I loathed. The letter worked beautifully. Thomas returned to England and his appeal to Mary I earned him a respite. On 23 October a patent was issued to give 'Thomas Stucley gentleman, son of Sir Hugh Stucley knight of Devonshire,' security and freedom from arrest from November 1554 to April 1555. This gave him six months to settle his debts before he could be arrested.[8]

Once his temporary pardon ran out, Thomas seems to have been in trouble again. On 13 May 1555, a warrant was issued against him for circulating counterfeit money. However, this charge was never proved or even pursued. Neither is there any record of Thomas being arrested for debt.

At some point Thomas married Anne, granddaughter and sole heiress of Sir Thomas Curtis (or Curteis), a wealthy London alderman and merchant. The exact date of their marriage is not recorded, but in 1552 Henri II is said to have offered the bribe of an advantageous marriage when trying to persuade Thomas to act as his agent. A play performed in Spain in 1570 dealt with scenes from Thomas's life in which he took part in Wyatt's rebellion (which he actually missed), operated as a pirate (which he did) and married Anne Curtis.

Thomas's next appearance was in 1557, once again in the service of the Duke of Savoy, as part of an English company under the leadership of the Earl of Pembroke; in 1557 Pembroke's men took part in the Battle of San Quentin, where the French army of Henri II was defeated. At this point, Thomas seems to have been in favour with the Spanish and in November 1558 one of the Spanish admirals wrote to the Queen about Thomas:

'I have since heard that there remain five brothers, for whose education the rents of his father are necessary; I humbly beseech your Majesty, if it can be done without injustice, that you would order that the captain [Thomas

Stukeley] should be assisted with these during the usual time, that he may educate them conformably with their quality, and that he may better serve your Majesty, for, to my mind, he is of sufficient parts to deserve employment ..."[9]

This definitely looks like one of Thomas's inventions in order to acquire money. He was certainly one of five, but two of his brothers were older than him, and both would have been in their mid-to-late twenties. Lewis, the eldest, was already married and the father of several children. Their father was very well off and, therefore, not likely to need financial assistance from his middle son in supporting the family, especially a son who was notorious as a debtor.

Thomas did gain one advantage through the approval of the Queen and the Spanish Court; in 1558 a warrant was issued from the Queen to Sir Francis Englefield, Master of the Wards, ordering that:

'Our right well-beloved cousin the Marquis of Saria [the Imperial Ambassador] hath made earnest suit unto us that it might like us to grant unto this bearer, our servant Thomas Stucley, Esq., freely the wardship and marriage of the son and heir of Sergeant Prideaux, lately deceased.'[10]

Prideaux had married Thomas's sister, Mary, and it was their son whose wardship he was awarded. Thomas got to take funds from the Prideaux estate and the wardship stayed within the family and went to a member who was enjoying remarkable favour at Court.

No sooner had Thomas become the Prideaux boy's guardian than he began looting the child's estate. The Privy Council issued a Note that since, 'order was heretofore given him to forbeare to enter the houses, open the chests, or meddell with the goods of serjeant Prideaux deceased, he hath contrary to that order sithens so don, he is eftsoones required to abstaine from the meddling therewith, until the lawe shall have determined the right herin …'[11] The Council ordered Edward Drew and John Bodley to 'keep safe from spoyle' the goods and chattels of the Prideaux estate until the courts had decided what should be done and what Thomas might be entitled to.

In 1559 Alderman Curtis died and Thomas's wife, Anne, came into her full inheritance. Thomas should now have been comfortably off. According to Dr Oliver in his *Views of Devonshire*, 'by rich matches he [Thomas] got so good an estate as might have qualified a moderate mind to have lived bountifully and in great esteem, equal to the chief of his house.' Thomas, however, was not a 'moderate mind'. In Lord Burghley's State Papers there was an anonymous account of Thomas's life that Burghley had edited. One part read that Thomas was, '… commonly pretending himself to be a man of value and livelihood, when in truth he never had in his own right one foot of land, but by borrowing in every place and paying nowhere …'[12]

By 1559 Thomas had managed to change his allegiance again and was now in the service of Sir Thomas Parry, Elizabeth I's Treasurer and Master of Wards, and Sir Henry Neville, Sheriff of Berkshire. The wardship of his nephew may have proved insufficiently lucrative and now Thomas applied again. In May 1560 he wrote to Parry, asking if he might purchase the wardship and marriage of 'Mr Brent's daughter'. If Anne Curtis was already dead and her money almost spent, Thomas would be looking for a second wealthy wife. Neville also wrote to Parry, praising Thomas but there is no record that Thomas gained the wardship of Mr Brent's daughter or that he married her. Perhaps on this occasion he failed to direct things his own way.

By 1561 Thomas, based on his growing reputation as an excellent soldier and commander, was captain of the forces at Berwick, and living very comfortably. However, his lavish lifestyle used up the last of his wife's money and he left Berwick a poor man

127

again. It was here that he met and became friendly with Shane O'Neill, an Irish nobleman, who wrote to Elizabeth I of his time in Berwick:

> 'Many of the nobles, magnates and gentlemen of that kingdom treated me kindly and ingenuously, and namely one of the gentlemen of your realm, Master Thomas Stucley, entertained me with his whole heart, and with all the favour he could. But I perceived that his whole intention, and the benevolence he showed me, tended to this: to show me the magnificence and the honour of your Majesty and your realm.'[13]

It was not just Shane O'Neill who appreciated Thomas's talents. When the King of Sweden was seeking the Elizabeth I's hand in marriage in 1562, he chose Mr Keyle, an Englishman, to act as his intermediary. Of course, Robert Dudley, Earl of Leicester, (who hoped to marry the Queen himself) was against the scheme, and Mr Keyle was forced to report to the King: 'Lord Robert ... wrought marvellously to have had me in prison ... he made his old friends Stucley and Allen his means to trouble me, thinking thereby to have had me in prison. '[14]

By 1563 Thomas was a licensed privateer. He decided to found a colony in the newly discovered lands of Florida, although he was not so much intending to set up a colony as found a kingdom. Thomas is supposed to have said, 'I would rather be king of a molehill than subject to a mountain.' The record of a meeting between Thomas and Elizabeth I recounted: '... that Queen Elizabeth ... demanded him pleasantly whether he would remember her when he settled his kingdom. "Yes," saieth he, "and write unto you also." "And what style wilt thou use?" "To my loving sister, as one prince write to another".'[15]

Thomas set about putting together a small fleet, five ships and a pinnace (a small vessel used in support of larger ships), to pursue his grand plan at colonisation. He even persuaded Elizabeth to provide him with one ship. Oliver Leeson wrote to Thomas Challoner, English Ambassador to Spain: 'They say the Queen has delivered certain of her ships to Mr Stucley, and he is bound to Florida with four or five ships.'[16]

The ships he assembled, however, turned out to be for privateering, not colonising. Thomas never got to Florida; in fact he got no further than Ireland. He used his warrant to become a privateer, although he attacked Spanish ships as well as the French vessels he was authorized to take. At the end of the year John Cureton in Bilbao wrote to Challoner in Madrid that English ships were seizing French ships carrying Spanish goods, including two French ships taken out of port in Galicia by Stukeley, carrying Spanish goods worth 30,000 ducats. Two charges were recorded of piracy, one being:

'... a ship called the Trinity, Captain Martin de Goyas from Zeeland to Biscay, fell in with two English ships of war commanded, one by James Spenser, the other by a man of the Stucley family, about June 1563, and was robbed of linen cloths and other wares to the value of 3,000 pounds Flemish'[17]

Thomas's attacks on friendly shipping were becoming embarrassing, especially at a time when Elizabeth I was trying to keep on reasonably friendly terms with other European rulers. Challoner wrote from Madrid to William Cecil: 'Stucley's piracies are much railed at here on all parts. I hang down my head with shame enough. Alas, though it cost the Queen roundly, let him for honours sake be fetched in.'[18] Elizabeth I responded to Challoner's request and the Council sent two ships after the pirates said to be operating in Irish waters. This small force was under the command of Sir Peter Carew, who happened to be Thomas's 'cousin' (Thomas's aunt, Thomasine, married Sir George Carew; Peter was his younger brother). Carew managed to seize one of Stukeley's ships in the Irish port of Cork Haven, but the man himself evaded capture and had left the port before their arrival.

On 22 June 1565, the Privy Council wrote to Lord Justice Arnold setting out rewards and punishments, and the current situation regarding illegal privateers including, 'grievous complaints by the King of Spain against T Stucley the pirate.'[19] In April 1565 Thomas sent a letter to Cecil from Dublin, agreeing to place himself in custody, 'I insure your honour I have little left at this present but mine honesty, which I shall most humbly desire you to think well of, not doubting but when I shall by your good means be heard I shall be better judged of than I am at this present …'[20]

—◦◦◦—

Cecil wished it to be known that the Queen took piracy very seriously but miraculously, far from being imprisoned or hanged, Thomas was released. Lord Justice Arnold who examined the case of piracy against him recorded that he 'did not understand that he had committed any piracy upon the coast of Ireland or elsewhere' and being 'recommended to mercy as having done no harm' Thomas should be discharged.[21] The Admiralty Court, however, was prepared to proceed against him until he was finally released on bail. There was trouble brewing in Ireland and Thomas had made a most valuable connection there. In June and again in July 1565 Shane O'Neill wrote to the Queen:

> 'In return for all he did for me in England, I cannot do less than with all my might requite him [Thomas] with love the fervency of whose love I then enjoyed. But it has been lately shown me that you are persuaded that he has done something that offends you and your laws. If it be true, alas and alas! … I wish you would send Stucley to me that I might use his aid and counsel against your Majesty's enemies and rebels, and then I doubt not that your service

in the North of Ireland will flourish so as has not been seen for many years past.'[22]

The Queen and Cecil decided to use Thomas's talents in Ireland. Cecil, the canniest of statesmen, supported Thomas in his new endeavours; so did his old commander, Pembroke, and his friend, the Earl of Leicester. Thus, Cecil wrote to Sir Henry Sydney, Lord Deputy in Ireland, praising Thomas's courage and his ability to serve.

Thomas started work as a liaison officer between Shane O'Neill and Sir Henry Sydney, but O'Neill was soon making himself unpopular with the Governors of Ireland with his Irish sympathies, his local strength and popularity. Sydney wrote to Cecil complaining that O'Neill would not meet with him. O'Neill was not wholly to blame for the circumstances. After many instances of treachery on the part of the English, he was loath to meet with Sydney in case he was arrested or even murdered. O'Neill would not trust any safe conduct and when he offered to meet Sydney in the open somewhere so that there could be no danger of an ambush, Sydney refused.

Once more Thomas appeared with letters and a 'first-hand' account of a conversation he claimed to have had with O'Neill who said:

> 'And whom would you have me trust, Mr Stucley? I came in to the Earl of Sussex, upon the safe-conduct of two Earls, and protection under the great seal, and the first courtesy that he offered me was to put me in a hand-lock [handcuffs] and to send me into England. And so held me till I had agreed to such inconveniences against my honour and profit as I would never perform while I live; and that made me make war … Ulster is mine, and shall be mine … with this sword I won them, with this sword I will keep them. This is my answer. Commend me to my gossip [neighbour] the Deputy.'[23]

131

The conversation was the kind of inflammatory rhetoric that the Lord Deputy wanted to hear since it supported his interpretation of events. Thomas was commended by Sydney who joined the ranks of his well-wishers.

Even now, things did not go all Stukeley's way. In March 1566, Sydney wrote to Cecil asking if Sir Nicholas Bagenall might sell the office of Marshall of Ireland along with his estates to Thomas Stukeley for £3,000. The offer, however, was not approved. Cecil and the Queen might be prepared to make use of Thomas's skills, but that was a far cry from letting him take an influential place amongst the landed gentry in Ireland. Cecil wrote back to Sydney on 27 March, saying that the transaction was not well spoken of at Court. On 31 March, Elizabeth I wrote to Sydney saying that the purchase of the estates and offices should not go ahead, 'considering the general discredit wherein he [Thomas] remaineth, not only in our own realm, but also in other countries ...'.

In May 1566 Thomas was still in Ireland, hoping to salvage something out of the ruins of his efforts. He may have been at the defence of Dundalk, fighting for Sydney against his old friend and ally, Shane O'Neill. He may have been marrying; it looks as if he married a rich Irish widow named Elizabeth Peppard. In 1562 and again in 1566 a lease was given to Walter Peppard, a Gentleman Usher of the King's Chamber, for the lands of St Mary's Abbey in Dublin. Walter had a wife, Elizabeth, and a son, Anthony, and another lease was issued in 1583 to 'Elizabeth Stukeley, widow' and her son, 'Anthony Peppard', indicating that Thomas married Elizabeth after the death of Walter Peppard. It was Elizabeth's money that funded all Thomas's extravagant attempts to purchase titles, lands and posts.[24]

In June 1567 Thomas made a last attempt to establish his fortunes, buying land and the post of Seneschal of Wexford from Nicholas Heron. Once again, the purchase was forbidden by the Council in London. It had actually been completed and Thomas was settled in the forts at Laghlin and Carlogh, but the Queen was adamant; within a year they had been handed back to Heron. The Barony of Odrone, which Thomas had purchased as part of the package, went to Sir Peter Carew.

Elizabeth had become annoyed with O'Neill and wrote to Sydney to say that O'Neill should be brought down and a Council in Munster set up; she also stated that Thomas should return to England 'to answer the charges against him' in the Admiralty Court.[25] Thomas had been at his old habits again; part of the charge against him related to his purchasing hides and skins from Edward Cook, a known pirate who operated out of Southampton. By October 1568, Thomas was officially removed from all the posts he had bought during his alliance with O'Neill, by order of the Crown.

Thomas was not one to go down without a battle – of words at least. On 10 March 1569 Nicholas White, Heron's successor, wrote to Cecil, complaining that Thomas had been criticising him and poisoning the Lord Deputy against him. White got his revenge when he sent Cecil a deposition from Richard Stafford, 'as to expressions of Stucley undutiful to her Majesty, in the presence of himself and William Hore.'[26] Amongst other offences, Thomas was reported to have said of the Queen, 'I care not a fart for her nor yet for her office.' In June 1569 Thomas was arrested, sent to Dublin Castle and charged with speaking against the Queen and raising troops to oppose her. It looked as if Thomas was in serious trouble – but yet again, after 17 weeks in prison, he was released on parole.

While it seemed that the English Royal Family were prepared to forgive and forget yet again, this time it was Thomas who had had enough. His servant, Alessandro Fideli, had used his nephew, Cristofero, as a messenger for liaising with Italian Catholics on his master's behalf and, through them, with the Spanish Ambassador. Four days after Thomas was arrested in Ireland, the Ambassador wrote to Philip II of Spain:

'Thomas Stucley, an English Captain residing in Ireland, who, in consequences of his being Catholic, this Queen has

133

deprived of the charge of all the horses she has there, pretends that with his friends he is prepared to give that Island to your Majesty, or another Catholic Prince. And he and some noblemen wish to pass into Spain to beseech you to accept their offer.'[27]

In October 1569 Thomas was in London, supposedly to present his case to the Privy Council, although he actually had other plans. A letter from the French Ambassador, Fenelon, to the French Queen, Catherine de Medici, dated 17 February 1570, presents a real mystery. The French Ambassador, Bertrand de Salignac Fénelon, seigneur de la Mothe had been approached by a gentleman whose name he does not give:

'... to say that if the king pleased to receive him he will willingly pass to his service, with such a good plot in hand, that when the king please to put it into action, he will find it very conducive to his greatness; adding many occasions of his discontent, and of that of the principle lords of this realm. Thereupon, not knowing if he came to try me, I answered that I knew not that the king had any other but a very good intention to keep peace with the Queen of England and her realm; On which he said he would return in a little time to know the answer of your Majesty.'

Catherine de Medici replied on 3 March and she was not so reticent in naming this mysterious gentleman:

'I have received your cypher containing your opinion of affairs there, and what Stucley came to say to you, likewise your good and prudent answer, in fear that he had been guilefully sent to you by the Queen or her ministers to discover whether there was any ill will against them ... It seems to me, that, to keep the said Lady from suspecting, instead of letting him come over here, it will be better for you to keep in him his present good will and affection to do service to the king my Lord and son ... '[28]

With France blowing hot and cold, but promising nothing, Thomas contacted the Spanish again, although they seem better at cloak and dagger work as no letters relating to this matter survive. However, Thomas went back to Ireland briefly, then by ship from Wexford to Vimiero in Spain, arriving on 23 April 1570. The welcome was less than ecstatic. The servant Fideli, and another servant, Reynald Digby, went on to Madrid to present Thomas's compliments to the King. Philip II sent back a letter telling Thomas to stay where he was, along with a gift of 2,000 ducats. Thomas immediately sent messages to the King recording his plan for the invasion and annexation of Ireland without a single life being lost. He pointed out what a wonderful, wealthy country Ireland was, a jewel for Philip's crown. He reported that the English were hated, were few in numbers (about 1,500) and that their fortifications were almost non-existent.

Maurice Fitzgibbon, the Archbishop of Cashel, elected by the Pope and burning to go to Ireland and take up his post, wrote to Philip in support of the soldier he saw as instrumental to the winning of Ireland, a country that was, he believed, ripe for the taking: '... and you have an excellent opportunity for this in the coming of this Englishman Thomas Stucley, who surely has received such wrongs from his countrymen that he will not fail to do them all the harm he can. He is a man of great courage and knowledge of war ... He ... knows the fortresses and the ports.'[29]

Cashel wanted Ireland to be free, ruled either by the Pope or by Philip II (with the Pope's blessing), and with himself in a leading role, the saviour of his nation. He was supported by a number of Catholic Irish nobles in exile who wanted to return to a free Ireland where they could resume their rights and lands. In the event that Philip let them down by making peace with Elizabeth, they had a secondary plan to invite Don John of Austria, the King's bastard brother, to become their leader and the next King of Ireland. What all parties wanted was immediate action, Thomas not least of all.

Finally, in August 1570, Thomas was summoned to Madrid and given 3,000 ducats in expenses. Thomas wrote to Philip II, complaining of his treatment at the hands of his 'sister', Elizabeth I. Philip was so impressed with him that he awarded him a pension. It looked as if Thomas would be a major influence with Philip, but Nicholas White, writing to Cecil, thought that he had 'more malice than power with the King of Spain.'

After a promising beginning, Philip had been receiving adverse comments about Thomas from Cashel, in a series of letters. The Archbishop saw himself as the leader of the invasion of Ireland, and was most put out to find his glory being stolen by this enthusiastic English soldier. Thomas's plans indicated he expected to be made an Irish duke at the very least, and Cashel may have suspected, as Thomas had already hinted, that he saw himself as a possible king. The two became bitter rivals, splitting those who supported an Irish invasion into two weaker factions.

In May 1571, Lord Justice 'Fytzwylliam' [Sir William Fitzwilliam] wrote to Cecil (now Lord Burghley) that he had had word from an old servant of Thomas that he had been in Spain, well received by Philip II at first, but that he had antagonised the Archbishop of Cashel and had lost some of his popularity. He had, however, spoken with Philip about taking the Isles of Scilly to use as a Spanish jumping-off point for invasion. A week later Fitzwilliam wrote again to say that he had heard that an army was being assembled at 'Vivero' in Spain, to invade Ireland; this army was to be under the command of Thomas. He enclosed a copy of a letter from John Morgans of Cork, reporting that 2,000 soldiers were promised by Philip and that Thomas was now known as Duke of Ireland; however, he had also heard that Philip planned to withdraw his offer.

The Archbishop of Cashel wrote one last letter to Philip, condemning Thomas. He recorded a remarkably accurate life history and ended by saying that Thomas had agreed to help with the conquest of Ireland because he wanted revenge on Elizabeth I and wanted his lands back, not at all because he was a good Catholic who wanted a free Catholic Ireland. Philip, probably tired of the squabbling, ignored the letter. Cashel, seeing that he had lost the King's support, left Spain for France where he met Walsingham, who was Ambassador to the Court of Charles IX. Cashel told Walsingham the whole story so far.

At last it seemed that Philip II might be taking the initiative. Thomas was moved to Arosso, close to Madrid with a retinue of 30 servants, all expenses paid by the Crown. Thomas must have been further reassured when he was invited to Madrid and knighted by the King.

———*♪♪♪*———

Finally, in January 1571, Philip set matters in motion. He issued Thomas with a warrant to proceed to Rome where he should seek the support of the Pope for their endeavour. A month later Elizabeth I wrote to Walsingham in Paris, ordering him to lay a complaint with the Spanish Ambassador in France about the Irish rebels who had taken refuge in Spain.

Whether or not Philip had doubts about Thomas's ability or veracity, once again things slowed to a halt. The rumour in England was that Philip finally believed all the stories about Thomas's past (his 'lewdness and insufficiency'). At that time Philip was putting his energies into his campaign against the Turks, led by Don John of Austria. During the preparations, in April, Thomas took his warrant and travelled to Rome where he had an audience with Pope Pius V. Thomas was very well received by the Pope, and spent long periods talking with him. He was said to have discussed his plan to invade Ireland with 3,000 men and reclaim it for the Papacy.

As it was, Pius V was also concentrating on the war with the Turks, so Thomas cut short his visit and returned to Spain where he joined Don John's forces. The two men fought together at the

Battle of Lepanto, 7 October 1571, and Thomas acquitted himself superbly as always. There was a contingent of Englishmen fighting against the Turks; one of them, Nicholas Rice, reported that Thomas Stucley, 'an Irish Merchant', had captained three galleys under Don John. In April 1572 merchants coming into Galway reported that Thomas had done so well that he was back in favour with Philip II and was 'with him in great estimation and credit.'[30]

The plans for an invasion of Ireland were only suspended as Philip intended to look at such an invasion at a later date. The secrecy of such a plan was compromised by an English counterspy. Amongst the disaffected Englishmen recruited for the enterprise was Sir John Hawkins who, as a loyal subject, was working for Burghley; he promptly turned over all the information he gathered.

In late 1571 to early 1572 Thomas was back at Court in Madrid. Hawkins reported that it seemed that he was indeed back in royal favour: 'He has already taught the Spaniards to frame their ships after our manner, which they are persuaded will annoy us greatly in a short time, and it is reported that he will be made Admiral or Vice-Admiral of the whole.'[31]

In May 1572 Pope Pius V died and Philip II found himself as the sole leader of the war against the Turks. Without the Vatican, the war stalled. The Spanish fleet under Don John was at Messina and here it stayed until October when it was brought back to harbour in Spain. One can only imagine Thomas's frustration as his chance of glory and wealth slipped away, but once again he appeared with highly controversial documents at a crucial moment.

His first note was supposed to have come from Dr Nicholas Sander, one of the leaders of the English in exile (in June 1573, these exiles wrote to the Pope to ask if a representative could be accredited by the Papacy as English spokesman in the Spanish Court to try and get Philip II to act; they suggested Sander as it was he who advocated Spain's invasion of England). The letter stated that the French, apparently going to England to arrange the marriage of Elizabeth I and the King's brother, the duc d'Alençon, were really going to arrange the death of Mary Stewart, so as to keep Spain and England enemies because it suited England, France and Scotland. The second document was from Englefield. It suggested that what was needed was a Franco–Spanish alliance against England, and that Thomas should be sent to France to negotiate it.

It is quite amazing to consider how many times Thomas's plans were progressed by his coming up with a relevant document at just the right moment. As these documents were usually copies of the original, there was no question of matching handwriting or checking signatures; the recipient had to take the word of the messenger. Philip II, however, was less amenable than others had been; he, or one of his servants, had noticed that 'they are in Spanish and not scaled, when the others came in Latin and sealed.' Thomas may have been a skilled forger, but he lacked the attention to detail that would have convinced a shrewd conspirator like Philip of Spain.

In March 1573 Venice made a separate peace with Constantinople, and the Turkish war was effectively over. Don John briefly invaded Tunis instead; given their previous campaigns together, Thomas may well have been with him. This was a brief interlude before the plans for the invasion of England were reactivated. This time Spain was to invade England, arrest Elizabeth I, and put Mary, Queen of Scots, on the throne in her place.

The taking of England into sympathetic rule would be of double benefit to Spain; it would mean an end to the support the English had been giving to Holland, a Protestant country fighting to be free of Catholic Imperial control. Once again, Thomas was mentioned in the planning, a valuable participant in the invasion as he could use his popularity, influence and charm to bring the English sea captains over to the Catholic alliance.

Thomas was high in Philip's favour once again as, 'The king hath given to Thomas Stucley at times from his first coming into Spain in anno 1570 to this time of August 1574 ... the whole sum to 27,576 ducats. The King doth give to Thomas Stucley for his pension by the year 600 ducats, and to William Stucley [his son] 400 ducats.³² However, despite the rumours that abounded, Philip II failed to act decisively.

Gerald, Earl of Desmond was said to have sent to France for munitions and Thomas 'Stewkeley' was to lead 100 Spanish ships to conquer Ireland. It was said that Spanish sailors were spies, Desmond had received a cargo of Spanish swords and Thomas's popularity was being revitalised; the Mayor of Waterford had heard that his own local watermen were being recruited as pilots to bring in the foreign ships. So serious were the rumours that the Irish nobility, including the Earls of Kildare and Ormonde, were ordered home, 2,000 men and 'a mass of victuals' were sent to Ireland, and Waterford, Cork and Kinsale were to be well fortified. The Lord Deputy wrote to the Privy Council, 'Stucley's invasion hath a show almost of undoubted certainty.'

Panic reigned in Ireland and London. From April to July 1574 letters flew between the Court and Dublin. The Mayor and officers of Waterford wrote to the Lord Deputy about preparations of a fleet in Andalusia, 'of Spaniards, Portuguese and Flemings.' 'Stucley,' they reported, was threatening to come into Ireland at any time. They enclosed a letter from Roger Winston to the Lord Deputy to the effect that a ship from Calais reported that Thomas was coming to Waterford with his men and a fleet of 100 ships.³³

The following year, 1575, Thomas was once more in Rome, seeking the approval of the new Pope, Gregory XIII, to bring forward the plans to fruition. The year of 1577 saw Thomas rarely still. He was in Rome, then Flanders, then Lisbon with the Irish nobleman, James Fitzgerald Fitzmorris, the Earl of Desmond's kinsman. He had been waiting for the promised, rumoured help, but now had almost given up. In November Thomas wrote to the Cardinal of Como that he would return to Ireland: '... without arms, without ships, without men, in the name of our Lord Jesus Christ, relying on the Pope's authority, and trusting much in your prayers to obtain victory against the enemies of the Church.'³⁴

Still the talk in Madrid and Rome was that the Pope would send men and ships, and that Thomas would command them. At the end of November, the figure of 2,000 men was mentioned. There is also a suggestion that the Pope wished the throne of Ireland to go to his bastard son, Giacomo Buoncompagno, Duke of Sora (born before Gregory XIII became Pope). There were a mass of reports and rumours about attacks on England and Ireland, some to be led by Thomas.

Suddenly, in early 1578, things seemed to be moving. One of the Fugger papers held in the Vienna Library is a memorial from Fitzgerald and Thomas to the Pope. It said that Ireland was firmly Catholic and that it needed only a small, determined army to wrest it away from English control. The Pope was convinced and gave 40,000 scudi towards buying ships and men. Philip II, although he would not get involved personally, gave another 20,000 scudi, and persuaded other exiled Englishmen, like Leonard Dacres and Charles Goade, to join the expedition.

One story reported that James Fitzgerald recruited Italian bandits, who had been troubling the Roman district, with the grant of a pardon. In February 1578, when Thomas and Fitzgerald had gathered together around 1,000 troops, Thomas went to Lisbon with the soldiers and ships, and Fitzgerald went to France to fetch his wife. This diversion to Portugal would prove to be Thomas's undoing.

The ships given so generously turned out to be rotten and worm-eaten. Thomas needed a port to carry out repairs, but at that time Philip was still unwilling to be seen publicly supporting the invasion. He ordered Thomas and his fleet out of Cadiz; they sailed slowly and painfully to the nearest friendly port, Lisbon. By 28 May, Thomas was in Lisbon waiting to meet Fitzgerald, but he was never to see his comrade again. In July 1578 the great invasion by Thomas and his Spanish fleet was known to have been called off. The Lord Deputy wrote to the Privy Council that 'Stucley is diverted from Ireland.'

Thomas's fate was sealed when he sailed into Lisbon and into the clutches of Sebastian, the young King of Portugal, who had a desperate need for Thomas and his army. Sebastian was the grandson of King John II of Portugal, son of Don John the Crown Prince and his wife, Joanna, daughter of Charles V of Spain. Don John died when his son was less than a year old and Sebastian ascended the throne when he was three years old. He was brought up by his aunt, Catharina, sister of Charles V, and Aleixo de Meneses, a Jesuit. The boy was brought up more as a monk than a king; on the advice of his confessors he never married. He was, however, under pressure from the Cortes, the Portuguese government, to do something about attacks on their shipping by the Ottoman Turkish navy.

Sebastian's chance came when the Morrocan emperor died. His heir was his nephew, Abu Abdallah Mohammed II Saadi (Mohammed Saadi), but the throne had been taken by Mohammed's uncle, Abd Al-Malik Saadi (Al-Malik). Mohammed Saadi turned to Portugal for help and was promised an army to assist him in retaking his throne. Al-Malik sought support from the Ottoman Empire. Sebastian was determined to set a friendly king on the throne of Morocco and to deal a blow to the power of the Ottoman Turks. He met with his uncle Philip II, but found him lukewarm on the question, so Sebastian decided he would go forward on his own. The Papacy supported Sebastian, and a comet appeared in the sign of Libra, near the station of Mars on 9 November – this was taken as a sign that the war would go well.

In Lisbon harbour Thomas was on board the San Juan of Genoa, 800 tons, with 700 troops. According to stories, Sebastian saw Thomas's troops and admired their efficiency and courage. He pressured Thomas into committing his troops to join the foray into Africa. Philip did not interfere because he was trying to avoid any obvious connection with the enterprise, and the Pope was too far away to intervene. Thomas agreed to join Sebastian when he in turn agreed to give aid in the Irish invasion.

The Portuguese invasion force was a mix of nationalities. There were 3,000 Germans contributed by the Prince of Orange, a few Spanish professional soldiers (Philip had forbidden his subjects from joining the expedition, possibly hoping to discourage Sebastian) and now Thomas's professional Italian soldiers. The Portuguese troops, however, were less valuable. The Portuguese historian, Juan de Mariana (1537?–1624) wrote:

'... the gentlemen, instead of scouring their arms, guarded their habits; for corselets they provided doublets of silk and gold; they were charged with sugar and conserves instead of water and biscuit; the vessels of silver, and the tents lined with silk and satin, were without number; every gentleman went furnished like a king, and the poor soldiers died for hunger.'[35]

On 17 June, after receiving his consecrated battle standard from the cathedral, Sebastian boarded his ship, stayed eight days in port, and then sailed for Africa on 24 June 1578. He landed at Arzila, in Portuguese-controlled Morocco, where Mohammed Saadi and his soldiers joined the army. Al-Malik was seriously ill, but he led an army of 100,000 men against the invaders. The armies met at a place that was called Alcazar by the Europeans, but was more correctly known as Alcácer Quibir, in northern Morocco between Tangier and Fez.

On 4 August, battle was joined. Al-Malik sent Moorish troops into his centre (men who had been driven out of Spain and were particularly bitter against the Portuguese), with cavalry on the wings, encircling the Portuguese forces. It was said either that the Portuguese advanced too fast, or that their allies held back, but in the event there was a massacre. Some 8,000 Portuguese and their allies were killed, with an additional 15,000 taken prisoner. Sebastian was killed, as were nearly all the young nobles who had come with him on this glorious enterprise. The King was last seen leading a charge into the heart of the opposing army; he must have been hacked to death, as his remains were never conclusively identified.

This battle was commonly called the Battle of the Three Kings. Sebastian died. Al-Malik, who was terminally ill, died of natural causes during the battle; his brother and successor, Ahmad al-Mansur, had the body propped up in a chair and carried about the field as if he were still alive. Mohammed Saadi, once he saw the battle was lost, attempted to flee and was drowned when he tried to escape across the river.

Thomas Stukeley, probably their best professional soldier, commanded the centre, where his Italians took the brunt of the fighting. He died almost at once, hit by a cannon ball. It was reported that both his legs were shot off and that he bled to death in moments. Westcote, in his *Views of Devon*, recorded that Thomas:

'... failed nothing to perform the part both of a skilful leader and valiant soldier; and as it was vulgarly reported, had the Council of war approved, and the King followed his advice, and forborne the fight for that day, the victory had been clearly his; but otherwise persuaded by his inexperienced nobles, young and full of courage, who also taxed Stucley with cowardice for giving procrastinating counsel; to whom he replied, "Out of your inexperience and ignorance in the stratagems of war you deem me a coward; yet this advice would prove safe and victorious, and your great haste be your overthrow; yet proceed, and when you come into action you will look after me, and shall apparently see that Englishmen are no cowards." All which he verified in his proceedings, and died nobly ...'

Back in Madrid, Philip continued to favour Thomas Stukeley's son, William, who was at the Spanish Court in 1584. In 1630 James Wadsworth wrote that, 'At Milan there resides Sir Thomas Stucley, who hath 100 crowns a month pension from the King of Spain. This Stucley is a grand traitor and enemy to his country, and were it not for the Duke of Feria, who entertains him at his own table, he might long since have rode back to Madrid on an ass as he came.'[58] This could be one of Thomas's sons, grown old in the Spanish Court, or even his grandson, William's child, fated to spend his life in Spain, refused entry to England because of his grandfather's history. It may even be that Thomas's descendents made a new life for themselves in the Catholic world.

On his death, two versions of the life of Thomas Stukeley arose. One is best typified by a biography that was produced for Burghley in 1583 and was edited in his own hand. Burghley said of Thomas:

'Out of Ireland ran away one Thomas Stucley, a defamed person almost through all Christendom, and a faithless beast rather than a man, fleeing first out of England for notable piracies, and out of Ireland for treacheries not pardonable ... Of this man might be written whole volumes to paint out the life of a man in the highest degree of vain-glory, prodigality, falsehood, and vile and filthy conversation of life, and altogether without faith, conscience, or religion.'[36]

This, however, was not the public opinion. It was only a matter of a few years before plays and epic poems surfaced with Thomas as the hero. George Peele wrote a play titled, *The Battell of Alcazar, fought in Barbarie, between Sebastian King of Portugal, Abdelmelec King of Marocco, with the death of Captain Stukeley.* It was performed in the late 1580s by the Lord Admiral's Men. Their 'star' was Edward Alleyn, one of the most illustrious Tudor actors; he may well have played the lead role of Thomas Stukeley.[37]

An anonymous author penned, *The Famous History of the life and death of Captain Thomas Stukeley with his marriage to Alderman Curteis Daughter and valiant ending of his life at the Battle of Alcazar*. This version of events starts with Thomas winning the hand of Anne Curtis from Vernon, who was to have been her husband. Vernon, crossed in love, goes adventuring to get over his loss until both he and Thomas die at Alcazar.

In the Roxburgh collection, in the British Museum, is a copy of a ballad by an unknown author telling the story of 'lusty Stucley,' which is to be sung to the tune of 'King Henry's going to Boulogne'. Another, earlier ballad was written before Thomas's abortive plan to settle Florida. It is called, 'A Commendation of the adventurous voyage of the worthy captain, Thomas Stutley Esquire and others towards the land called Terra Florida'.

Finally, Westcote, in his *Views of Devonshire*, quotes two verses from yet another early rhyme, a 'ditty, made by him [Thomas Stukeley] or of him':

> *Have over the waters to Florida*
> *Farewell good London now*
> *Through long delays on land and seas*
> *I'm brought, I cannot tell how.*

Thomas is portrayed as a hero, a valiant warrior, a victim of fate and the machinations of villains like Philip II. Here and there are references to the secret of Thomas's birth:

> *I am a gentleman, and well deriv'd*
> *Equal, I may say, in all true respects*
> *With higher fortune that I aim at now ...*

> *What a high spirit hath this Englishman*
> *He tunes his speeches to a kingly key*
> *Conquers the world, and casts it at his heels ...*[38]

As Thomas's character lies dying on the stage, he tells his English companion:

Yet with this blood of ours the blood of kings
Shall be co-mixed, and with their fame our fame
Shall be eternis'd in the mouths of men

The author was right; Thomas's fame has crossed the centuries and his bloodline may survive today.

THE FAMILY OF SIR JOHN PERROT

- ◆ mistress of Henry VIII
- ✚ illegitimate child of Henry VIII
- = married

Thomas Perrot
=
1) Janet, daughter of John Wise
2) Isabella, daughter of Sir Henry Wogan

Sir William Perrot

Joanna, daughter of Sir Henry Wogan

Sir Owen Perrot
=
Catherine, daughter of Sir Robert Poyntz

Sir James Berkeley
=
Isabel, daughter of Thomas Mowbray, Duke of Norfolk

Maurice Berkeley (?–1506)
=
Isabel d. of Philip Meade

James (1466–c.1515) Lord Berkeley
=
Susan, daughter of William Fitzalan

◆ **Mary Berkeley** (c.1480–?) = 1) Sir Thomas Perrot (c.1505–?) 2) Sir Thomas Jones

Jane
=
William Philips

Elizabeth
=
John Price

✚ **Sir John Perrot**
(c.1520–83)
=
1) Anne Cheyney
2) Jane Pruett

Sir Harry Jones
=
1) Elizabeth Herbert
2) Catherine Morgan

Katherine
=
N Vaughan

Ellenor
=
Griffith Rice

Sir Thomas Perrot
=
Dorothy Devereaux

William Perrot

Anne
=
Sir John Philips

Lettice
=
1) Roland Lacharn
2) Walter Vaughan
3) Arthur Chichester, Baron

Elizabeth
=
Hugh Butler

Sir James Perrot
=
Mary, daughter of Robert Ashfield

John Perrot

Thomas Perrot

The Huntsman's Wife
and the Blustering Diplomat

———◦/◦◦————

John Perrot was born at Haroldston, Pembrokeshire, somewhere between 1527 and 1530. He was the son of Mary, the wife of Sir Thomas Perrot, and although he passed for the offspring of her husband, he was widely believed to be the son of Henry VIII.

John's mother's maiden name was Berkeley, and she had been one of Catherine of Aragon's ladies. Mary came from an old and illustrious family based at Berkeley Castle in Somerset. Her father was James Berkeley and her mother Susan Fitzalan. The Berkeleys were one of the great families in the west of England. One of her cousins was married to the Earl of Ormonde, and her Berkeley great-grandfather had married the daughter of one of the Mowbray Dukes of Norfolk. One can assume that she was well-bred and possessed the talents that Henry found so attractive: she was a good musician, poetess, literate, lively, witty and pretty.

Henry VIII obviously knew both bride and groom since he knighted Thomas on the occasion of the Perrots' marriage. Sir Thomas Perrot was a renowned huntsman and he would have played host to the King, who came to his house to hunt, a sport they both really enjoyed.

In Edmund Spenser's famous epic poem, *The Faerie Queene*, the reason for Mary's brief affair with Henry VIII is explained. The poem was an allegory based on the life of Elizabeth I and the various characters in the poem were based on those surrounding the Queen. John Perrot was personified as Sir Satyrane, whose character and parentage are described as follows:

> ... *begotten of a Lady myld*
> *Faire Thyamis, the daughter of Labryde,*
> *That was in sacred bands of Wedlocke tyde*
> *To Therion, a lose unruly swayne;*
> *Who had more ioy to raunge the forrest wyde,*
> *And chase the salvage beast with busie payne,*
> *Then serve his Ladies love and wast in pleasures vayne.*[1]

In the poem, Mary Perrot was said to have been married to a man who cared more about hunting than his wife. It is no surprise that the King, invited to hunt with Perrot, should notice the charming Mary and dally in one of the several affairs with married ladies that seem to have so delighted him in middle age. It also meant, of course, that in the event of a pregnancy from the liaison there was a ready-made father, willing to accept the child.

150

According to his own biography, young John was educated at St Davids, Pembrokeshire,[2] and at the age of 18 he joined the household of William Paulet, Marquis of Winchester. John was a large, tall, strong, auburn-haired youth, and it was said that he much resembled Henry VIII. Unlike the stereotypical image of the gentle giant, he had a quarrelsome nature and a short temper. However, his Tudor 'family' seemed to like him. John came to the King's attention in a rather remarkable way. He was found brawling with two of the King's Yeoman of the Guard within a palace precinct, a crime that normally required the aggressor to lose a hand. The King, however, obviously found the sight of his bastard son, battling with two men and fighting on despite his injuries, highly gratifying. Henry VIII may well have believed John was his son, not least because of the young man's resemblance to the Tudors rather than to the Perrots. The King gave him a Promise of Preferment (that he would be put forward for a position or office at Court) instead of a visit to the nearest jail cell. Henry meant to do great things for John, had his own death not intervened.

In an even more bizarre twist of fate, shy, repressed Edward VI counted John Perrot as a friend. He was made a Knight of the Bath at Edward's coronation and Sir John recalled that he entertained the young King with tales of his bad temper (he admitted to Edward that he 'could not brook any crosses'), drinking, swearing, fighting and wenching. Instead of being horrified, Edward enjoyed these swaggering boasts. Perhaps Edward liked this image of a big brother, one who refused to stand on ceremony with a lonely little boy, treating him more like a real human being than a regal figurehead. One story featured Sir John and Lord Abergavenny. They had planned a party for a group of their friends, but: '... before their guests arrived they came to some contention, and so to blows, that they took the glasses and brake them about one another's ears; when the guests came thither, they found, instead of claret wine, blood besprinkled about the chamber.'[3] Sir John, being somewhat older, could also tell tales of Henry VIII, and these seemed to give particular pleasure to Edward VI who was only 10 years old when he lost his magnificent father.

In 1548, Sir John became an MP for the first time, for Carmarthenshire in south west Wales. In 1551, he was one of the party led by the Marquis of Northampton that went to France to start the negotiations for the marriage of Edward VI with Elizabeth, the daughter of Henri II. Sir John charmed everyone there and Henri II particularly loved his skill and enthusiasm for hunting. The King tried to bribe him to stay in France and enter his personal service but to no avail.

On his return to England, Sir John enthusiastically entered into Court life, but he soon found himself seriously in debt to the sum of around £8,000 – an enormous amount for the time. Not one to give in meekly, he is reputed to have come up with a brilliant stratagem. In the words of his biography:

'He walked into a place where commonly the King used to come about that hour, and there he began to complain, as it were, against himself, to himself – how unfortunate and how unwise he was, so to consume his living … "Must I be the man that shall overthrow my house, which hath continued so long? It had been better I had never been born. What shall I do? … Had I best leave the Court and follow the wars? Shall I retire into the country?'"

As planned, the King came in, just in time to overhear this sad lament. Edward VI then asked Sir John if he had spent his money in the service of the King. When Sir John stated that he had, Edward agreed to recompense him and the bulk of the £8,000 debt was paid by the young King. Sir John went on to enjoy Edward's favour until the young man died in 1553.[4]

Mary I also liked Sir John. He was a strong Protestant, and when he hid 'heretics' in his house he was denounced by a man called Catherne. Mary may have felt his sin to be fairly minor, given that one of those he hid was his own uncle, Robert Perrot, who had been Reader in Greek to Edward VI and so she was quite lenient in his punishment. Sir John spent a short time imprisoned in the Fleet, and when released, he found it prudent to retire to the continent. He joined his friend the Earl of Pembroke as part of the forces in the French Wars, being present at the capture of St Quentin in 1557 (along with Thomas Stukeley). However, as Mary lay ill and dying, John returned to England, to enjoy a profitable friendship with Elizabeth I.

At Elizabeth I's coronation, tall, handsome Sir John was one of the four gentlemen chosen to carry the canopy of state. In 1562 he was appointed Vice-Admiral of the coast of south Wales and keeper of the gaol at Haverfordwest. In 1563 he was rapidly becoming a political force in Pembrokeshire including serving as the local MP. In 1570 he was Mayor of Haverfordwest. Unfortunately he was also involved in a large number of disputes and lawsuits with his neighbours, which did nothing to make him a popular figure.

In 1571, Elizabeth wanted to settle Munster with a presidency. Sir John was specifically requested for the job by the Earl of Ormonde and Ossory, rival of the powerful Earl of Desmond, who wanted a firm hand in Ireland. Sir John set about suppressing a rebellion headed by James Fitzmaurice, nephew of the Earl of Desmond; his campaign was one of severity and brutality. It was calculated that he had ordered the hanging of more than 800 rebels, losing only 18 of his own men during his campaigns and founding his reputation as an Irish expert.[5]

A series of letters were sent from Ireland to England, reporting on the activities of an English rebel who had once served in Ireland and was now in the service of the King of Spain and the Pope – a certain Thomas Stukeley. He was reported to be gathering an army for invasion and Sir John was ordered to be in readiness for their coming.

By 1573, Sir John was in poor health and he resigned the presidency to return to Wales. He was tired and sick, and particularly angry that Elizabeth I seemed bent on restoring Gerald Fitzgerald, Earl of Desmond, despite his family's rebellious history. He had received word that the rising star at Court, the Earl of Essex, was interfering with his Welsh holdings, and that he was to be questioned by the Privy Council about his having illegally held a French ship, the *Peter and Paul*, at Cork.[6]

The Queen, however, knew her man and valued him accordingly. One of Sir John's rewards was land and the 13th-century Carew Castle at Milford Haven, which, suitably modernised, became his second residence. Much of the Tudor Carew Castle was destroyed during the Civil War.

Having returned from Ireland, Sir John wrote to Lord Burghley that he wished to live a 'countryman's life.' As it happened, this meant 10 years of legal cases and attempts to increase his land holdings in Pembrokeshire. He tried to acquire lands lately held by Haverfordwest Priory, and was suspected of unfairly influencing a jury to find in his favour. In fact he lost on this occasion, and had to wait many years before he could buy the much-desired lands.[7] His behaviour tended to polarise people into those who supported him and those who didn't; it was very difficult to remain neutral on the subject of Sir John Perrot.

Even though he was back in Wales, his reputation in Irish affairs remained strong. During the first half of 1574 there were numerous communications relating to the need for a strong hand in control in Ireland, and Sir John's name came up many times. In January, Patrick Sherlok, Sheriff of Waterford, was writing to Lord Burghley to advise him that the Earl of Desmond had allied with Turlough Lynaugh O'Neill and the 'gentlemen of Thomond' so that the potential rebels numbered 3,000. Sherlock requested that the Earl of Ormonde and Sir John Perrot be sent with a force of 1,000 English soldiers to avert any rebellion.[8] The Queen added her opinion to Burghley, acknowledging that the Earl of Desmond's behaviour was unacceptable. She was annoyed that the current Lord Deputy in Ireland had let matters get out of hand. She decided to send forces there under the command of Sir John. By March a memorial had been produced on the situation in Ireland. The Earl of Essex was to stay at his post there, despite having asked to be allowed to resign; Sir John was to be ordered to recover Munster and to pacify Leinster and Connaught.

However, instead of taking up a post in Ireland, Sir John joined the Council in the Marches of Wales, and became involved with suppression of piracy along the Welsh coast. The following year the Privy Council set up a commission to deal with piracy of which Sir John, with his experience, was made chief commissioner. Within 12 months Glamorgan and Monmouthshire followed suit and offered the post of chief commissioner to Sir John. By this time, however, he was forced to refuse on the grounds of ill health.

According to the *Dictionary of National Biography*, 'His [Sir John's] anti-piracy activities are chiefly of interest because of the bitter feud which they created between him and Richard Vaughan, deputy-admiral in Wales and chief commissioner for piracy in Carmarthenshire, who deeply resented Perrot's interference in his sphere of influence.' Vaughan ended up accusing the irascible Sir John of acting the tyrant, having illicit dealings with pirates himself, and subverting justice. Happily Sir John had no trouble convincing his judges of his innocence and was able to continue his activities.

In 1575, he became Mayor of Haverfordwest again, this time after establishing better relations with the corporation. In 1580, Sir John made a bequest of land and property valued at £30 to the town of Haverfordwest. This was the Perrot Trust that was still active in the late 1980s, yielding around £400 a year. The revenue from the Trust was used for civic improvement, including providing the first pavements in Haverfordwest.[9]

In 1579 Sir John was given command of five ships and on 29 August he set sail with his son Thomas. His orders were to wait off the coast of Ireland and watch for Spanish shipping trying to land. In September he was moored in Baltimore Bay, from where he sailed to Cork and then along the coast to Waterford. There, he met Sir William Drury, the Irish president, who had taken the job when Sir John retired. They never saw any Spaniards, but Sir John's fleet chased and captured a pirate ship, the *Derifold*.

In his absence, and following failure to come up with more than one small prize, Sir John's enemies had started a campaign to discredit him. They claimed that, far from pursuing the pirates, he was in league with them; his houses at Haroldston and Carew were said to be full of contraband goods, including looted Gascon wine. Certainly, the pirates seem to have been brazen when it came to selling on their stolen goods, and captures of pirates were few and far between. This time Sir John found it difficult to clear his name.

In 1581, in response to a request from the Queen for information, Sir John wrote a 'Discourse' on the action most suited to governing Ireland. In 1584, he was again appointed to Ireland as Lord Deputy. Elizabeth had admired his first tour of duty in

Munster and, after the 'Discourse', held him to be something of an expert on Ireland. He spent four years in Ireland this time, but it did not go well. He was hampered by his own quarrelsome bad temper, the tortuous complexities of Irish politics and enmity from a range of people, including his own officials and Adam Loftus, Archbishop of Dublin. Ireland was a political nightmare, a true poisoned chalice for a Lord Deputy. If he was lenient towards the Irish, he was branded a traitor to his own people. If he favoured the English, he was hated by the Irish. Trying to be fair to both sides usually meant that both sides hated their governor.

Sir John took his time in going out to Ireland in 1584. In March of that year the Earl of Ormonde wrote to Burghley that Sir William Fitzwilliam should to be sent as a temporary Deputy if Sir John was delayed any further. After the matter of Sir John's establishment was addressed, with a final estimate of £3,900 settled as the necessary sum to set up his household in Ireland, things somehow sorted themselves out.

In June 1584, Sir John arrived in Ireland and on 21 June he was formally inducted, receiving the sword of state as Lord Deputy. On 22 June an Order was sent out from Dublin Castle in the name of the Lord Deputy, Council and Grand Council for a general assembly, to begin 10 August next, and to assemble at the Hill of Tara. There were to be general musters in every county and for every barony. The following day Sir Richard Byngham, governor of Connaught, wrote to Walsingham, 'The country is in very good state and likely to continue so.' It was hoped that 'the Lord Deputy will do much good', but at the same time the arrival was noted of 1,700 Scots (illegal settlers) in the province.[10]

Even before his arrival Sir John was aware of trouble brewing with Lord Justice Wallop in Athlone. On 9 April 1584, Wallop wrote to Burghley about the rule of Athlone. He feared that it was Sir John's intention to displace him. He had saved Her Majesty £10,000, he said, and now was obliged to yield Athlone to the Lord Deputy. Sir John, he suspected, wished to carry out the pacification of Munster. The leaders of the rebels in Munster would be pardoned, but if this were done there would be little land confiscated for the English Crown. This last dig was aimed at discrediting Sir John; one thing the Queen and every noble lord and gentleman who had acquired land in Ireland wanted was more land and more money derived from that land.

In an uncharacteristic move, Sir John seems to have tried a little diplomacy, writing that he found Wallop to be well respected by the people he governed. He complimented Wallop both for his careful government and sound policy. It seemed to work. On 13 July, Wallop, now Treasurer, wrote to Walsingham supporting Sir John's requests for funding, and a note was attached to the letter for the disbursement of £10,000. Sir John's inauguration, when he officially received his sword of office, was an ideal occasion for him to speak to the Irish lords. He declared the Queen's 'care and love' of the Irish people, and his commission to bring them to the same state of peace and prosperity as her English subjects.

Sir John made one enormously popular, yet quite simple pronouncement; he abolished 'the name of churl' to great applause. Perrot decreed that the term 'churl' should be replaced with 'yeoman' or 'husbandman'. The word 'churl' had servile, serf-like connotations; 'yeoman' sounded free and English, and the Irish peasantry thanked Sir John for it. William Johnes, one of Sir John's officers, wrote to Walsingham on 14 July, to advise him that a steady stream of rebels was surrendering, submitting to the Crown. Already it was being recognised that Perrot's word was 'as much credited as his hand and seal.'[11]

Sir John got straight to work. In August, he issued a proclamation that appealed to both sides, that any Irish who had fled the country had six months to return voluntarily before their goods, chattels and lands were forfeit. If they came back, they would prove themselves loyal and be able to resume their lands, which would please the Irish. If they failed to return, they were obviously rebels and traitors, and their lands would be seized and given to the Crown, which would please the Queen and the English.

For Sir John, Scotland was a hostile kingdom. He wrote to Walsingham that he was sorry he had so few spies in Spain and Scotland, and could only report that 120 more galleys were ready to invade from Scotland carrying troops. By mid-August, Sir John was planning his move against the Scotts invaders, reporting that his officials were preparing to send soldiers, money and food to supply his troops. A couple of days later a letter was sent to Burghley by Mr Fenton concerning the danger of an invading army of 4,000 Scots. The Deputy, he reported, would have 2,000 men besides any Irish who would fight on the English side. Sir John wrote to Burghley to describe the current situation, his intention to 'look through his fingers' [spy] at Ulster, whose people he could not trust. He believed that the Scots planned to help the Irish to set up Shane O'Neill against the English. Sir John planned to move his more trusted Irish allies (the O'Mara's, O'Connor's and Kavanaugh's) into Munster and to the Outer Isles to act as a first line of defence against a Scots invasion. Enclosed was a report by Gerald Hay of Wexford, a merchant arrived from Spain, concerning English and Irish rebels abroad who included 'young Stucley' (Thomas Stukeley).

On 25 August, Sir John set out, with the intelligence that several Irish lords had joined the Scots and that there was to be a naval invasion. He planned to intercept their galleys at Loughfoyle and by 30 August Sir Richard Byngham was able to report to Walsingham from Roscommon that the Scots forces had returned home. Six of their galleys were reported as taken or sunk by Elizabeth I's ships. On 31 August 1584 the Privy Council wrote to the Lord Deputy approving his actions; they believed the Scots would think twice before trying something like that again. In fact, very few Scots landed in Ireland. The Queen herself wrote sharply to her Lord Deputy, 'Your Lordship is not ignorant how loth we are to be carried into charges, and how we would rather spend a pound, forced by necessity, than a penny for prevention.'[12] This view was to hamper Sir John's time in Ireland; Elizabeth would only respond with funds during a crisis,but would give him nothing to prevent crises from occurring.

By October, Sir John felt confident enough to report that all seemed to be going well. He wrote to Walsingham of his plan for maintaining 1,100 soldiers in the heart of Ulster. He estimated that he needed £50,000 a year for three years. To sweeten the message he sent his hostages to Elizabeth: Clanrycard's heir, the young Lord of Dunkellen and O'Rourke's son. He also enclosed his plan for the government of Ulster.[13] Burghley also received a missive from Sir John including plans to erect seven towns, seven castles and seven bridges, and to found two universities. Sir John sent a mazer (a large dish) garnished with silver gilt, with the arms of 'Sorley Boy' (one of the rebels) graven in the bottom, a nice gift to the Queen's most influential adviser.

Writing from Dublin Castle, Sir John sent a detailed report to the Privy Council, demonstrating how some money invested now could bring about peace and prosperity. Once again, Perrot suggested that as the Queen had already spent between £30,000 and £40,000 per annum in Ireland (and sometimes £50,000 to £60,000), if she would allow him £50,000 per annum for three years, over and above the natural revenue of the country, he would be able to keep the peace and set things up so that the payments could be stopped after the period (hiring and training troops, building towns, castles and bridges). His letter crossed one from Elizabeth, presumably before she had seen the amount of money he wanted her to provide. Walsingham wrote to Sir John that the Queen was pleased with his service in Ulster; she would like to know about his plot for maintenance of 500 soldiers there, and how far the young Scottish King had been involved in the invasion. Elizabeth's concerns ran far further than the state of the government of Ireland.

The year 1585 opened with news, sent to Burghley, of the Scots plan of another invasion of Ulster. Sir John regretted that the

Privy Council had not yet sent him the 600 men he requested, reminding them that, as warriors, the Scots were superior to his native Irish troops.

Sir John was determined to do the best he could for the people of Ireland, whether English or Irish. On 4 March 1585, he sent a circular to the Bishop, Sheriff and Justices throughout the country. He wanted to set up a commission of inquiry into the decay and ruin of churches, chancels and bridges and the neglect of free schools. He ordered that these details must be returned to him by mid-summer under threat of penalties.

In March 1585 began one of those epic struggles between two stubborn men that often blights public life. On 18 March, Adam Loftus, Archbishop of Dublin, sent a letter to Burghley to try to persuade the Queen to expressly to forbid the dissolution of St Patrick's Cathedral (in November 1584 there is the first mention by Sir John of plans for converting St Patrick's into a university). Loftus wrote that he would not endure seeing his church lands or buildings misappropriated and if Sir John's plan was supported, he would resign. Within three weeks a second letter followed: Loftus reported, with some exaggeration, that there were only three Protestant preachers in Ireland apart from those provided by the training seminary at St Patrick's. Loftus argued that he was not being obstructive to the Lord Deputy, nor acting for his own personal benefit, but rather to protect the Protestant spiritual well-being of Ireland, by maintaining a religious seminary, based in the Cathedral, rather than creating a university.

This was a bad time for Sir John to battle against such an important figure as the Archbishop as he was ill. Wallop wrote to Walsingham that Perrot was ill with colic and gallstones. The stones could pass through the system, with agonising pain; otherwise there were such cures on offer as a concoction of cooked and crushed snail shells and bees mixed in bonemeal water.

1. Henry VIII, (1491–1547; reigned 1509–1547).

2. Elizabeth of York,
(1466–1503).

3. Henry VII,
(1457–1509; reigned 1485–1509).

4. *Catherine of Aragon,*
(1485–1536).

5. *Mary Boleyn,*
(1499–1543).

6. *Anne Boleyn,*
(1501–36).

7. *Jane Seymour,*
(c.1509–37).

8. *Catherine Howard,*
   (1522–42).

9. *Katharine d'Eresby,*
   (1520–80).

10. *Henry Fitzroy, Duke of Richmond*
and Somerset, (1519–36).

11. Thomas Stukeley, (c.1530–78) at the Battle of the Three Kings at Alcazar, Morocco, on 4 August 1578. Stukeley is depicted as one of the two figures behind Sebastian, King of Portugal, on horseback in the centre.

12. John Perrot,
(1527–92).

13. Henry Carey,
(c.1524–96).

Not everyone disliked Sir John, however. Doctor John Long, Archbishop of Armagh, wrote to Walsingham in June 1585 with good news about the Lord Deputy's actions. The Ulster lords had apparently come to Dublin Castle dressed in English attire. A leading Catholic churchman had converted to Protestantism:

'Owen O'Hart, Bishop of Achamore, committed to me by his Lordship to be conferred with ... is brought by the Lord's good direction to acknowledge his blindness, to prostrate himself before Her Majesty ... And I assure your Honour, if we used not this people more for gain than for conscience, here would the Lord's work be mightily preferred.'[14]

Archbishop Long had found good in Sir John; Loftus still did not. He wrote again to Burghley saying that the two had met and that Sir John had reiterated his plan to turn St Patrick's into a university and had informed the frustrated prelate that he would be his enemy if the Archbishop opposed him. Loftus, however, had found a new ally, one who detested Sir John quite as much as he did. Loftus wrote to Burghley, commending a gentleman named Jacomo di Francesqui, a servant to 'Mr Vice-Chamberlain Hatton', 'a forward and valiant gentleman.'[15] Romantic myth would have it that Sir Christopher Hatton had never married because of his love for Elizabeth I, with whom he was a favourite. Certainly, he never married. His heir was William Newport, son of Sir Christopher's sister Dorothy, although he did have an illegitimate daughter, Elizabeth. She became Sir John Perrot's mistress, which was the cause of the emnity between the two men. Elizabeth had a daughter by Perrot, also named Elizabeth. Sadly, there is no record of Elizabeth Hatton ever marrying. Their daughter, Elizabeth Perrot, married Hugh Butler of Johnston.

Once again, Loftus wrote to Walsingham, more in sorrow than anger, shedding crocodile tears. He had always wanted to live at peace with the Lord Deputy, he said, but had heard that Sir John meant to complain to the Court about him. However, not all the Irish prelates were against Sir John. In July 1585, John Long once again wrote to Walsingham concerning the refusal of the Justices of the Peace to take the oath of supremacy and added that he found Sir John to be of a good Protestant persuasion.

The animosity of Loftus continued, though. He wrote, again and again, about the impertinences that he suffered at Sir John's hands. He found an ally in the newly appointed Thomas Jones, Bishop of Meath, who wrote to thank Walsingham for his recent promotion. Sir John had already acted against Bishop Jones, granting a commission to many enemies of Jones to inspect all the churches in Ireland, admonish churchmen who failed to come up to standard and even deprive them of their living or send them to prison, if necessary. Jones added his weight to the call by Loftus that the English Council should mediate between Loftus and Sir John to bring peace to the government of Ireland. Walsingham wrote back to say that he held both Loftus and Perrot in esteem, and would seek to reconcile the pair.

The constant sniping by some of the Irish officials and ill will by some of the Queen's advisers came to a head in September 1585. The Council were bombarded with a list of the expenses of the Lord Deputy's household; a 'brief note ... particularly discovering the small expenses and the strict and pinching parsimony of the Lord Deputy's house, what great show of expense so ever he may advertise' and a 'Book of the objections that can be charged against Sir John Perrot, and the answer thereunto.'[16] Despite this, Sir John stayed put. The Queen had complete faith both in his loyalty and in his abilities. Sir John, however, was feeling the strain.

He wrote to Burghley that he had received no reply to his letters. He wished Burghley and the Queen to know that he was not alone in his desire to turn St Patrick's into a university. He added that, far from being miserly, he opened his house to anyone who might wish to partake of a good and hearty supper with him, even though Sir John himself had been unable to enjoy such good food for some 23 years due to his poor health. A second letter followed, in which he demanded to be sent a copy of Loftus's accusations: the record of his expenses was quite accurate and any money he spent was necessary. In fact, although he had been promised £16,000, only £1,200 had arrived so far. He made the first of what was to be many requests that he should be relieved of his office.

January 1586 began with more orders from London and a note of explanation from Sir John. He wrote to the Privy Council explaining why he had been unable, as yet, to carry out the orders in recent letters from the Council on behalf of a number of petitioners; including Richard Sheeth (who had requested his freedom; Sir John had already freed him).

On a more positive note, of three Irish lords, Slane, Howth and Louth, who had previously written letters complaining about Sir John, the former two had now retracted them, and Sir John asked that Louth be obliged to prove his accusations and, when he failed, that he should be punished accordingly. Oliver Plunkett, Baron Louth, was made of sterner stuff, however. He wrote to Burghley telling of how the Lord Deputy had threatened him with disgrace to compel him to recant his previous complaint about Sir John's financial irregularities. He also sent a lengthy report to Walsingham on the same subject, claiming that Perrot demanded recompense for his lavish life style, but in fact spent very little on his official status, pocketing the difference. Louth suggested that Perrot looked down on those he saw as lesser than himself, saying: 'I confess my wealth is not so great as his, which maketh him in truth to despise all men without measure.'[17]

One of the major worries for the Council of Ireland was the threat of invasion from Spain. A Barbary merchant, Challis, had reported that Spain was amassing an invasion fleet, with 20,000 men, to sail against Ireland. Sir John was able to advise the Queen and Walsingham that he was keeping his ear to the ground.

All the while he kept up a steady stream of reports on the planned Spanish invasion and requests for men, money, food and clothing. He was active, however, in his attempts to protect Ireland. He had hired a spy, Davy Duke, although he had to share these services with Walsingham:

'I have made a choice of one I take to be a very fit instrument for that purpose. He hath the Italian and Spanish tongue … and been at Rome accepted for one to the fraternity of the Jesuits, and goeth thence as it were, disgraced by me and recommended by a supposed Bishop of the Pope's … The man is of good carriage, born in this land, and his name is Davy Duke … I have concluded with him upon a figure and tripartite indented piece of parchment, whereof I send you one part herein closed. If he write unto you in that figure, and send unto you his counterpart of the indenture, you are to consider of it and I take it, to give credit to it, for I think he will deal both wisely and honestly.'[18]

164

Back at the English Court, Sir John's enemies were busy. Walsingham told him that Elizabeth I was unhappy that there were so many complaints about him and that he should be careful how he behaved. She had been told that Sir John had taken greater care of his own affairs than he had of the Queen's. However, both Walsingham and Burghley were still prepared to support Sir John against these rumours and calumnies. The Queen also wrote, in her own hand, but with less conciliation, reprimanding Sir John for producing yet another scare story about invasions.

It is difficult not to feel sorry for Sir John. He was in an impossible situation, obliged to protect the land, but reprimanded if he suggested an invasion might actually happen. He had to keep the Irish people happy, but continue to reward the English. He was in a permanent state of poverty and the orders kept coming from London. After receiving one such bundle of orders and requests, he wrote to Burghley that he felt worn down and disgraced: 'For first there is such a kind of superintendence of this Council set over me, as I do not see how I may henceforth without fear enter into consultation much less action of any importance ...'[19]

His feelings were presumably known as in May 1586 Loftus and Sir William Stanley started a rumour that Perrot was leaving Ireland and the Earl of Ormonde replacing him. By July, Wallop further demonstrated his opposition to Sir John by sending a document to Walsingham detailing financial irregularities in the Lord Deputy's budget, including that he had claimed stable charges of £1,700 for horses, when the actual fee was £400. However, in that same month a list of the household wages, liveries and stable for the Lord Deputy was sent home. Unfortunately for Sir John, according to the figures and taking into account what the Queen had allowed him, he suffered a financial loss of £3,021 16s 6d.

Whilst Wallop was belittling Sir John, Sir Nicholas White, Master of the Rolls in Dublin, had a better report for Burghley, although he could not confess to like him:

'The Lord Deputy Perrot hath been so many ways interrupted in his intended good purposes for settling of this realm, which (in his judgment) ought first to have been begun in the North ... he stands to prove upon the forfeiture of so much of his own wealth, that his journeys into the North hath cost Her Highness little or nothing, and would have brought to pass that Her Highness should have a resident garrison of 400 men maintained there for ever without any charge to her crown; by which both the inland and outland Scots might have been always mastered. I must confess to your Lordship that the manners of the man are far contrary to my nature, and yet the success of his government makes me to follow it and not him.'[20]

Sir John's gift for making enemies was not helped by foolish actions on behalf of the families of his officers. In November, Sir Nicholas White reported to Burghley of a disagreement between Sir John and the Marshall, Sir Nicholas Bagenall. Bagenall was furious about the arrest of his son, Dudley, for failing to appear on the Lord Deputy's summons to answer a complaint, and for beating the party that delivered the summons.

Sir Nicholas Bagenall, still smarting from his son's arrest, wrote a scathing letter in December, stating that everyone was dissatisfied with Sir John, that his supporters were villains and that he treated his own Crown officers badly, calling them 'beggars, squibs, puppies'. He finished his letter by claiming that, should there be an invasion, the troops hated Sir John so much that they would refuse to fight under him.

Loftus, as ever, was there at Sir Nicholas's side. He sent a supporting missive stating that Sir John still acted against him when he could, so much so that Loftus was in fear for his life. He claimed that the Council was being ignored and if a case was brought before them, 'his Lordship's common answer is this, with great fury, "What tellest thou me of the Council?" "What care I for the Council?", "They are all of them, but a sort of beggars and squibs, puppies, dogs, dunghill churls – yea, even the proudest of them come hither with their hose patched on the heels".' A third letter, in the same vein, came from Sir Geoffrey Fenton, although rather primly he declined to repeat the names that the Lord Deputy had used towards his colleagues.[21]

Sir John was aware that his enemies were amassing against him. He wrote to the new secretary to the Council, William Davison:

'I am most glad to learn that her Majesty hath chosen you to be one of her principal secretaries ... There was never any Governor here, that held my place, but was subject to malicious tongues; I pray you therefore if any man say ought of me there ... let him set it down in writing and set his hand to it, for wind hath more hurt me, delivered in corners, than matter.'

Sir John was able to enjoy a small revenge. On 7 December Roger Wilbraham, Solicitor General for Ireland, and Charles Calthorpe, Attorney General, submitted their statement of expected payment of first fruits (a fee payable to the Crown from anyone taking up a new Government or Church post). The first name on the list was that of 'A Loftus, Archbishop of Dublin'; Sir John Perrot endorsed the document. Wallop commented: 'I know your Lordship cannot but be advertised by sundry means of the continual jarring and mislike that is between the Lord Deputy and the Lord Chancellor, wherein I can commend neither of them ... and here I see none that can appease it.'[22]

The year 1587 began with a rumour that Sir John was to be recalled to England. Both Sir Geoffrey Fenton and Sir Richard Byngham signalled their approval. The Auditor, Mr Jenyson, wrote to Burghley that the nobles of Ireland were delighted that they would now be governed by someone of noble rank and not someone who, no matter how experienced or well meaning, was a mere knight.

Sir John then made a tactical error. In January 1587 he authorised the arrest of Sir Geoffrey Fenton for the debt of the trifling sum of £70. Fenton, a noted author and also the son-in-law of Dr Robert Weston, former Lord Chancellor of Ireland, immediately sent a note to Burghley. In remarkably quick time a reply came back to Sir John from Elizabeth I herself (to whom one of Fenton's books had been dedicated). Since Fenton had been arrested for such a small sum and he had, of course, meant to repay it in good time: '... we cannot but advise you not only to enlarge the said Fenton that he may attend upon his ordinary calling there for our service ... but also to forbear those hard kind of proceedings in like cases hereafter. And considering how inconvenient it is at all times ... to have you and the rest of our Council there divided, as we hear you are by factions and partialities ...'[23]

However, it appears that Sir John did not learn from this lesson. He apparently challenged Sir Richard Byngham, another competent officer with royal support, to a duel. Sir Richard could not believe that Sir John was behaving like a bully and begged Burghley either to recall him or the Lord Deputy.

The battle lines were well and truly drawn. Geoffrey Fenton supported Justice Gardiner in his request to be recalled to England, on the grounds that he was unable to work under the continued harassment and lack of support of the Lord Deputy. He reported that the Attorney General supported the Lord Deputy, and was prone to take the part of the Irish against the English. Fenton went on the offensive in March, suggesting to Burghley that the Council was too cumbersome and too much under the control of the Lord Deputy, so that even those who were not his supporters were afraid to stand up to him. Fenton suggested that a Council of three or four men would make decisions much faster. The Councillors presently numbered 18, of who 3 usually failed to appear. Fenton was himself secretary.

In May, it looked as if Sir John had been given permission to return to England, at least temporarily. He wrote to Burghley, '… yet seeing Her Highness hath appointed me to come over at Michaelmas, I would gladly leave the country quiet in all respects, to him that shall come after me …' He hoped to receive some small sum of money before he left, to sort out a couple of persistent rebels and troublemakers, and he was hopeful that the Spanish would take no action that summer.[24]

Before he could get too complacent, another serious problem arose following an argument between Sir John and Sir Nicholas Bagenall. In May 1587, Patrick Cullen, a servant of Turlough O'Neil, had been arrested and Sir John decided that he should not carry out the interrogation, since O'Neil had already complained about him and Cullen had carried his letters. Presumably before he could let his Council know, Bagenall approached Sir John and ordered him not to carry out the questioning. Sir John lost his temper and words were exchanged. According to one account:

> '... with that he [Sir John] rose and went toward the Marshal [Bagenall], and with his flat hand touched his cheek, once or twice, staying his other hand on his right shoulder, saying, Well, well, Marshall (not striking him as he could have done) if you defied a man in my place, in any other country, he would hang you. Wherewithal the Marshall, having a staff in his hand, did threateningly raise up the same, as though he would have stroken the Deputy; wherewith the Justice, Sir Nicholas White and Mr. Fenton went between them.'

Sir Nicholas gave his version of events. The accusations against Cullen had involved his son, Sir Henry Bagenall, and Sir Nicholas, believing Sir John had an vendetta against him and his family, was keen that the Lord Deputy should have nothing to do with the matter. In his version, he had courteously asked Sir John to step down, but had been told by the Lord Deputy that he would do what he liked, when he liked.

Of course Gardiner and Fenton supported Sir Nicholas Bagenall. They added that Sir Nicholas White had approached them to retract their support and when they refused, he had asked to see their written statements; when he was given them, he promptly tore the papers up. White, in his account, agreed largely with Sir John.

—◦◦◦—

The question of invasion was active as always. In August Sir John reported that he had spoken with James Tirrell, a Dublin merchant who had returned from Bilboa, who had information about the Spanish preparation for war. Sir John was in increasingly poor health, but at last release was in sight. In September he was able to write to Walsingham, thanking him for arranging with the Queen that Sir John might be recalled. In December it was clear that Sir John had had enough, partly due to illness: 'I daily look for an easterly wind to bring over another governor, according to the constant bruit that runneth generally in the realm here ... For my own part my disease doth so increase upon me as I am daily worse and worse.'[25]

He had some reason to breathe a sigh of relief. In the same month his successor, Sir William Fitzwilliam, was receiving his orders from the Queen. In the New Year Sir John wrote to the Queen with pleasure at his recall, but stating his willingness to defend his actions in the face of his accusers, even when wracked with disease. Sir John was not going to be allowed to escape so easily, however. Almost before the ink was dry on Sir William Fitzwilliam's commission to the post, Loftus, Gardiner and Fenton were reporting that the new Lord Deputy's household was having trouble gathering provisions as the outgoing incumbent had already stripped the place bare. Sir John, however, was glad to be going home finally: 'I remain here daily expecting the coming over of the new governor, that I may take the advantage of this spring to help my swollen legs and the grating stone that lieth in my kidneys ...'[26]

If Loftus and his cronies sought to denigrate Sir John, others were more generous. The Attorney Charles Calthorpe wrote in March to Burghley: 'This Lord Deputy's departing is much lamented, by reason of his good and happy government, both for the Prince and people, as specially may appear by the great increase of Her Majesty's revenue, the decrease of Her Majesty's charge, and keeping of Her Majesty's subjects in justice and peace ...'[27]

As Sir John's homecoming seemed so close, his contentment grew. He had written to the Queen about his plans to deal with his health problems but days and weeks passed and still there was no sign of his replacement. A growing anxiety in Sir John led him to write to Walsingham in April 1588, begging that the new Lord

Deputy might be hurried to Dublin. Sir John's health was deteriorating and he longed to take up the treatment he needed. He was also in financial limbo, as the Treasurer had been told to stop paying his personal expenses, in anticipation of the arrival of his successor. He wrote again in May, but it was 25 June 1588 before Sir William Fitzwilliam finally arrived in Dublin. Fitzwilliam's journey had been broken by ill health, and he was now obliged to wait for Sir John's better health before they could meet.

The ailing Fitzwilliam went on to report that he was suffering from a 'tertian ague' (bouts of malaria with attacks at three-day intervals) and was subject to fits. He also stated that there was a remarkable lack of ready money available. On 29 June Sir John was finally able to make his declaration relating to the state of Ireland before the Council and its new Lord Deputy.

In July, Sir John began his journey home. At the end of July, Fitzwilliam asked for Burghley's help. When he left, Sir John had, against instructions, taken the state robes with him, and he claimed to have them at his house in Wales and would send them on later. Fitzwilliam also noted that of £12,000 that had been sent over from Elizabeth I, which was not to be spent until he had agreed, it appeared that only £46 13s 4d was left.

Sir John responded to the Privy Council in September from Carew Castle. He admitted that he had, indeed, taken the official robes, but they were old and shabby and he was planning to turn them into stool covers. As soon as he had received the new Lord Deputy's letter, he had sent them back, 'wishing that His Lordship would upon my promise have forborne to write to your Lordships for such a trifle, but I hope his Lordship will leave them to his successor.'[28]

On 12 December 1588, the Privy Council discussed matters relating to the rule of Ireland and they wanted answers from Sir John, particularly his opinion of the situation in the north of Ireland. The month saw Sir John provide a variety of documents to the Council; including 14 memorials, covering issues from his

171

service in Ireland to the reasons behind the disagreement between Perrot and some of his Council. In response Sir John wrote, 'A brief declaration of part of the services done to your Majesty by Sir John Perrot, knight, during the time of his deputation in the realm of Ireland', an exceedingly lengthy document, listing and justifying all he had done, with names of witnesses who could confirm his version of events. Another declaration covered his expenses for travel and accommodation. The dates covered were from when he 'received the sword' on 21 June 1584, until he was relieved on 16 April, and left Dublin on 2 July 1588; the total days in Dublin were 122 weeks 4 days, and 'On journeys' he spent 24 weeks 3 days.'[29]

The first of the serious accusations against Sir John was recorded late in 1588, although it appears that nothing was done about it at that time. The declarations against him remained to haunt him later on. These included the ridiculous charge that he took the Lord Deputy's robes home with him, he took food and wine belonging to the office of Lord Deputy, he made decisions against the orders and interests of the Queen and that he appointed unqualified and lazy Justices and Sheriffs without the Council's approval. The charges were for the most part trivial, already resolved or just well-rehearsed spite on the part of his enemies. In March 1589 Sir John produced a rebuttal of those charges that he referred to as being from an unknown informer. Later charges would have more substance and be irrefutable, however.

Not all his erstwhile colleagues were prepared to denigrate their departed leader. At least two of his supporters held firm. Fitzwilliam wrote to the Privy Council and added a brief note to Burghley, 'It may please your Lordship, I cannot obtain Sir Lucas Dillon's hand nor Sir Nic. White's to any letter wherein Sir John Perrot is mentioned not to their liking.'[30]

In May came a detailed account of lengthy dialogue between Sir John and his successor, Fitzwilliam. Fitzwilliam was in a difficult position. It was easy to blame Sir John for anything that was wrong, but no Lord Deputy wanted to admit that all the good was down to his predecessor. Fitzwilliam had said that he was under no obligation, nor would he follow all the rules and directions of Sir John's government. Sir John's response was, 'If his Lordship hath found a better course than I did follow it shall no whit displease me, for I did my best and I hope he will do so too.' Fitzwilliam responded that he might follow some of Sir John's policies, but that he would not be bound to necessarily follow all of them. Sir John then produced another rebuttal on the matter to Burghley that began:

> 'My purpose in delivering to your Lordship [Burghley] what I heard from men of good credit out of Ireland of the causeless, malicious and inconsiderate speeches of the Deputy towards me, was not that I need care for his good or evil will, but rather to show his unthankfulness. I had written unto him four or five letters, whereof he disdained to answer any. Were it not to satisfy others, I would to make a rejoin to such mad replies, for to such a spirit as he carries, silence were the best answer.'

173

Sir John was determined to set the record straight and prove that he had governed in a fair and judicious manner. He was particularly determined to show that he had treated both the Irish and English with equal favour and punishment, when necessary.

By August 1589 the Queen had made Sir John a member of the Privy Council, and he was now on the receiving end of such letters from Ireland as he had formerly sent. Sir Richard Byngham wrote concerning malicious complaints and reports sent to England against him that he claimed were the work of rebels and malcontents. He begged that Sir John would acknowledge his service during his time of office, and how he 'justified' himself from the slanders against him.[31]

Now that he was a member of the Privy Council, Sir John became the resident expert on Irish matters. A docquet (list) of the opinions of the Earl of Ormonde, the Lord Grey and Sir John

Perrot relating to the defence of Ireland was committed to the consideration of the Council. The following month Sir John set out a series of notes for the Lord Treasurer on how to reduce Sir John Norris's pay to the Irish.

In April 1590 Sir John wrote to Burghley, giving an update on the state of his health and then moving to a lengthy analysis of Irish affairs. He reminded Burghley that Irish lands were held by custom and should be dealt with accordingly, adding that the Crown should not interfere in this. He supported his favourable impression of O'Connor of Sligo, who he held in esteem. It was Sir John's opinion that a recent case against him had gone badly 'for Sir R[ichard] Byngham had a great mind to have Sligo, and to place himself there, and his brother Sir George Byngham at Ballymote.' Sir John then commended his own son, Thomas, aged 37, to be governor of Connaught, if Sir Richard was dead (presumably there was a rumour to this effect).[32]

174

Fitzwilliam was finding out at first hand how troublesome the rule of Ireland could be. In early 1590, Sir Edward Moore wrote to Sir John Perrot, asking that he might be assigned the muster of cattle in the north. He added some wider news; in his opinion, Ireland might be lost through bad government. Whereas Sir John had gone out of his way to try and act honourably, his successor seemed to be throwing all that goodwill away. In January, Owen Woodde wrote to Sir John about the Lord Deputy's attempts to pacify Galway by meeting the rebels. A safe passage was guaranteed into the meeting – but not out – and therefore most of those invited refused to attend. A number of notable Irish lords, Woodde said, were now dead or hanged. He finished on the rather depressing note, 'The Lord Chancellor's quartan ague [malaria bouts at four-day intervals] and the Lord Deputy's quotidian fits [daily attacks of fever] have this term nonsuited many a poor man.'[33]

—◦◦◦—

Out of sight, however, was not out of mind. Before long, new accusations of treasonable activity began to arise against Sir John. Much of the trouble lay in the fact that John never held his tongue nor considered his words when he was in a passion. One particularly dangerous enemy was Sir Christopher Hatton, who was now able to give full reign to his animosity. Sir Christopher was sensitive on the subject of his rise to power. Sir John is supposed to have said that Hatton had caught the Queen's attention because of his dancing (that he had 'risen by the galliard'); Elizabeth I is supposed to have first been attracted to Hatton as he danced at a masque.

In 1590, matters became serious for Sir John. An ex-priest, Denis Roughan (also called O'Roughan), produced a letter that appeared to be from Sir John to Philip of Spain, promising to help Spain conquer England if he was promised the governorship of Wales. On 16 February of that year, Fitzwilliam wrote to Burghley from Dublin Castle. He sent his son, John, to deliver the letter, presumably for added security, that it might be passed to the Queen. He reported that Roughan and his wife had brought him the incriminating letter and that Roughan was in fear of his life from Sir John's supporters in Ireland. According to Fitzwilliam, public report had it that Sir John's popularity amongst the Irish was not due to his fair dealing or honesty, but to his support of Spain – and also because he was Catholic. Roughan reported that he said Mass for Sir John and that he had given him confession.

A copy of the letter to Philip of Spain was enclosed, in Fitzwilliam's handwriting. The writer, apparently Sir John, acknowledged Philip's letters to him and offered that if Philip would give him 'the whole land of Wales for ever' then Sir John would undertake to get him the two lands of England and Ireland. The address on the letter was, 'Out of the Castle of Dublin, the 25 June 1585'.

It was a good time for Roughan to bring forward his plot. On 17 February 1590, Robert Legge, Deputy Remembrancer in the

Exchequer in Ireland, made his report to Burghley on the revenues and debts appertaining to Ireland. He attached a certificate from Sir Henry Wallop and Justice Gardiner relating to this petition. His opinion was that the revenues and debts needed close scrutiny. In the enclosed report by Legge was all the information 'touching the debts of the Lord Chancellor (Adam Loftus), the Bishop of Meath, Sir Robert Dillon, Sir N[icholas] White, and other principal officers when Sir John Perrot came over from Ireland in July 1588.' Legge found that Loftus had cheated the Queen out of revenues, as well as running up debts to the Crown. He held on to churches and livings, using the revenues to support his young children who were not then or ever likely to be church ministers. When Legge faced Loftus, he was insulted by the furious Archbishop. The others were the same, insulting and threatening Legge and refusing to pay what they owed. It was an ideal moment to divert attention to the misdeeds of Sir John.[34]

Of course Sir John's enemies pretended to believe in the letter, but Roughan had actually already been prosecuted by Sir John – for forgery. The letter might muddy the waters and shift attention to England, but it never had any real chance of being believed. In March the Privy Council ordered Fitzwilliam to deliver Roughan to the Bishop of Meath and the Bishop of Leighlin or Sir Lucas Dillon. They were to set out the particulars of the convictions of Roughan for previous acts of forging Sir John's signature. Roughan was to be handed over to John Worsley, appointed by the Privy Council to oversee the interrogation of the prisoner. The Privy Council wrote to the Bishops of Meath and Leighlin, Sir Lucas Dillon, Sir Nicholas White, Sir Edward Moore, Sir Edward Waterhous, Justice Walshe and Charles Calthorpe to appoint them commissioners 'to examine Sir Dennis O'Rowghan, priest, who had been formerly condemned in the Castle Chamber for counterfeiting Sir John Perot's hand to a certain letter purporting to be addressed to the King of Spain, importing a foul and disloyal intent'. Also they were to look into the matter of his forging Sir John's signature to three warrants whilst he was Lord Deputy.

Fitzwilliam sent over a lengthy letter dated 30 April to Burghley. It dealt with his actions relating to Roughan. He then went on to cover himself in case the matter proved false: 'If there be any cause of doubt in Sir Denis O'Rawghane's book, it shall be his fault, and not mine, who have delivered but what I received from him'. Apparently, even Fitzwilliam could see that the story was weak. The Lord Deputy ended his letter by saying that he was having great difficulty in allowing any of the Council to try the evidence of the priest, Roughan. They were either favourites of Sir John's (like Dillon and White) or confidently expected his return to Ireland and were therefore totally unwilling to put their names to anything that slandered him. An attempt was made to find other witnesses. Mr John Ball made a declaration, 'About a three or four days before my coming for England, James Reynolds, late servant of Mr Michael Kettlewell, told me that his brother, John Reynolds, had received a message from one Charles Trevor (Travares) saying that if he would get his protection from my Lord Deputy he would reprove the letter which the priest did charge Sir John Perrot withal ...'[35] As a witness, a man who said his brother had told him that a friend of his might confirm Roughan's story, was plainly ridiculous.

By May even the participants in the plot were giving up. Loftus, the Archbishop of Dublin and Chancellor, wrote to the Bishop of Meath and others Commissioners that Roughan should go to trial. Loftus told Fitzwilliam on his return from Connaught that Roughan was a 'lewd, dishonest man, void of the truth.' An array of documents was forwarded to England relating to previous trials for forgery, where the accused counterfeited Sir John's name to illegally seize property.

And so the matter dragged on. Sir John noted his opinion that he believed Ireland to be the most unfortunate country in the world. He knew of no 'good Governor who sincerely served there

177

but who was stung, maligned, or bitten by some means.' Still Sir John was to have no peace concerning Ireland. In May Roughan escaped from prison in Dublin and the Privy Council demanded a number of persons should be sent over to England to take part in a hearing into the events. In the event, 46 persons were to be examined in Ireland touching the disclosures of Roughan. A number of selected persons were to be sent to England for questioning, including the Bishop of Leighlin, Sir Nicholas White, Philip the gaoler, the priest Rice ap Hugh, and Margaret Leonard, the wife of Roughan. Sir Nicholas White was certainly not prepared to take this lying down; he wrote to Burghley, 'the bad priest, Roughane, hath told many malicious tales of the Commissioners to the Lord Deputy.' Sir Nicholas found himself under restraint, which, he believed, was dangerous for his health. He begged Burghley for parole to go into the country.[36]

By July, Fitzwilliam was writing to Hatton and Burghley, the former of whom hated Sir John and the latter who supported him. The Lord Deputy told both men he would not make any further accusations until he heard how the Privy Council felt about what had been presented so far. However, to maintain his case against Sir John he enclosed a note dated 30 June, which was an account by Sir Robert Dillon, Chief Justice of the Common Pleas, that 'Sir John Perrot, in time of his government, was desirous to have pardoned himself, but that the Lord Chancellor demurred to seal the warrant.' The suggestion was that Sir John wanted to give himself a formal pardon for unspecified crimes, but that Loftus refused to authorise it.[37]

By August, the Court was at Oatlands Palace in Weybridge, where the Lord Chancellor, the Treasurer, Admiral and Chamberlain sent a response to the Lord Deputy. They raised a series of comments on the examinations, indicating that there had been 'palpable concealments of truths and variances in the several answers of the Commissioners'; only the Bishop of Meath seemed to have been wholly and truthfully forthcoming. Fitzwilliam replied by expressing his wish that Sir John, the Bishop of Leighlin, Sir Nicholas White and the rest might come by their just deserts.

Back in Ireland, Archbishop Loftus added his weight to the accusations when he answered Burghley's letter of 21 October, requiring Loftus's testimony for the examination of Sir John. Loftus reported that in his government he had 'showed himself void of pity and compassion and without measure in his punishment.' He added that Sir John had remarked on one occasion that he would 'send the Council out of Dublin Castle riding upon cabbage stalks.' This foolish remark was remembered and used to show Sir John's contempt for his colleagues and, through them, for the Privy Council and the Queen. Fitzwilliam joined in with the story of the cabbage stalks, although he changed it to 'cole staffs' (a pole carried between two people on their shoulders, hung with goods).

On 31 January 1591 Loftus sent a lengthy letter to Burghley laying out the bones of his information against Sir John:

'I have lately received a joint letter from your Lordship, and others, of the Lords reproving me for my last answer sent unto you, both for the generality and doubtfulness thereof, and requiring me in more particular manner to signify to Her Majesty, and your Lordships my knowledge of Sir John Perrot's behaviour towards her Majesty, and the State in his late government ... I humbly crave your Lordship's pardon, protesting that no other respects in the world stayed me hitherto from informing your Lordship against Sir John Perrot ... but the remembrance of that known mislike between us, which made me very unwilling to intermeddle in his causes.'[38]

⸻❧⸻

More accusations surfaced against Sir John as his enemies sensed that he was now vulnerable. Loftus added to his dossier and reported that Sir John once said to Sir Henry Bagenall, 'You shall see that shortly I shall pull the Bishop in as small pieces as I would do yonder grass, if I had it between my fingers', and pointed out of a window. Mathew Smith, who had witnessed the cole staff incident, gave a statement concerning Sir John's answer to John Kilcarte, a Scot, who brought a letter on his own behalf from the Scottish King, and importuned Sir John for an answer, to whom Sir John said, 'Thy King! Thy King! What tellest thou me of the King! I will give thee an answer when I will, and as I see cause.'[39]

In the climate of fear generated by the threat of a Spanish invasion and plans uncovered for Elizabeth I's assassination, the forged letter focused attention on Sir John and even the Queen may have had her doubts about his temper, if not about his loyalty. Above all, she could not let it be imagined she took such matters lightly. Sir John's adversaries changed tack; they brought forward testimony from his Irish colleagues and servants that he had frequently spoken rudely and disparagingly of the Council, of the Scottish King and even of the Queen herself. Such a thing was unforgivable and, if true, could not go unpunished. Despite support from Lord Burghley, Sir John was arrested, as were his supporters, 'for Sir John Perrot's cause, *viz*. the bishop of Leighlin [a close prisoner in the Fleet, but 'merry as ever he was'], Sir Nicholas White [in the Marshalsea, and in a depressed state], Philip Williams, Theobald Dillon, Francis Barkeley, Nicholas Halye, Wm Lombard, Thos Clynton, Leonard Walker, John Evans, Walter Androwes, all prisoners, and Sir Edward Moore depending upon bond.'[40]

After spending a short period under house arrest at Lord Burghley's London home, Sir John was sent to the Tower of London in March 1591. In April 1592 he was tried for treason before a panel comprising Lord Hunsdon, Lord Buckhurst, Sir Robert Cecil (Burghley's son) and others. A note in Burghley's own hand dated to 15 November, listed the material points against Sir John. Along the margin are the names of those who gave evidence for each article. These ranged from his favouring of Catholics to making contemptuous references to the Queen. He was supposed to have railed against Elizabeth I's letters when she took him to task or reprimanded him. He allegedly claimed that he failed in his government of Ireland because the Queen would not support him. He also is alleged to have poured scorn on her courage. According to one witness, John Garland, he had called the Queen a 'base bastard piss-kytching'. Elizabeth I was prepared to forgive a lot, but not anyone who doubted her courage or the strength and authority of her rule.[41]

The charge of treasonable correspondence was dropped (no one really believed in the Roughan letter), but the charge of speaking disrespectfully about the Queen was upheld, and this was treason. Sir John was now in poor health, having spent over a year in prison. Though he hardly remembered the incidents, he admitted that he might, in the heat of the moment, have said something along the lines of the reported words, but that they were out of context and had been misinterpreted. He was found guilty of treason and returned to the Tower. Even then, he could not control his tongue. He is reputed to have exclaimed as he was led into captivity, 'God's death! Will the Queen suffer her brother to be offered up a sacrifice to the envy of his frisking adversary?'[42] This is probably apocryphal, but it does have the ring of Sir John about it; mentioning his supposed paternity before witnesses and questioning the Queen's decision when he had just been found guilty of insulting her.

On 23 December 1591, Sir John wrote to Burghley from the Tower. He complained that his memory had become impaired through his lengthy imprisonment and his misery, and the incommodity of the lodging he was in. Even now, however, he could not resist his work, responding presumably to Burghley's query. He had some comments to make on Mr Fowle's dealing for a very large charter of incorporation for the town of Athenry. Fowle had suffered expenses in bringing in men for mineral extraction for the benefit of Athenry and should be recompensed with £30 or £40 a year.[43]

181

In May, Sir John drew up his will and in June he was brought before the Court for sentence. Found guilty of treason, there was only one punishment – death. It is doubtful that the Queen believed him to be a traitor, and it is possible that she would have pardoned him or allowed him to pay a fine in return for his freedom. His health, however, proved his undoing. In September 1592 he died in the Tower, either from an exacerbated pre-existing medical condition or from the ever-present gaol fever, typhus. Given the sustained attacks by his enemies, and the real possibility that Sir John might be pardoned and released, it was rumoured that he had been poisoned. Sir John technically died destitute since, as a convicted traitor, his lands and possessions had already been seized by the Crown. The suggestion that Elizabeth planned to forgive him is reinforced by the fact that he was not executed immediately and that she allowed his estate to pass intact to his eldest son, Thomas Perrot.

Thomas was the son of Sir John's first wife, Ann, daughter of Sir Thomas Cheyney. Sir John's second wife, Jane Pruett, was a widow when they married and she bore Sir John another son, William (who died unmarried) and two daughters, Lettice and Ann. Jane Pruett's first husband had been Sir Lewis Pollard, Judge of the Common Pleas. By his first wife, Anne Hext, he had had 11 children, 5 sons and 6 daughters – Grace, Elizabeth, Agnes, Thomasin, Philippa and Jane. Mistress Jane Pollard would later marry Sir Hugh Stukeley and was the mother of Thomas Stukeley, another of Henry VIII's illegitimate sons. Jane's son William died a bare five years after his father. Lettice married three times, to Roland Lacharn of St Brides, Walter Vaughan of St Brides and Arthur Chichester, Baron Chichester of Belfast and eventually Lord Deputy of Ireland. Ann married John Philips.

Sir John also had a number of natural children. He had a son, James Perrot, by Sybil Jones of Radnorshire, as well as a daughter, Elizabeth, by Elizabeth Hatton. Sir James tried unsuccessfully to claim part of the Perrot estate but he did receive a knighthood in

1603. He was MP for Haverfordwest, a town alderman, Vice Admiral for Pembrokeshire (like his father) and an author – his most famous work was *Meditations and Prayers on the Lord's Prayer and the Ten Commandments*, published in 1630. An unnamed natural daughter of Sir John's married a gentleman called David Morgan.

In around 1980, an elderly man named Robert Perrot bought the ruined castle at Narbeth in Pembrokeshire, once the home of Sir John. He lived there less than 10 years, and was found dead one day. He had tried to excavate and rebuild parts of the castle of his ancestors. Robert's heir, his sister's grandson, a dentist from Chelmsford in Essex, inherited the castle – and the bloodline of Henry VIII.

THE PATERNAL FAMILY TREE OF ANNE BOLEYN

Geoffery Boleyn
=
Anne, daughter of Thomas Lord Hoo and Hastings

Sir William Boleyn
=
Margaret, daughter of Thomas Butler Earl of Ormonde

Sir Thomas Boleyn = Elizabeth Howard

Margaret = Sir John Sackville

Alice = Robert Clere

Anne = Sir John Shelton

Edward = Anne Tempest

James = Elizabeth Woode

William

George (1502–36) = Jane Parker

◆ Mary Boleyn (c.1499–1543) = 1) William Carey 2) William Stafford

◆ Anne Boleyn (c.1507–36) = Henry VIII

Henry VIII

Elizabeth I (1533–1605)

◆ Margaret Shelton (c.1505–1583) = Thomas Wodhouse

Mary Shelton (c.1510–1570) = Sir Anthony Heveningham

Catherine Carey (c.1526–68)

✚ Henry Carey Baron Hunsdon (c.1524–96)

◆	mistress of Henry VIII
✚	illegitimate child of Henry VIII
=	married

From Mistress to Queen
to the Executioner's Block

The Boleyns came from humble beginnings to rise to the lofty and dangerous heights of producing a queen of England. In the mid-15th century Geoffery Boleyn began the family's social advance when he married the daughter and co-heiress of Lord Hoo and Hastings. Geoffery was a farmer's son and had come to London to make his fortune, rising to the trade of hatter and then mercer (trader in fine cloth, often imported). By 1446, he was Sheriff; by 1457, he was Alderman and Lord Mayor. He made his fortune and bought Blickling Hall in Norfolk and also Hever Castle with its manor, in Kent. His son, Sir William, went one better and married Margaret Butler, the daughter and co-heiress of the Anglo-Irish Thomas Butler, Earl of Ormonde. Sir William was one of the newly made Knights of the Bath at Richard III's coronation in 1483. He had a daughter Margaret who married Sir John Shelton, and two sons – James who married Elizabeth, daughter and co-heiress of John Wood, and Thomas.[1] Birth and marriage into the nobility, coupled with considerable wealth, meant that young Thomas Boleyn was able to marry Elizabeth Howard, daughter of Thomas Howard, Earl of Surrey, who later became Duke of Norfolk. Thomas Boleyn had more than noble relatives and wealth to commend him; he showed enormous social talents and began an impressive diplomatic career when he was quite young.

Thomas Boleyn's position was advanced by the fact that he was related by marriage to a number of prominent English noble families. His father-in-law, Thomas Howard, Earl of Surrey, had married twice. By his first wife, Elizabeth Bourchier, his children and grandchildren married into the families of Bryan, Carewe, Guildford, Culpepper and Boleyn. By his second wife, Agnes Tylney, his offspring gave him connections with the Radcliffes and Stanleys.

Thomas and Elizabeth Boleyn settled down to raise their family. It is assumed that Anne was their third child, born around 1507, after Mary and George. Given the extent of the Boleyn estates, it is also not known for certain where the Boleyn children were born. Anne was most probably born at Blickling. Eventually, Hever Castle became the family's principal residence. Although Anne's mother did not have a large dowry – as the Howards were short of money at the time – her father managed to get a place at Court. Thomas Boleyn attended Prince Arthur's wedding to Catherine of Aragon, and was one of the escort that took Princess Margaret to her marriage to James V of Scotland in 1503. He spoke excellent French and was a good jouster; he ran a course against the young Henry VIII at Greenwich in May 1510.

186

Apart from his sporting prowess, Thomas Boleyn was also a skilled and easy negotiator, a man of enormous charm. In 1512 he went on a diplomatic mission to Brussels. Shortly after his arrival he made a bet with the Regent of the Netherlands, Margaret of Austria, that within 10 days they would make progress in their negotiations. So easy was their relationship that Thomas bet his horse against Margaret's fine Spanish mount, and they were seen to 'clap hands' (shake hands) on the bargain.[2]

Back at the English Court, Henry VIII had his 'chamber', divided into three parts – the Privy Chamber, his private suite of rooms, with access only for the Gentlemen of the Privy Chamber; the Presence Chamber, for the principal courtiers, and where the King held his audiences; and the Great or Watching Chamber, which all his household 'above stairs' had access to. The Gentlemen of the Privy Chamber were his tight group of favourites; his chosen companions and had the most influence with him. Thomas Boleyn was one of this inner circle, his son George was the King's page and his wife, Elizabeth, was one of Catherine of Aragon's ladies.

In 1513, Thomas Boleyn placed his younger daughter, Anne, at the court of Margaret of Austria with whom he had established a friendly and respectful relationship. Margaret was bringing up her nephews and nieces, and her Court was home to the highest born children in Europe who would be brought up alongside its future rulers. Margaret of Austria was Catherine of Aragon's sister-in-law, and had taught her French. If Anne Boleyn were brought up in such a court, it would place her in a good position to get a post with Catherine at the English Court, and to be at the forefront of Court life. Margaret of Austria wrote to Sir Thomas: 'I have received your letter by the Esquire Bouton who has presented your daughter to me, who is very welcome, and I am confident of being able to deal with her in a way which will give you satisfaction, so that on your return the two of us will need no intermediary other than she. I find her so bright and pleasant for her young age that I am more beholden to you for sending her to me than you are to me.'[3]

Anne was aware of the importance of learning all she could. She wrote to her father, in French, from La Vure, the palace near Brussels: 'Sir, I understand from your letter that you desire me to be a woman of good reputation when I come to court, and you tell me that the queen [Catherine of Aragon] will take the trouble to converse with me, and it gives me great joy to think of talking with such a wise and virtuous person.'[4]

It was essential in any Court that had pretensions to greatness that the ladies were its ornament. They had to dance, sing, play musical instruments, ride, shoot with a bow, write poetry and prose, thus providing the stately court entertainment. A lady should be able to perform the dancing, singing and reciting necessary for a masque or 'disguising'. These performances were relatively new to England, but part of the European courts; Margaret of Austria was recognised as a skilled planner, director and performer of such events. Margaret kept a strict eye on the behaviour of her ladies. Whereas she would not allow immoral behaviour, she was someone who enjoyed courtly love – forlorn and chaste devotion of a lady by her gentleman admirer. Under Margaret's supervision, this was all very romantic and entirely harmless, however.

Margaret had spent her childhood in France, from the age of 3 to 13, as the proposed bride of Charles VIII. In the event, the marriage never happened; she married John, the only son of Ferdinand and Isabella, and, after he died, Philibert, Duke of Savoy. Both marriages left her childless, and she became her brother Philip the Fair's Regent in the Low Countries for his infant son, Charles V. Margaret was a good musician, particularly on the virginals (a keyboard instrument); Anne may well have picked up or improved her musical skills here. Cavendish later said of Anne, 'when she composed her hands to play and her voice to sing, it was joined with that sweetness of countenance that three harmonies concurred.'[5]

In 1513, when Henry and Maximilian met Margaret and her ladies at Lille, while campaigning in France, Anne was probably there; however, Henry was a powerful, lusty, 22-year-old man and she was little more than a child. He was probably not even aware of her. Henry took a companion, Etionette de la Baume and Anne Boleyn would most probably have watched from the sidelines.

On 14 August 1514, Thomas Boleyn wrote to Margaret of Austria to say that he was sending a messenger to collect Anne and bring her back to England. The long-arranged marriage between Henry VIII's sister, Princess Mary, and Charles V was now officially cancelled, and Mary was to marry Louis XII of France instead. It was, therefore, important that she should have ladies about her who spoke French, such as Anne. Thomas was apologetic, as Princess Mary's spurned suitor was Margaret's nephew, but explained that it was Henry VIII's wish that Anne Boleyn join Mary Tudor's household in France.[6]

However, although Mary Boleyn was included as one of Princess Mary's ladies, Anne was not. Anne may well have arrived late from the Netherlands, and since the French marriage lasted a mere 82 days, she was not in Princess Mary's household for long. The new king, Francis I, supported Princess Mary in her marriage to Henry VIII's friend, Charles Brandon, and by April 1515 Princess Mary, now the Duchess of Suffolk, was back in England. Anne, however, remained in France with her father, in the household of one of the French royal ladies. George Cavendish, a Gentleman Usher in the Cardinal's household, wrote in his *History of the Life of Wolsey*, that Anne was 'made one of the French Queen's women', but does not specify which queen.[7] There were two possibilities – that she was either part of the household of Queen Claude, or that of the King's sister, Margaret of Angoulême, Queen of Navarre. There is no direct evidence for either, however.

Queen Claude was the only surviving child of Louis XII by his second wife, Anne of Brittany, and was her father's eldest surviving child. When her father married Princess Mary, Claude would have valued an interpreter in order to communicate with her stepmother and Anne Boleyn could have been such a person, arriving just in time to be taken into Claude's service. The year before her father's death, Claude married Francis, her cousin, and the heir to the throne. He confirmed his right to rule by marrying the royal heiress. Queen Claude gave her husband a succession of children and died in 1524. If Anne had been part of Claude's household, she would have attended her at her coronation in St Denis in May 1516, and would have been under her protection, away from the looser morals of Francis I's court circle.

189

Anne Boleyn would have acted as interpreter when the English came to Paris to finalise the marriage treaty between the infant dauphin Francis and Princess Mary (the future Mary I), Henry VIII's daughter, in December 1518. Her services would also have been in demand at another event at the Field of the Cloth of Gold, in France in June 1520. If Anne had indeed been present with the French household of Queen Claude, she would have been reunited with her father, her mother and sister (Queen Catherine's ladies), and her brother as Henry VIII's page.

In 1521 Anne left Paris on her father's orders as France became involved in Scottish political affairs. The Imperial Ambassador recorded that Anne's departure was mentioned by Francis I, and that she was one of Queen Claude's ladies. The reason for Anne leaving may be indicated by a letter from Francis I complaining of England's aggressive intentions towards France, as evidence for which he sites the English scholars leaving Paris and 'Mr Boleyn's' daughter returning to England.[8] If she was born in 1507, Anne would then have been 15 years old.

Back in England, Thomas Boleyn and Piers Butler were in conflict over the vacant Earldom of Ormonde. Thomas had right of inheritance through his mother, but Butler was in possession of it. The Earl of Surrey, Thomas's brother-in-law, suggested that the whole matter could be settled if Piers' son, James Butler, a young gentleman in Wolsey's household, married Thomas's daughter. Although this daughter is never mentioned by name, it is Anne who is referred to rather than Mary, who had already married William Carey in February 1520. Piers Butler approved; the Irish lords approved, Henry VIII and Wolsey approved. In October 1521, Wolsey wrote to Henry: 'I shall ... devise with Your Grace how the marriage betwixt him [James Butler] and Sir Thomas Boleyn's daughter may be brought to pass ... '[9] As it turned out, the suggestion came to nothing. The marriage proposal foundered when each party thought he could succeed without it. Piers Butler succeeded in aligning the Irish lords with him and held the Irish estates, paying Thomas Boleyn a small rent. He surrendered the title of Earl of Ormonde in return for the title of Earl of Ossory. In 1529, after Wolsey's fall, the Ormonde title was finally awarded to Thomas Boleyn.

From the time she was 6 until she was 15, Anne was brought up in the glittering Renaissance courts of Europe where she learned French manners that gave her a cosmopolitan sparkle amongst the English ladies. The French were leaders in fashion, and court ladies were expected to be elegant, learned, witty and talented. Like other ladies of her time, Anne Boleyn wrote poetry, played and sang her own compositions, and even assisted in the design of her own dresses. In March 1522 Anne's first post at the English Court was with the Royal Wardrobe. Thanks to her father's position, his closeness to Henry VIII, and her sister Mary's relationship with the King, Anne soon became one of Catherine of Aragon's ladies-in-waiting. Although formally one of the Queen's ladies, Anne also became part of the group who glittered around Mary, Duchess of Suffolk, Henry VIII's beloved sister and one of the Court's most merry and glamorous ladies. As the years passed, Catherine of Aragon's immediate circle became older, more worthy and religious – Mary's comprised gay and charming young people.

It was to this circle that Henry VIII gravitated. Within that group Anne, her brother George and the poet Thomas Wyatt formed a clique. Although Wyatt was married, he fell passionately in love with Anne and they played out their courtly 'romances' (all poems, sighs, tokens, service by the men and coy acceptance or rejection by the ladies), until Henry VIII joined in and fell in love with Anne in earnest. Thomas Wyatt was married to Lord Cobham's daughter, Elizabeth Brooke, when he wrote a poem entitled, 'Of his Love, called Anna':

> *What word is that, that changeth not*
> *Though it be turn'd and made in twain?*
> *It is mine Anna, God it wot,*
> *And eke the causes of my pain,*
> *Who love rewardeth with distain* ...[10]

Anne made an instant impact on the Court. She had glossy dark hair, was a good musician, a graceful dancer and possessed exquisite French manners. She also dressed well, which was important since Tudor ladies were expected to show off the latest fashions. She invented a hanging sleeve to hide a blemish on one hand and a high collar that hid a mark on her neck (a birthmark or mole). She was reputed to be a wit, and men seemed to find her irresistible. Since she caused so much interest, we are fortunate to have several descriptions of Anne. The Venetian Ambassador said of her:

> 'Mistress Anne is not one of the handsomest women in the world. She is of middling stature, swarthy complexion, long neck, wide mouth, bosom not much raised and in fact has nothing but the king's great appetite – and her eyes which are black and beautiful.'[11]

Nicholas Sander, a Catholic exile, born in 1527 and living abroad in 1561, wrote of what he had heard about Anne, a rather honest assessment:

> 'Anne Boleyn was rather tall of stature with black hair and an oval face of sallow complexion, as if troubled with jaundice. She had a projecting tooth under her upper lip, and on her right hand, six fingers. There was a large wen (tumour or wart) under her chin, and therefore to hide its ugliness, she wore a high dress covering her throat. She was handsome to look at … She was the model and the mirror of those who were at court, for she was always well dressed, and every day made some change in the fashion of her garments.'[12]

George Wyatt, grandson of the poet who had loved Anne, wrote concerning that 'extra finger' and her other attributes:

> 'There was found, indeed, upon the side of her nail, upon one of her fingers, some little show of a nail, which yet was so small … albeit in beauty she was to many inferior, but for behaviour, manners, attire and tongue she excelled them all … she was indeed a very wilful woman … but yet that and other things cost her after dear.'[13]

Anne found herself in a strangely ambiguous position at Court. Although she was niece to the country's premier Duke and daughter of a leading diplomat, she was also the sister of Henry VIII's current mistress. Despite this, in September 1523, a year after her return to England, Anne was loved and solicited in marriage by Henry Percy, the son and heir of the Earl of Northumberland. George Cavendish wrote of the meeting of Percy and Anne, that he was a visitor to the Queen's chambers where he met her ladies: '... when it chanced the Lord Cardinal at any time to repair to the Court, the Lord Percy would then resort for his pastime unto the Queen's chamber, and there would fall in dalliance among the Queen's maidens, being at the last more conversant with Mistress Anne Boleyn than with any other; so that there grew such a secret love between them that at length they were insured together, intending to marry ...'[14]

This was a formidably good match for the daughter of Sir Thomas Boleyn. Despite its noble connections to Ormonde and Norfolk, the Boleyn family was not particularly rich or of the first rank of nobility. The marriage would have placed Anne Boleyn at the very centre of English society, and established her as a wealthy and powerful woman. Her suitor was young, quite good looking and very much in love – Anne could hardly have expected to do better.

193

However, the match was broken by Wolsey, who did not consider her to be good enough for the Percys. In the end, the young man was very unhappily married to a daughter of the Earl of Shrewsbury. A record exists, written by Cavendish, of Wolsey's approach to the young Percy. He started by pointing out that both the King and Percy's father, the Earl of Northumberland, were angry at his clandestine behaviour and about the young lady he had chosen. Percy responded by listing Anne's noble connections and saying that he had hoped his father would approve of his choice; he had not known that the King had any interest in the matter. According to Cavendish, the great Cardinal would not allow one of the country's premier earls to throw himself away. He reminded Percy that the King had made his feelings known and the whole matter should be at an end. Percy tried to counter that he had already promised marriage to Anne, but Wolsey assured him that this was irrelevant. What mattered was that Percy should do as he was told. Realising he would have to give in, Percy agreed and so the betrothal was broken off.

There is no suggestion that Henry VIII was himself in love with Anne at this point, only that he, Wolsey and the Earl had all decided – somewhat ironically – that she was not of suitable rank to become the bride to the heir to the Earl of Northumberland. Anne had her affair with Percy in 1523; she left Court shortly after that, possibly ordered home by the Cardinal to keep her away from Percy, and just possibly in a fit of pique at being humiliated, rejected as an unsuitable bride in front of the Court. She returned to Court in late 1525 or early 1526.

This affair is said to have been at the root of Anne's hatred for Wolsey. Anne saw that her chance of making a remarkably good marriage to a young man who sincerely loved her had been ruined. Since we have no way of knowing and no direct evidence, Anne may well have loved Percy in return or at least held him in great affection. She had been left in no doubt as to the reason for Wolsey's intervention – she simply wasn't good enough for Percy. In retrospect, it was a most unfortunate decision. On a personal level, she and Percy might have lived happily together, with a large family and Anne as a harmless ornament to the Court. As it was, Percy's marriage was extremely unhappy: he and his wife loathed each other. She deliberately aborted her one pregnancy and they had no children.

In later years, when Anne and Henry were considering marriage, Percy stated that there had never been any formal engagement or contract between him and Anne Boleyn. This was an important issue as at the time there were considered to be three stages of marriage. The first was a *de futuro* Promise of Marriage (saying 'I will' rather than 'I do'), which could be made between infants and children; this could be revoked if one or both of the parties requested it. Only cohabitation could bar a couple from withdrawing from a *de futuro* promise so it particularly applied to matches arranged between minors. The second stage was the *de praesenti* betrothal; a solemn and binding promise to marry. It could be done publicly or privately in front of witnesses. Whilst in this state, neither participant could marry anyone else; such a marriage would be illegal, and any children born would be illegitimate. It was at this point that the banns were called, allowing anyone who had any knowledge of any prior commitments to make their objections known. The final stage was the actual marriage, a religious ceremony to sanctify the union. This had to be done by a priest and before witnesses. The vows were now, 'I do', and wedding gifts were given.[15]

A precontract or betrothal was a serious matter; it was almost as binding as marriage itself. If there had been any formal promise of marriage between Anne and Percy, this would have put her marriage to Henry in jeopardy. If they had a son, in later years his legitimacy could be challenged by anyone who could prove that there had been a preconnection with another man. This explains Percy's vehement insistence that there had never been anything formal between him and Anne. Wolsey could not have foreseen the events to come, but Anne was in a perfect position to cause him trouble. When it came to Henry's world, Anne was related to, or friendly with, many of his circle – Charles Brandon was a friend, as were William Compton and Thomas Wyatt; Francis Bryan was Anne's cousin and Henry Norris was a distant relation. Anne was, through her mother, related to the widespread Howard family. It was incredibly easy for her to become part of Henry's intimate group.

In July 1527, Cardinal Wolsey wrote to the King, and made the first mention of his 'great matter' – his proposal for a divorce from Catherine of Aragon. In 1518 Catherine had been pregnant for the last time and Henry saw he now had little chance of a lawful male heir from her. Unfortunately, in June, Rome had been sacked by a

Spanish army, and the Pope was the prisoner of Charles V, Catherine of Aragon's nephew. Henry VIII was now highly unlikely to get papal dispensation to end his marriage.

The divorce was suggested by Wolsey, partly to further reduce Catherine's influence with Henry regarding Charles V, since the Cardinal was pro-French. Catherine had shown herself to be Wolsey's enemy, and this was his chance to get rid of her. More importantly Henry wanted a son. Once Henry had been shown a way, nothing could save Catherine from divorce, leaving Henry free to take another, younger wife. Whether before or after making the decision to obtain a divorce, when Henry first fell in love with Anne Boleyn, he did not think in terms of marrying her. Like her sister Mary, he saw her as a potential mistress. Anne's refusal to become just another passing fancy spurred him on with the thought that, if he were free, he could marry her. Anne also refused to have a sexual relationship with Henry since the prospect of marriage was before her as it had never been for her predecessors. The depth of Henry's passion for Anne only served to emphasise his need for the divorce and made him more determined then he might otherwise have been.

In June 1528, Sir Thomas Heneage, the Cardinal's Gentleman Usher, wrote to Wolsey; he mentioned the Lady Anne and her rise in the King's esteem. However, even then, Henry was still appearing at public functions with Catherine, apparently in harmony. For some time it was uncertain as to whether the divorce would happen, and it was certainly unclear as to whom the next queen would be, if it occurred. If Anne Boleyn was considered at all, it would have been as the King's mistress at this stage.

It was almost certainly in 1526, after her return to Court, that Henry first fell in love with Anne. A letter survives, from Anne to the King:

> 'Inexhaustible as is the treasury of your majesty's bounties, I pray you to consider that it cannot be sufficient to your generosity; for, if you recompense so slight a conversation by

gifts so great, what would you be able to do for those who are ready to consecrate their entire obedience to your desires? How great soever may be the bounties I have received, the joy that I feel in being loved by a king who I adore, and to whom I would with pleasure make a sacrifice of my heart ... will ever be infinitely greater. The warrant of maid of honour to the queen induces me to think that your majesty has some regard for me, since it gives me a means of seeing you oftener, and of assuring you by my own lips ... that I am, Your Majesty's very obliged and very obedient servant ..."[16]

Her sister had already been Henry's mistress, but Anne had no intention of being used and discarded. At first, she may just have been holding Henry off so as to make the best possible bargain when she followed Mary's example; with the Queen's influence in decline, Anne might have hoped to be the sole mistress and wield enormous power. If Anne had a son, he would be made a duke, like Richmond had been, and might even become heir to the throne.

197

One of Henry's early letters to Anne makes it quite clear that, at least to begin with, Henry had no thoughts of marriage with her: '... if it shall please you to do me the office of true, loyal mistress and friend, and to give yourself up, body and soul, to me who will be and have been your very loyal servant ... I promise you... that also I will take you for my only mistress, rejecting from thoughts and affection all others save yourself, to serve you only.'[17]

At some point, however, Henry mentioned marriage and Anne realised that this was a real possibility; after all, Edward IV had married Elizabeth Woodville and made her Queen of England. She too had had nothing but the desire of the King, and she had been the daughter of a knight. All Anne had to do was maintain Henry's interest and keep her honour intact. Once she saw the glittering prize, Anne kept Henry interested in her for six years – it was marriage or nothing.

Seventeen of Henry's love letters to Anne survive, ten in French and seven in English. When Henry courted Anne, the World was interested. Thankfully, Cardinal Campeggio, on his visits to England, managed to acquire several love letters written by the King to Anne, which he passed to the Pope to let him see how things were developing. They can now be found in the Vatican Library.

———◦∾◦———

Henry and Anne also exchanged brief notes in a Book of Hours belonging to Anne, probably passing the book from one to the other during chapel services. Henry wrote, 'If you remember my love in your prayers as strongly as I adore you, I shall hardly be forgotten, for I am yours, Henry R forever', and Anne wrote, 'By daily proof you shall me find/To be to you both loving and kind.'[18]

Wolsey began discussions on the divorce and on 18 June the trial opened at Blackfriars to decide the legality of Henry and Catherine's marriage, although it closed in July without reaching a conclusion. A second attack on the Church that was now unable or unwilling to grant Henry's divorce was mounted by Parliament. Much was made of spiritual failings and frauds in the Church. Thomas Cranmer, a rising cleric in the King's service, suggested to Stephen Gardiner, Bishop of Winchester, another of the King's clerical servants, that an appeal should be made, not to fellow churchmen, but to the academics of the Universities. They would look at the question of whether the marriage was correct in civil law as opposed to church law. While these legal niceties were being addressed, there must have been rumours about Henry and Anne. However, at this time the fiction of marriage was maintained; Catherine still lived with Henry in their apartments while Anne had separate rooms nearby.

Henry's love for Anne continued and increased. In an early dispatch from the Imperial Ambassador, Chapuys wrote, 'The king's affection for La Bolaing [*sic*] increases daily. It is so great just now that it can hardly be greater; such is the intimacy and familiarities in which they live at present.'[19]

By November 1529 Wolsey was in the sad position of writing to Cromwell that he was under Anne's displeasure. She wrote a personal letter to the Cardinal:

'My Lord, though you are a man of great understanding, you cannot avoid being censured by every body for having drawn on yourself the hatred of a King who had raised you to the highest degree ... I cannot comprehend, and the King still less, how your reverent lordship, after having allured us by so many fine promises about divorce, can have repented of your purpose ... What, then, is your mode of proceeding? You quarrelled with the Queen to favour me at the time when I was less advanced in the King's good graces; and after, having therein given me the strongest mark of your affection, your lordship abandons my interests to embrace those of the Queen ... But, for the future, I shall rely on nothing but the protection of Heaven and the love of my dear King, which alone will be able to set right again those plans which you have broken and spoiled, and to place me in that happy station which God wills, the King so much wishes, and which will be entirely to the advantage of the kingdom.'[20]

In October 1528, William Tyndale published *The Obedience of the Christian Man and How Christian Rulers Ought to Govern*, and copies came into England printed in English. According to Anne Zouche (née Gainsford), one of the Queen's ladies, recording the event many years later, Anne Boleyn got hold of a copy. She lent it to one of her ladies, Anne Gainsford, whose fiancée George Zouche took it as a joke. He was caught reading it by the Dean of the Chapel Royal, who confiscated it as a proscribed book and gave it to Cardinal Wolsey. Anne told Henry who ordered Wolsey to give it back to Anne. She then showed it to Henry, particularly the passages that said that the King, as God's Anointed, should be the sole temporal and spiritual ruler of a country ('One king, one law is God's ordinance in every realm'). Although Henry strongly disapproved of most of Tyndale's ideas, he found this particular one most appealing.[21]

The divorce was supposed to proceed as follows: Henry would be called before a court. He would be found to have married his brother's widow in error. The marriage would be annulled, with a papal bull confirming this, leaving the King free to remarry.

In fact, William Warham, Archbishop of Canterbury, declined to make a ruling and referred the matter to Rome. With the Papal City under the control of Charles V's Imperial army, Pope Clement VII was unlikely to go against the wishes of the Holy Roman Emperor, also Catherine's nephew. While Wolsey was negotiating to have a separate papal court set up in England under his authority, Henry privately sent Dr William Knight as his envoy to the Pope. He asked for two things. The first was a dispensation to take a second wife without divorcing, for the purpose of getting an heir; the second was a dispensation for this second wife if she were within the proscribed bounds of consanguinity. The problem addressed by the second bull was that since Mary Boleyn had been Henry's mistress, marrying Anne Boleyn was technically like marrying his wife's sister (a publicly acknowledged mistress had the same legal standing as a wife under church law), which was equally as proscribed as marrying his brother's wife. This request confirmed that Henry was indeed considering marrying Anne at this point. Wolsey now saw clearly that Henry planned to make Anne his queen, and not take a French princess as his wife as Wolsey wanted. Against public opinion, Wolsey backed a French army to drive the Imperial forces out of Italy and out of Rome. Once they had done this and he was free from Imperial control, the Pope issued a warrant for Wolsey and Cardinal Campeggio to try Henry's case in London.

When it came to the divorce, the Pope sought only to delay matters. He did not wish to alienate either Henry VIII or Charles

V. He instructed the cardinals to examine only relevant issues of canon law, and that any result should be kept secret, to be ratified by Rome. Lorenzo Campeggio, the Papal Envoy, was a diplomat and a professor of canon law from Bologna. While Campeggio, racked with gout, travelled to England, the French army fell victim to disease and the Imperial army again invaded Italy: once more papal power was under the control of Charles V. Arriving in England, Campeggio at first tried reconciliation. He was forced to report, 'He [Henry VIII] told me briefly that he wished nothing except a declaration whether his marriage was valid or not, always presuming it was not, and I think that an angel descending from heaven could not persuade him otherwise.'[22]

The King met with the Lord Mayor of London, aldermen, burgesses, assorted worthies and commons, one of whom was Edward Hall, the historian, who made a record of the event. Henry said he sought divorce only for the succession, not for his own pleasure, and because he had been brought to believe that he had broken canon law. In public he had only praise for Catherine[23]

On 18 June 1529 Catherine of Aragon came to court at Blackfriars and appealed against the case proceeding since a) the location and b) the composition of the court were prejudicial towards her, and c) the case was still pending in Rome. On 24 June she appeared again, and made a speech before Henry. After proclaiming herself 'your true wife, and by me ye have had divers children, although it hath pleased God to call them from this world', she then played her strongest card, '… and when ye had me at the first, I take God to be my judge, I was a true maid, without touch of man, and whether this be true or not, I put it to your conscience.' After the speech, she walked out, despite being called back to attend the court.[24] Henry ignored the point about Catherine being a virgin at the time of their marriage. It may be that he could not commit perjury. Possibly the only defence Henry could have put forward was that he didn't know if she was a virgin or not, because he was very inexperienced at the time of his marriage. This would have been unbelievably embarrassing, especially if people believed it were true.

Back in Rome, with the Papacy once more under the influence of Charles V, on 13 July, Clement VII and the papal court decided that the case should be heard by them, and that the London court should be closed. There were also indications that Charles V and Francis I were considering peace between them, which came about at the beginning of August. Henry had lost his ally against Charles and his ability to rescue the Papacy and get the decision he needed.

On 22 July, Campeggio explained that in Rome it was a papal holiday, and adjourned the papal court in London until 1 October, yet another delaying tactic, although the court would never reconvene. Wolsey was now doomed. Everyone was against him; Anne Boleyn's supporters, Catherine's supporters, the dukes, the nobility who resented his power coupled with his working class origins, the Church, almost everyone in fact. His fall was sudden, and absolute, and virtually unlamented.

By late 1529, Wolsey had lost the King's favour and resigned his court posts when he was accused of praemunire, the crime of acting in ecclesiastical matters without the royal consent. In Wolsey's case, this was plainly ridiculous, but it was enough to lose him his posts and place in the King's Privy Council. His resignation, however, could not save him; in 1530 Wolsey was arrested and died in November, on his way to prison. The irony was that the nobleman sent to arrest him was Henry Percy, now Earl of Northumberland on his father's death, whose engagement to Anne Boleyn had been ended by Wolsey years before. In the last months before his death, Wolsey thought he could end the crisis by persuading the Pope to order Henry to put aside Anne. In the event, his arrest for treason and his death occurred too soon. Once they knew of his death, the Boleyns ordered an entertainment for Anne and Henry, with a performance of a farce entitled, 'Of the Cardinal's going to Hell'.[25]

Some time in November, Henry quarrelled with Catherine. They had spoken and Catherine had effectively told Henry that he knew very well she was his wife and a virgin when they married. Henry said the lawyers and scholars meeting at the University of Paris would find in his favour; if the Pope didn't annul the marriage, he would call the Pope a heretic, and marry where he pleased anyway. Catherine said the decisions in Paris were irrelevant. If Henry's experts said one thing, she could find a thousand more to say another. Henry went straight to Anne for reassurance; what he got instead was tears. Anne claimed that she had given up the best years of her life for him, given up other chances to get married; if he went on talking to Catherine she would convince him to go back to her, and then where would Anne be for all her love, fidelity and devotion?

Henry's response was to take immediate action: Catherine was told to stay in her rooms or go to Richmond. A ball was held at which Anne acted as if she were the queen, taking precedence over the Duchesses of Suffolk and Norfolk. By January 1530, Catherine was now virtually separated from her husband, with Henry refusing to see her or behave kindly towards her. By February he was living with Anne at York Place. The Pope insisted that the divorce case could only be heard in Rome and ordered Henry not to interfere; the academics might be bullied into supporting the divorce, but there was still popular support for Catherine.

By July, Henry was going on a summer progress with Catherine and the whole affair seemed to blow hot and cold. There were almost as many opinions around Court as there were people asked; the English nobles signed a letter to the Pope asking for the divorce, and the Pope responded by reminding Henry that this was a matter of canon law, not a popularity contest. Some advisers simply didn't want to give an opinion; some said leave it all to Rome; some said, marry Anne and then trust to making it right later.[26]

It was Thomas Cromwell, formerly one of Wolsey's agents, who gave Henry's plans a new direction. Why should the Church in England have effectively two heads: God's Vicar and God's Anointed King? Why should Henry not be sole Head of the Church in England? All this needed was agreement from the Church Council and from Parliament. By these means, he could stay within the Catholic Church, but would have overall control over both Church and State. This appealed not only to Henry's desire for a divorce, but also his constant need for money. Cromwell had been responsible, under Wolsey, for closing down some of the smaller monastic sites so that Wolsey could use their revenue to found colleges; Cromwell knew how wealthy the monasteries were, and how that wealth could be liberated for the Crown. His first step was to persuade the clergy at Convocation that they were guilty of treason in publishing papal bulls without the King's permission. They responded by voting a subsidy (actually a bribe) of over £100,000 to Henry. He agreed to take it if they acknowledged him as Supreme Head of the Church and Clergy of England. The Pope was the Supreme Head of the Christian Catholic Church, after Christ. Henry was currently Head of the Church in England and Protector of the Faith. In the end they compromised: Henry was to be voted Supreme Head 'as far as the law of Christ allows.'

Catherine had a lot of support from the church, nobles and commons; the Boleyns had very little. However, the nobles and commons thought little of the Pope as he refrained from taking any action on her behalf. Clement VII had become mentally ill and was incapable of making decisions or initiating action. When asked for a decision, the Pope would breathe rapidly and unevenly, rub his hands together and cry. He was also playing politics, to save the authority of the Church and win back ground lost to the Protestant reformers. For this he needed the support of France and England. So he did nothing, hoping that Henry would remain, at least to all appearances, a supporter of the Catholic Church.

In 1530, Henry began suffering the first signs of the ill health that was to dog him for the rest of his life. He suffered from bad headaches and pains and ulcers in his legs. These were believed to be the result of earlier jousting and hunting injuries. This suggested to him that he had to get his divorce and remarry as soon as possible. To make matters worse, on 21 March Pope Clement issued a bull forbidding any criticism of Henry's marriage to Catherine, thereby giving it the full backing of the Catholic Church and forcing Henry to look for another way out of his marital predicament.

Finally a petition was drawn up and signed by most of the nobles and a few senior churchmen, begging the Pope to issue a divorce for the good of England and offering veiled threats about alternative options. It was circulated for signature by nobles who were away from London by William Brereton, Groom of the Privy Chamber, and Thomas Wroithesley, a protégée of Stephen Gardiner. Edward Fox, Bishop of Durham, led a team collecting scriptural and historical precedents for the King to make decisions separately from Rome (the *Collectanea satis copiosa*). They came up with two possibilities. One was that in the early days of Christianity, each province of the Church had had its own powers, under the loose authority of the Pope. This meant the Church in England could settle its own problems. The second was that the king was (as Tyndale had suggested) the sole representative of God in his own country. Thus it was the Popish Church that was corrupting the intention of the founding fathers, not Henry seeking to overthrow the authority of the Mother Church.

205

The formal ending of the marriage of Henry and Catherine finally came in June 1531. The court moved from Greenwich to Hampton Court, then to Windsor. From there Henry moved away, leaving Catherine without any explanation. When she wrote to him, Henry claimed that the whole mess was her fault for being so unreasonable. He ordered her to leave Windsor before he returned; she could go to The More (Wolsey's old house), a nunnery, or any small manor – anywhere away from him. She was to cut down on her household and would not see their daughter Mary again.

Catherine moved to The More, then to Easthampstead, then back to The More again. The threat to reduce her staff was lifted for a time (in November 1531 she had a staff of 200), partly because of the intervention of Chapuys who gave the impression that Charles V would go to war for Catherine if she were treated too badly. In fact, Charles thought she was a nuisance to his political plans.[27]

On New Year's Day 1532 Henry gave Anne a set of room and bed hangings made of crimson satin, cloth of silver and cloth of gold. At the same time, he forbade anyone to give Catherine presents; he gave her nothing, and returned a gold cup she sent him before it could be formally presented in the name of the Queen.[28]

On 11 May 1532, Henry raised the question of whether the clergy were loyal to him, or to Rome. On 15 May the clergy responded by passing the Act of Submission of the Clergy, giving their support to the King. Cromwell, meanwhile, also encouraged Parliament to attack the abuses of the Church, which culminated in the Commons' Supplication against the Ordinaries, in January 1532. This petition complained about the Church's expense, delays and corruption, the abuses of Church law, and the fact that it was not under the control of the King and Parliament. This was closely followed by squeezing a bill through to stop annates or first fruits (taxes raised) of bishoprics being sent to Rome without the King's express permission. This hurt the Papacy, which enjoyed vast revenues from England. In the end, the churchmen agreed to the Submission of the Clergy, on 15 May 1532, that the Church should make no new laws and all the existing ones should be ratified or rejected by Henry.

On 23 August 1532, William Warham, 82-year-old Archbishop of Canterbury, died. With the prospect of putting an agreeable replacement in office, Anne finally surrendered to Henry and they moved on to a physical relationship. She had held out for six years. On 1 September she was created Anne Rochford, Marquess of Pembroke, owning her title in her own right. To support her title, Anne was given Crown lands with a value of £1,000 a year. Her title and possessions were to pass to her 'heirs male of her body', but the usual accompanying phrase 'lawfully begotten' was left out.[29] This supports the fact that Anne was having sexual relations with Henry that might end in pregnancy before they could be married.

On 11 October 1532, Henry visited the English-controlled Calais to meet with Francis I, and took Anne with him. Originally it had been hoped that some royal or high-ranking noble French lady could have come as hostess to welcome Anne and give her credibility as the queen-presumptive. In the event, the Queen Eleanor (Catherine of Aragon's niece) refused; the King's sister, Marguerite, backed out due to 'illness', and the only lady who would agree to come was the King's own mistress. Francis I didn't want to cause trouble in public. He had recently arranged the marriage of his second son, Henri, to Catherine de Medici, a wealthy heiress and the niece of the Pope; so he hardly wanted to offend the Papacy by formally recognising Anne's relationship with the English King.

Anne was attended by some 20 ladies-in-waiting and robed like a queen; she was also decked out in Catherine's jewels, which Henry had ordered his wife to surrender (the first request was met with the reminder that at New Year Henry had forbidden Catherine to give him anything, and anyway it would be wrong to give her jewels into the possession of a woman she described as 'the scandal of Christendom'). At the great banquet that night Anne made her appearance, leading a noble dance troupe, comprising her ladies: Mary Carey, her sister; Dorothy, Countess of Derby, her aunt; Elizabeth, Lady Fitzwalter, her aunt; Lady Jane Rochford, her sister-in-law; Honor, Lady Lisle (the wife of Henry's bastard uncle, Arthur Plantagenet, Lord Lisle, the illegitimate son of King Edward IV), and Lady Wallop, wife of the Ambassador to France. They wore cloth of gold gowns with gold lace over-dresses, crimson satin sashes ornamented with cloth of silver, and were masked. They led out various French nobles to dance, and Anne partnered Francis I.[30]

On 29 October Henry escorted Francis back to French soil. Bad weather intervened, and Henry and Anne had to stay at Calais until

207

12 November, lodging at the Exchequer, with adjoining bedrooms (linked by a door). It is believed that either in Calais, or on their return, Henry and Anne were definitely sleeping together. By the end of December, Anne believed she was pregnant, and some time around 25 January 1533 Henry and Anne were married at York Place. Anne had remarkably kept Henry interested in her for eight years now, only giving in when their marriage was imminent.

In February 1533, Thomas Cranmer was elected Archbishop of Canterbury and on 23 May, he wrote to Henry confirming that the divorce had been granted. On 9 April, the Dukes of Norfolk and Suffolk visited Catherine at Ampthill to tell her that her marriage had been annulled, that she was to be referred to as Dowager Princess, the late Prince Arthur's widow, and that her daughter was illegitimate, that Henry was free to remarry and her income was to be cut by three-quarters. Catherine responded by saying that all she needed was her confessor, her physician and two maids; if there was no money, she could always go out into the streets begging. Norfolk finally broke the news to her that Henry and Anne were married.

Time was now of the essence. On 12 April, the day before Easter Sunday 1533, Anne went to church as Queen of England, dressed in cloth of gold, dripping with jewels, attended by 60 maids of honour and with her cousin Mary Howard, the future Duchess of Richmond, holding her train. On 8 May 1533, Cranmer summoned a formal court at Dunstable, near Ampthill, and when Catherine failed to answer its summons, he publicly declared her marriage annulled on the grounds that she had had sex with Arthur and no man, including the Pope, had any right to override church law on this point. This was followed by a communiqué on 25 May when Cranmer publicly stated that Henry and Anne were married legally. Henry's latest marriage was therefore the only lawful one he had entered into. The child would be legitimate. On the same day, Cranmer hurried to Lambeth Palace where he carried out a marriage service, finally officially uniting Henry and Anne. She had achieved her aim, and, six months pregnant, she formally became queen.

On 1 June Anne Boleyn rode into London. A grand pageant had been organised, but even with the incentive of free wine there were a lot of adverse comments. Cromwell's spies reported that someone had called Anne a 'goggle eyed whore', that another had called 'God save Queen Catherine, our own righteous lady', while one man said he was not stupid enough 'to take that whore Nan Bullen to be queen.'[31] Anne was escorted to Westminster Abbey where she was crowned queen. The High Steward responsible for the coronation was Henry's old friend Charles Brandon. Henry seems to have gone to great lengths to make the event as magnificent as possible, with all the nobility in attendance, as well as representatives of the government and the London guilds. When she came by barge from Greenwich to the Tower she was met with a salute of a thousand guns, as well as those fired from ships as she passed.

Later there was a banquet at the Great Hall at Westminster, where Anne sat in state, served by the greatest nobles of the Court. One prominent member of the court was absent, however. Charles Brandon organised the celebrations, then hurried to his house at Westhorpe Hall, where his duchess lay dying. She had always been a partisan of Catherine of Aragon, and the terminal illness under which she was suffering was enough to excuse her from attending Anne Boleyn in her moment of glory. Despite her support for Catherine, Mary was reconciled with her brother before her death, which both he and Charles Brandon deeply mourned.

The secret marriage of Henry and Anne was attended by a small number of witnesses. Rumours reported that these included Henry Norris and Thomas Heneage of the privy chamber, Anne Savage (later Lady Berkeley) as Anne's attendant, and a groom (possibly William Brereton, who had a family connection with Anne Savage). The date may be significant, as Anne had probably just confirmed she was pregnant. On the occasion of Anne's coronation, 18 Knights of the Bath were created. These included Francis Weston (the King's page), Henry Parker (George Boleyn's

209

brother-in-law), Thomas Arundel (married to Anne's cousin), the Earl of Derby (married to Anne's aunt) and Lord Berkeley (husband of Anne's attendant at her secret marriage).[32]

The Act of Succession was passed to confirm that Henry's marriage to Catherine was annulled; his marriage to Anne was the only lawful one and the throne would go to their children, lawfully born. It was now a treasonable offence to question or deny the marriage. Not only that, everyone had to take an oath to abide by this Act. Catherine and her daughter Mary were now in real danger, but Catherine was prepared for martyrdom. She wrote to Charles V, 'I could not endure so much, did I not think these things suffered for God's sake … As long as I live I shall not fail to defend our rights.'

The Pope finally acted. In March 1534 the Papal Consistory found that Henry and Catherine's marriage was 'lawful and good'. It was too late for England and for the Queen, however. Catherine was now officially the Dowager Princess and her servants were being forced to take the Oath of the Act of Succession. When Dr Edward Lee, Archbishop of York, and Cuthbert Tunstall, Bishop of Durham, read the Act to her and warned her she must obey, she replied, 'If one of you has a commission to execute this penalty upon me, I am ready. I ask only that I be allowed to die in the sight of the people.'[33] In the face of such calm defiance, all Parliament could do was to order her removal to Kimbolton Castle in Huntingdon, even more bleak and remote than Buckden. Here, those of her servants who had already been arrested were replaced. Sir Edmund Bedingfield became her steward and Sir Edward Chamberlayne, her chamberlain. She was to receive no visitors without the King's written permission. Since Catheine would not receive anyone who refused to call her queen and her new servants were instructed to call her Dowager Princess, she remained in her private rooms with just a few of her old servants, all of whom had refused to take the Oath of Succession, risking imprisonment and death.

Henry certainly recognised Catherine's strength and her forbearance. He told the Council in 1535, 'The lady Katherine is a proud, stubborn woman of very high courage. If she took it into her head to take her daughter's part, she could quite easily take the field, muster a great array, and wage against me a war as fierce as any her mother Isabella ever waged in Spain.'[34]

Chapuys was finally allowed to see Catherine on 2 January 1536, when she was dying. She begged Chapuys to ask Henry to pay her debts, settle her servants' outstanding wages, and make some few small bequests out of the little she had left. She wished to be buried in a convent, and to have masses said for her soul. After three days Chapuys had to leave; Catherine seemed a little better, but still weak. On the last night, a visitor arrived without permission, and refused to go away; Maria de Salinas, widowed Countess Willoughby d'Eresby, was with her mistress once again. The next day, Chapuys went back to London leaving Maria attending her mistress. By the evening, Catherine's condition had deteriorated. At 10 a.m. the next morning she received extreme unction, and died at 2 p.m. on 7 January 1536. She was buried at Peterborough Abbey on 29 January, with the dignities of a Dowager Princess.

When Henry heard of Catherine's death, he organised a ball at Greenwich, dressed in yellow with a white feather in his cap, and carried his daughter Elizabeth shoulder high, telling those present, 'God be praised, the old harridan is dead, now there is no fear of war.'[35] On the day Catherine was buried Anne Boleyn had a miscarriage of a boy. She was in dire trouble. Had Henry divorced Anne while Catherine lived, he would have been under enormous pressure to take Catherine back. Now, if he were free of Anne, Henry would be able to marry again. She had to get pregnant again as quickly as possible and pray that this time she gave birth to a living, lusty boy. Even if Henry did not divorce her, Anne was realising that he no longer loved her so wholeheartedly. There was a very real danger that he would look for love with another Lady.

211

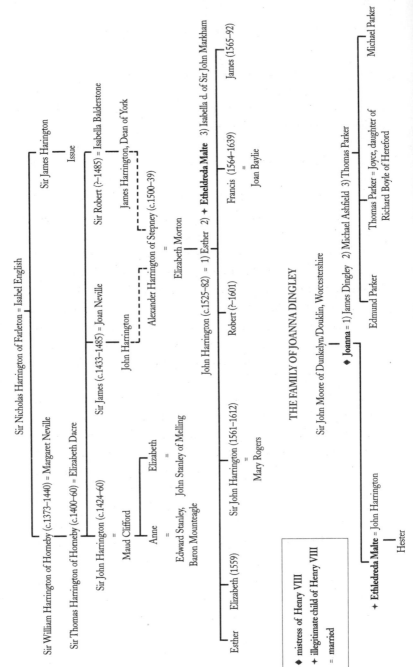

THE FAMILY OF JOHN HARRINGTON

Sir Nicholas Harrington of Farleton = Isabel English

Sir James Harrington

Issue

Sir William Harrington of Hornby (c.1373–1440) = Margaret Neville

Sir Thomas Harrington of Hornby (c.1400–60) = Elizabeth Dacre

Sir James (c.1433–1485) = Joan Neville

Sir Robert (?–1485) = Isabella Balderstone

James Harrington, Dean of York

John Harrington

Sir John Harrington (c.1424–60)
=
Maud Clifford

Alexander Harrington of Stepney (c.1500–39)

Anne   Elizabeth
=
Edward Stanley, John Stanley of Melling
Baron Mounteagle

Elizabeth Morton
=
John Harrington (c.1525–82) = 1) Esther 2) **+ Etheldreda Malte** 3) Isabella d. of Sir John Markham

Esther   Elizabeth (1559)

Sir John Harrington (1561–1612)
=
Mary Rogers

Robert (?–1601)

Francis (1564–1639)
=
Joan Baylie

James (1565–92)

THE FAMILY OF JOANNA DINGLEY

Sir John Moore of Dunkelyn/Douklin, Worcestershire

♦ Joanna = 1) James Dingley 2) Michael Ashfield 3) Thomas Parker

Edmund Parker

Thomas Parker = Joyce, daughter of Richard Boyle of Hereford

Michael Parker

+ Etheldreda Malte = John Harrington

Hester

♦ mistress of Henry VIII
+ illegitimate child of Henry VIII
= married

The Mysterious Mistress and the Tailor's Foster Daughter

―⟨ᴧᴧ⟩―

E theldreda Malte is one of the least well known of Henry's children, and her mother, Joanna Dingley, is an almost total enigma. The confusion over Etheldreda can be summarised in a letter written by J. Lesley in c.1656. It reads, 'The great King Henry the Eighth matched his darling daughter [Etheldreda] to John Harrington and, though a bastard, dowered her with the rich lands of Bath's Priory; and Queen Elizabeth affected these faithful servants so much, as to become godmother to their son, and made him a knight for his wit and valour.'[1] As will unfold in this chapter, most of the facts here are incorrect.

The story starts with a tailor. In 1527 the Wardrobe Account of Henry VIII recorded the tradesman supplying velvet and other fabrics was John Malte.[2] By 1529 came mention of 'wages to John Malte, the king's tailor', along with William Mortymer, the king's 'brouderer' [embroiderer]. They had purchased velvet, satin and damask to a value of £319 2s 1d for the King's wardrobe. In 1530 John Malte, Richard Gresham and William Ibgrave claimed £630 13s 4d paid for similar fabrics.[3]

In January 1532 came a grant of office to John Malte as the King's tailor, with a fee of 12d a day and Malte was listed amongst the creditors to the Wardrobe Account for that year. In such a privileged position, attached to the court, Malte was able to benefit from the Crown's need for revenue by disposing of its lands.[4] In April 1544 a number of property leases were sold to 'John Malte, the king's servant', for lands and manors in Somerset to a value of £1,824 16s 8d.

In September 1545, the following place was filled: 'Richard Egilston to be joint patent with John Malte, your Majesty's tailor in the office of cutter and botcher in your Great Wardrobe', with the wage of 6d a day. As cutter, Malte designed the patterns for the King's clothes, and as botcher he assembled the cut pieces – the modern term 'botch' means to patch over something and derives from the piecing together of various elements of the finished garment.[5] Thus John Malte became one of the two principal tailors to a king famed for his wardrobe. Malte purchased fabrics, as well as designing and cutting the clothes. Lesser journeymen would have stitched the garments, and embroiderers added the distinctive patterns, but it was Henry and Malte who worked together to create Henry's magnificent, distinctive and individual appearance.

In 1546 Henry VIII was sick, and probably realised that he was dying. He made one last request of a man who had served him faithfully for more than 20 years. He asked John Malte to take care of his bastard daughter, Etheldreda. An important point was that Malte was to pretend to the world that the girl was his own. Even with a foster father, the child would need a dowry to ensure that she married and led a comfortable and happy life and Henry VIII settled several estates on her in return for a cash payment. Should she fail to reach adulthood and marry, the lands would revert to the honest and loyal Malte and his own family.

A grant was made of land to, 'John Malte, tailor, and Etheldreda Malte, alias Dyngley, bastard daughter of the said John Malte by Joan Dyngley alias Dobson. Grant for £1,311 2d of the lordship and manor of Kelveston, Somerset, the lordship and manor of Easton and Kateryn, Somerset, the chief messuage called Katerns courte and lands in tenure of Wm. Hereford and Alice his wife of Eston and Kateryn, 400 ewes called "le yowe flocke of Charmerdon", in tenure of the said Wm. and Alice in Eston, Kateryn and Ford, Somerset – Bathe Priory. To hold to the said John Malte and Etheldreda and the heirs of the body of the said Etheldreda, with remainder to the right heirs of the said John.' In

January 1547 in a record of lands sold by the Crown, is the 'Docket of purchases xv to September xv, John Malte, tailor, and Awdrye, his base daughter, £1,312 12d.'[6]

Ten days after the transfer of the properties, during the night between 27 and 28 January 1547, Henry VIII died. He had settled his daughter with a man he trusted, and left her well provided for. Malte would see to her education and arrange a good marriage for her. Her education would have been a mixture of formal teaching and learning housewifely duties. Officially she was Malte's bastard child, but with her dowry and the open knowledge of her real parentage, she would marry well. Etheldreda had formal teaching in reading and writing. She probably never aspired to the dizzy intellectual heights of Lady Jane Grey or Elizabeth I, but she would have learned to translate Latin and possibly Greek, and to write a legible hand. Her reading material in her native language, thanks to her father's religious policy, would now have included Protestant literature and the English Bible.

Why was she called Etheldreda? She could have been born in the parish served by St. Etheldreda's Church, a Roman Catholic chapel in Ely Place, Holborn.[7] More likely she was named after St Etheldreda herself, the daughter of King Anna of East Anglia. This Etheldreda married twice, but contrived to live celibate; in 672 she founded a monastery and nunnery at Ely, where she died in 679 of the plague. She is the patron saint of those with throat and neck ailments, and her festival day is 23 June; another possibility is that this was Etheldreda Malte's birthday.[8]

However, as Henry Harrington recorded, 'This Esther [sic] was a natural daughter of the King's, to whom he gave as a dower the lands belonging to Bathe priory or a part thereof.'[9] The Rev. John Collinson, in the *History of Somerset*, recorded in 1791, 'The king's natural daughter, begotten upon the body of Joanna Dyngley, alias Dobson, which Etheldred was committed to the care of the said Malte, who was the king's tailor, for education; and the king, having special love and regard for her, granted these estates to her use and benefit; but she always passed for Malte's natural daughter. She was shortly after married to John Harrington, a confidential servant of the king, who thus obtained the several estates above mentioned.'[10]

John Malte also settled land upon his 'daughter'. In 1546 he gave her the manor of Watchenfield and Offynton, Berkshire, and referred to her as his illegitimate daughter in the title. The influx of lands for the girl, from both her adopted and natural fathers, coincided with a proposal for her marriage with the illegitimate son of Sir Robert Southwell, but this marriage never came about.

Marriage in Tudor England did not mean what it necessarily means to us today. Children, and even babies, could be betrothed or promised in marriage; this meant that they were to consider themselves as legally married until such time as the formal ceremonies could take place when they had reached a greater age. Prince Arthur was 18 months old when plans for his marriage to the four-year-old Catherine of Aragon were set up; in 1500, when he was 14 and his bride 16, a proxy marriage service was carried out in London, and it was not until the following year that the marriage actually took place. Sometimes the marriages failed to happen when one of the parties died. Likewise, as can be imagined, if a better bargain came along, a dispensation from the church could be acquired and the young couple declared free to choose another partner. This was particularly true of royal children, who could change partners as the need for political alliances changed. Even after the betrothal, consummation of the marriage could be delayed again, until they were physically ready. A child might stay with its own parents until the marriage was ready to begin in earnest, or go to the home of the parents of their intended spouse, so that the marriage, though arranged, did not unite two strangers.

John Malte was a good person to bring up a fatherless child. He already had two daughters, both married and with children of their own. He may very well have shared a household in London with his elder daughter, Bridget, and her husband John Scutte. A licence of 5 July 1547 mentions John Scutte, citizen and tailor of London, and Bridget his wife, one of the daughters and heiresses of John Malte (deceased), and the heirs of the body of Bridget. 'John Scutte' was another supplier to the Wardrobe in 1532. After Anne Boleyn's death in 1536, her unpaid debts included, 'To Tailors John Malte and Scutte, £34 9s 8d', so the two men, father-in-law and son-in-law, worked together as well as living together.[11]

Mention is also made of John Horner of Clofford, Somerset, esquire, and his wife Meriola ('late his wife'), another of John Malte's daughters. Although Meriola was dead by 1547, the licence mentions the heirs of her body (her children) by Horner.[12] John Horner, or Sir John as he became, would have kept an eye on Etheldreda and her lands. He was not one to let property slip through his fingers. His family had been at Clofford for several generations, but during the Dissolution of the Monasteries, in 1540 John ('Jack') and his father Thomas picked up a 'plum' property at Mells, and were the inspiration for the famous nursery rhyme, 'Little Jack Horner'. John had been the bailiff at Mells for the owners, the Abbey of Glastonbury, and was the one who surrendered the deeds to Thomas Cromwell in 1535. According to legend, the deeds were hidden under piecrust in a dish for their journey to London; John Horner was suspicious, lifted the piecrust and took out the deed to Mells, the best of the properties. In fact, it was Thomas Horner who bought the land at Mells from the Crown Commissioners, although his prior knowledge of the estate (given him by his son) may have given Horner an advantage on realising its worth. Since medieval times, Mells had grown prosperous on the woollen industry.

Malte died in 1547, and left to 'Audrey [a corruption of the name Elthedreda] Malte, my Bastard Daughter' a further estate at 'Andressy otherwise called Nyland' in his will. She was now a well-dowered heiress. The will also referred to her as being 'begotten on the body of Joane Dingley, now wife of one Dobson'. A further bequest of £20 was made, 'to Joane Dyngley, otherwise Joane Dobson.'[13] Looking for Joanna is a difficult problem. She was not a

217

noble lady like the well-recorded mistresses. The fact that Malte, rather than a great family, was asked to foster her daughter, suggests that the mother was not of noble rank, like Bessie Blount or Mary Boleyn. There are a number of Dingleys associated with the Court, and Joanna could be a sister or daughter of almost any of them. A gentleman, Henry Dyngley, received a royal annuity; in 1511 William Dingley was granted a pension from the monastery of St Peter, Gloucester, 'which the abbot elect is bound to give to a clerk, nominated by the king until the abbot promotes him to a competent benefice', while he was living at Sudeley Castle and trading in wool; Thomas Dingley, preceptor of Baddysley and Mayne, was Commander of the Order of the Knights of St John in England; John Dyngley was a Groom of the Privy Chamber at Greenwich in 1510 and Sewer of the Chamber in 1524.[14] At least the family of John Dyngley are well recorded at Charlton in Worcestershire. They do not, however, have a female called Jane, Joan or Joanna in the family in the reign of Henry VIII.

The identity of Joanna Dingley, Etheldreda's mother, rests on her being in a position to have met and had an affair with Henry. He must have seen her at close quarters; indeed, most of his mistresses (and wives) were ladies-in-waiting to one or more of the queens and therefore part of his immediate circle on a day-to-day basis. Bessie Blount, Anne Hastings, Jane Popincourt, Mary and Anne Boleyn, all served Catherine of Aragon; Jane Seymour and Margaret Shelton served Queen Anne, Anne Bassett served Queen Jane, and Catherine Howard served Anne of Cleves. Mary Berkeley's husband was a fanatical huntsman, and he entertained the King for hunting parties. Jane Pollard's husband had connections with the Royal Household and was an influential landowner.

Since Joanna Dingley was not a noble lady, she may have been of low enough rank for her not to be a risk politically. She would, however, have had to be sufficiently well born for Henry to have her as a sexual partner and for him to feel an attachment for her child.

One possible candidate is a lady called Joan Parker. A reference to her can be found in a lease of land made in 1546, the same year as the gift made to Etheldreda, to 'Thos. Parker of London and Joan, his wife, late wife of Jas. Dingley and of Mich. Asshefelde, dec.' of 'Northlatche Manor, Glouc.'[15] In the *Visitation of Worcestershire* Joan (or Jane), daughter of John Moore, is listed as having married James Dingley, and after the name of Dingley is the word 'Douklin', which may refer to the place that the Moores came from. In a list of Charters printed for Lord Sherborne, there occurs the entry, 'Letters patent 27 May 1586 to Thomas Parker, Gent., and Richard and Michael his sons, the site of the Manor of Northleach in tenure of William Dingley, Esq., James his son and Jane, Daughter of John Moore of Dunkelyn, co. Worster'.[16]

In the uncertain calligraphy of the time, Douklin/Dunkelyn could easily have been written as Dobson on the grant to Etheldreda, which would ideally have read 'Joan Dyngley alias Douklin/Dunkelyn', Douklin being used instead of Moore as her maiden name. The spelling of any person's name was idiosyncratic – Shakespeare, for example, has every spelling from Shakespear to Shagsper. The mother of Etheldreda could be Jane, Joan, Joanne or Joanna, with the spelling varying from reference to reference.

Since Joan was the daughter of Sir John Moore, and she had married an Ashfield and a Parker, kinsmen to each other and to Abbot Parker, a friend and supporter of the King, Joan would have been in a position to meet Henry VIII. She was a member of the minor nobility by birth, and a member of the ecclesiastical meritocracy by marriage. This was an age when, like Wolsey, a man from a modest background could rise through the church to achieve the favour of the King himself.

Abbot Thomas Parker (also known as Malvern) was a monk at St Peter's, Gloucester, in 1510, and Abbot in 1514. He took his seat in the House of Lords during the Dissolution of the Monasteries and supported the King. When he saw how the wind was blowing, he leased monastery lands at Northleach to his nephew, also

Thomas Parker (married to the twice-widowed Jane Moore) who lived at Notgrove, and leased land at Farmington to another relative, Michael Ashfield. Abbot Parker died in 1539, just failing to achieve the position of Bishop of Gloucester, created after Gloucester Abbey was surrendered in January 1540. On Abbot Parker's tomb are carved Tudor roses in honour of King Henry, and the pomegranate, emblem of Catherine of Aragon.[17]

If Joan Moore is indeed Etheldreda's mother, she would have been married to James Dingley (or had just become a widow) when she had her affair with Henry, perhaps in 1534; thus it is by the name of Dingley that she is listed on the document relating to Etheldreda's property. Whoever made Malte's will may have copied the reference to Etheldreda and her mother from the previous grant of land, and put 'now wife of one Dobson' because they had read 'alias Dobson', not because they had any firm knowledge of the current marital status of the lady. By 1540 she was married to Michael Ashfield, who in that year bought the manor of Farmington, previously the property of the monastery of Edington, after the Dissolution, only to die in the following year. His lands passed to his son, Robert Ashfield, who sold Farmington in 1608.

Thus, by 1546 Joan was married to Thomas Parker of Notgrove, and was to become the mother of his three sons, Edmund, Thomas and Michael; the Parker land eventually went to Thomas (who lived to be 100) and his children. It may have been on her mother's remarriage that Etheldreda was placed in the care of John Malte, so that she would remain in her father's orbit, while her mother made a new life in distant Gloucestershire.

As to when Joanna Dingley came into Henry's life – in spring 1534 Henry set up a 'new mistress'. The editor of the 'Letters and Papers, Foreign and Domestic', describes her: '[King] Henry was in love with another lady (not Jane Seymour, I rather think, but who she was must, for the present at least, remain uncertain), whom he refused to send away at Anne's request.'[18] Anne Boleyn was reported to have complained bitterly about this mistress, and

Henry is said to have told her to mind her own business and that she should remember how he had raised her. He stated that he could lower her just as quickly and that he might not choose to raise her again, given the choice. George Boleyn's wife, Jane Parker, tried to get Joanna sent away, but the King refused, and Jane herself was banished for interfering.

At that time, the Spanish Ambassador recorded that the life of the Princess Mary, made so wretched under the rule of Anne Boleyn, had improved and he mentioned the mysterious mistress. He wrote in a letter dated 27 September 1534: 'Since the king began to doubt whether his lady [Anne Boleyn] was enceinte [pregnant] or not, he has renewed and increased the love he formerly had for a very beautiful damsel of the Court.'[19] His next letter of 13 October records Jane Parker's banishment from court for interfering. He describes the mistress as one 'whose influence increases daily, while that of the Concubine [Anne Boleyn] diminishes ... The said young lady has lately sent to the Princess [Mary] to tell her to be of good cheer ... and that ... she would show herself her true and devoted friend.'[20] If the new mistress was indeed sympathetic to Mary's cause, and persuaded the King to be kinder and make her life easier, she would have found Mary I a devoted friend. Mary never forgot those who supported her before she became queen.

On 18 October, another letter was sent from the Count de Cifuentes to Charles V, reporting that Henry VIII was 'milder' towards Catherine of Aragon. Anne Boleyn was less popular: 'The King was entertaining another lady and many lords helped him with the object of separating him from Anne.'[21] The final letter is dated 24 October and says one might doubt the King's love for his eldest daughter 'were it not that the king is of amiable and cordial nature, and that the young lady his new mistress who is quite devoted to the Princess, has already busied herself on her behalf.'[22]

The dates and the fact that she is unknown all suggest that this could be Joanna Dingley. Even the date for the conception and birth of Etheldreda is possible. The editor of the state papers is right to be dubious that Jane Seymour is the lady referred to. Jane Seymour was well connected, and once Henry began to notice her, there was no bar to her being mentioned by name and their relationship recorded. To add to this, the mistress is described as being 'beautiful', an epithet that is never used to describe Jane Seymour, whose charm lay in her compliant and quiet prettiness. If Joanna is the mystery mistress, that would place their affair in mid to late 1534, and Etheldreda's birth in the following year, perhaps on 23 June. Thus in 1546 when she received her lands and passed into the care of John Malte, she would have been 11 years old, and 12 when Malte died.

In 1547, after Malte's death, Etheldreda would have continued living with Bridget Scutte in Malte's house, until she married John Harrington. Geoffrey Strutt, in his *History of St Catherine's Court*, wrote, 'At Malte's death, Etheldreda became a rich woman and in 1548 she married John Harrington of London.'[23] Etheldreda would have been about 13 years old. Given that she is unlikely to have arranged her own marriage, John Harrington must have approached her new guardians with the proposal, which they accepted.

At this time, Harrington must have appeared to be quite a good husband for the bastard daughter of a tailor, no matter how well endowed. He had been a servant to the late Henry VIII, he was related to the noble family of Harrington, and to the Greys (one of whom, Henry Grey, Marquis of Dorset, had married Henry VIII's niece, Frances Brandon). He was the servant of Thomas Seymour, Lord High Admiral and favourite uncle to the young Edward VI. He would be able to give Etheldreda the position in life that she deserved, at least in theory. The couple had several houses to choose from for their residence, including Harrington's house in Stepney, London. Their principal home outside London was the manor house of St Catherine's Court.

John Harrington came from a prolific and well-connected family. However, John's father was Alexander Harrington, believed to be the bastard son of James Harrington, Dean of York. Since Alexander is not mentioned in the Dean's will, it is possible that he was the bastard of James's cousin John, who was himself illegitimate. Illegitimacy did not have the same social stigma then as it did later. Marriages were usually arranged, at most social levels, and divorce was extremely difficult. This meant that love and marriage were not thought of as being necessarily connected, although each couple hoped love, or at least affection, would be part of their relationship. Love flourished, in and out of wedlock, and the presence of 'love children' was not uncommon. A good and responsible father would recognise all his offspring and make provision for them, regardless of their mother's formal status.

Alexander Harrington lived at the Prebendary House at Stepney, which became the home of the child John, probably born around 1520. The boy showed a musical talent, and was taught by Thomas Tallis, the great organist and composer and the father of English cathedral music. John Harrington was also a poet, and would go on to produce notable verses. His family background was a trifle confused, partly because of his father's disputed parentage (although he was definitely a Harrington), so when John applied for a coat of arms in 1546, a regnant of arms was issued to 'John Harrington of Kelston ... son of Alexander Harrington, descended of a younger brother of the Harringtons of Brierley in the County of York ... and yet, not knowing in what manner he ought to bear his arms, the time being now so long since his ancestors first descended from out of the said house of Brierley.'

Young John's career began at Court late in the reign of Henry VIII. By October 1538, the year after the birth of Prince Edward, he was an 18-year-old Gentleman of the King's Chapel,[24] and was brought to the King's attention by his musical talent. He wrote a song called 'The Black Sanctus, or Monk's Hymn to Satan', which 'King Henry was used in pleasant mood to sing'.[25] Henry still appreciated anyone who could entertain him with their own musical composition. A letter written by Sir John Harrington (John's son) to Lord Burghley in 1595 gives an interesting piece of information about John's early life. He writes, 'My father, who had

223

his [King Henry's] good countenance, and a goodlie office in his Courte, and also his goodlies Esther to wife, did sometime receive the honour of hearing his own song ...'[26] This indicates that John had a wife called Esther during the lifetime of the King, which may explain the choice of the name of his daughter. Henry Harrington suggests that Esther is one and the same as Etheldreda, but she and John only married after the death of King Henry, and Esther is not a corruption of Etheldreda; the alternative version of the name is Audrey. Sir John must have been well aware of the name of his father's previous wife, and was unlikely to mistake Etheldreda for Esther. The first wife, Esther, would have been married when John Harrington was a young man. She was neither nobly born nor wealthy, and died before they could have a family. This left him free to marry Etheldreda in 1548, when John was 28 years old.

John's marriage to Etheldreda has given rise to various unsupported statements, like those of Margaret Irwin, who wrote a romantic novel about Elizabeth I, and set one of her scenes in the Tower. Princess Elizabeth, her servant Isabella Markham, Robert Dudley and John Harrington are meeting together (which never happened). Irwin writes of John, 'He had been married to a bastard daughter of King Henry and had not much liked it, for Etheldreda (what a name!) had something of her father's temper and nothing of his charm.'[27] F. J. Paynton, in his *Memoranda of Kelston*, perpetuated this idea when he wrote, 'She [Etheldreda] who founded the fortune of the Harringtons of Kelston aroused no strong emotion in the passionate poet she married.'[28]

All descriptions of Henry VIII's mistresses agree that they had to be at least pretty, if not beautiful. Thus Etheldreda's mother was probably beautiful, certainly not plain or dull. Henry's children were all handsome – his sons Edward VI, Richmond, Henry Carey, John Perrot and Thomas Stukeley looked a great deal like him. His daughters, Mary and Elizabeth, were good-looking; his sisters, Margaret and Mary, were both beauties. It follows that any child of two such handsome parents would tend to be attractive; Etheldreda was probably pretty, possibly beautiful, and intelligent. This may have been one reason why John Harrington married her; her dowry may have been another incentive. It is a great pity that the only known portrait of Etheldreda has disappeared.

The couple spent much of their married life apart, serving the various households of which they were a part. It was common practice for couples like the Harringtons to attach themselves to patrons, in whose households they would act as superior servants, the equivalent of the modern-day personal assistant. The Harringtons served their noble masters and mistresses just as they, in turn, served the king or queen. Harrington was a servant to Thomas Seymour; on 27 April 1546, Edward Seymour (later Duke of Somerset and Lord Protector under Edward VI) wrote to Henry VIII, 'Here arrived yesternight Harrington, my brother's servant with letters.'[29] Harrington was one of the group who negotiated with Sir Henry Grey to arrange for Seymour to have the wardship of his daughter, Lady Jane Grey. Jane had gone to the household of Catherine Parr when she married Seymour, but had returned to her father's house on the Dowager's death in childbirth.

Seymour had promised Jane Grey's family that he would arrange a marriage between Jane and Edward VI. He therefore approached her father on two further occasions. At the first, Harrington had escorted Jane from Bradgate, her home, to Seymour at Hanworth, although she shortly returned to her parents when nothing happened in respect of the promised marriage. Seymour had praised Jane, saying 'She is as handsome a lady as any in England', to which Harrington added a comment about 'her excellent beauty.'[30]

Jane had two sisters. Mary Grey, born in 1545, was a hunchback. Katherine Grey, born in 1540, was described as being the pretty one, but Baptista Spinola, a Genovese merchant who witnessed Jane's procession to the Tower on her proclamation as queen on 10 July 1553, said of Jane that she was, 'very short and thin, but prettily shaped and graceful.'[31] Like most of Henry's female relatives, she was a pretty girl and very intelligent.

Edward VI himself was set on a foreign marriage and alliance. For many years, it was hoped that his wife would be Mary, Queen of Scots. Then there were discussions with the French Court, as a marriage was suggested between Edward and a French princess, and he sent her a large diamond ring as a betrothal gift. This did not stop Thomas Seymour intriguing for 'Queen Jane'.

In January 1549 Harrington was imprisoned in the Tower with Thomas Seymour, his friend and master. Seymour had capped a series of follies by persuading himself that he could lead a rebellion against his brother and the Council. Edward VI, he imagined, wished to be free of his brother's government and he went to the palace by night, attempting to kidnap the King out of his bedchamber. The plan, which involved Seymour becoming First Minister in place of Somerset and arranging the Grey marriage, failed when the King's dog barked and gave the alarm; Seymour's response was to shoot it with a pistol before fleeing the palace.

A document dating to 18 January says of Seymour, 'Harrington his man was sent to the Tower by decree of the Counsell.'[32] In January and February, Harrington was one of those questioned at Seymour's trial, about Seymour's relationship with the Princess Elizabeth whilst they were part of Catherine Parr's household. The Privy Council investigating Seymour's treason believed that he had had sex with Elizabeth, a treasonable crime in itself. The aim was to prove that he may even have contemplated seizing the throne for himself by marrying Elizabeth and disposing of Edward VI and Princess Mary.

Harrington remained faithful. He refused to implicate either Seymour or Elizabeth in any improper action, and returned to the Tower for his pains. The fact that Seymour had planned to seize the King, and had raised funds to support a rebellion to make himself Protector, was enough to seal his fate.

It is ironic that the Lieutenant responsible for the prisoners in the Tower was Sir John Markham, whose daughter Isabella would eventually marry Harrington. It might also explain why Sir John

Markham did not support his daughter's proposed marriage to Harrington when the question of it arose some years later.

Elizabeth I called Seymour, 'a man of much wit and little judgement', an assessment which has gone down through the centuries as a remarkably astute reading of his character. Seymour was executed for treason, beyond the help of Somerset and unlamented by his nephew, the King; Harrington was released in the spring of 1550. A portrait of Seymour, presently on the wall at Longleat, is decorated with a set of laudatory verses, written by Harrington. According to legend, Harrington had commissioned the picture to give to Elizabeth I; despite all his reversals, Harrington remained faithful to the memory of Seymour. The verse reads:

> *Of person rare, strong lymbes, and manly shape,*
> *By nature fram'd to serve on seas or lands;*
> *In friendship firme, in good state or ill hap,*
> *In peace, head-wise, in war-skill great, bolde hands,*
> *On hors or foot, in peril or in playe,*
> *None could excel, tho' many did assaye;*
> *A subjecte true to Kynge, a servant greate,*
> *Friend to God's truth, and foe to Rome's deceite …*
> *Yet against nature, reason and just lawes,*
> *His blood was spilt, guiltless, without just cause.* [33]

Before this first imprisonment in the Tower, Harrington seems to have fallen in love with Isabella Markham. He wrote a sonnet, 'On Isabella Markhame, when I first thought her fayre as she stood at the Princess's Windowe in goodlye Attyre, and talkede of dyvers in the Courte-Yard'. It is believed that this sonnet dates to 1548 when the Princess Elizabeth had her household at Hatfield, and Harrington would have visited her as Seymour's messenger. He also wrote a poem, 'The prayse of six gentle Women attending of the Ladye Elizabeth, her grace at Hatfield then … Grey, Willobie, Markhams, Norwyche, Seintloe, Skypwith'.[34]

It may be that even now Etheldreda, a dearly loved wife, was suffering from some illness and Harrington knew he was going to lose her sooner rather than later. He was married to a child, while he was a man in his prime, so it is entirely possible that his eye should turn to a more mature woman. As the years passed, however, he seems to have made the most of the situation, and at some point between 1548 and 1555 when she died, Etheldreda gave birth to a daughter called Esther (also referred to as Hester).

In 1553 Harrington was imprisoned again, as part of the conspiracy to make Jane Grey the queen. He was kept at first in the Tower, but moved to the Fleet prison in June. Bishop Gardiner wrote that he had ordered the arrest of 'Harrington ... who confesses to having been in correspondence with Lord John Grey.'[35] This treasonable correspondence took place during Wyatt's rebellion, a further attempt to usurp Mary I and replace Jane Grey on the throne. As a plot, it was doomed to failure from the outset, and Harrington seems to have been involved only as far as he supported his new patron, Henry Grey, Duke of Suffolk, to whom he was distantly related.

Edward VI died on 6 July 1553, and Jane Grey was proclaimed queen. By 12 February 1554, however, Jane had ruled, been overthrown, imprisoned and executed. John Harrington was in the Fleet in January 1554. He was then removed and sent back to the Tower on 8 February. On this occasion, his fellow prisoner in the Tower was Princess Elizabeth, also implicated by rumour in Wyatt's rebellion. She had been at Ashridge at the time of the rebellion and, hoping to distance herself from any suspicion of complicity, in January 1554 she wrote to Mary I explaining that her poor health kept her from leaving the manor. Mary listened to her claims of sickness, and then insisted that she travel, even if only for a few miles a day, to join the Queen in London for her own safety.

Once in London, Mary ordered that Elizabeth be transferred to the Tower, on the suspicion of treason. She came to the Tower on 18 March 1554 (Palm Sunday) with a modest household of two yeoman of the chamber, two of the robe, two of the pantry, two of the kitchen, one of the buttery, the cellar and the larder, along with six ladies and two gentlemen. One of the ladies was Etheldreda Malte. When John Harrington wrote to Bishop Gardiner, requesting his freedom, in one letter he wrote,

> 'My wife is her [Princess Elizabeth's] servant, and doth but rejoice in this our misery, when we look with whom we are holden in bondage. Our gracious King Henry did ever advance our families good estate ... Mine poor Lady [Princess Elizabeth] hath greater cause to wail than we of such small degree, but her rare example affordeth comfort to us, and shameth our complaint.'[36]

Later statements that the wife in question was Isabella Markham are confounded by the fact that in 1554 Harrington's wife was Etheldreda; we also have a letter written many years later by Sir John Harrington, Isabella's son, referring to the time that Elizabeth was in the Tower, 'My mother [Isabella], that then served the said Lady Elizabeth, he [Bishop Gardiner] causeth to be sequestered from her as an heretick ...'[37] Isabella, therefore, was not allowed to stay with Elizabeth in the Tower.

Etheldreda would have made a sound choice as an attendant for the Princess. She was the daughter of the mistress who had tried to help Mary I while she had been under her father's displeasure and the malice of Anne Boleyn in the early 1530s. Mary would feel deeply obligated to the daughter of her friend. Such a woman could be trusted to remain faithful to Mary I in the presence of her rival, Elizabeth. Edward VI, Mary I and Elizabeth I all seem to have got on well with their bastard brothers and sisters, and there is no reason to suppose that Elizabeth was any less pleased to have Etheldreda close to her; Elizabeth, too, felt she could trust her father's daughter. Though still a young woman, perhaps Etheldreda did, indeed, resemble the old King, in a way that reassured Mary and Elizabeth.

John Harrington spent 11 months in the Tower on this occasion; he eventually got out on 18 January 1555 by expending over £1,000 in bribes, and when this failed to have effect, he wrote an impudent verse about Bishop Gardiner, who laughed heartily at his wit and released the author. Harrington's son, Sir John, wrote in later years, concerning the verse, 'He [Gardiner] would say that my father was worthy to have lain in prison a year longer for the saucy sonnet he wrote to him from out of the Tower.'[38]

Sadly there is no surviving description of Etheldreda. There is a portrait of John Harrington in the Victoria Art Gallery in Bath, in south west England, bought in 1942 when the Harrington collection of pictures was sold at auction by Sotheby's. Portraits of Etheldreda and their daughter Esther were sold, but their new owners' identities are not known. In the first catalogue of the family portraits, the picture of Etheldreda is recorded as being by Hans Holbein; however, the later sale catalogue records 'British School'. Etheldreda's portrait is a three-quarter length (47 x 33-in panel) 'in embroidered dress'; that of Esther is entitled 'Child holding a book, embroidered dress' (23 x 19-in panel) and a Victoria Gallery note says the dress is brown.

If the picture had been by Holbein, it would have had to have been painted before the artist's death in 1543, which would mean that it was completed more than five years before Etheldreda married. If the picture were available, it might be possible to estimate the age of the subject, and therefore the possible date of Etheldreda's birth; Holbein usually gave the date of the painting in one corner, and sometimes the sitter's age. If, as seems more likely, it was by an artist influenced by Holbein, this would also give a clue to the period in which it was painted.

In St Catherine's Church, adjacent to St Catherine's Court, are printed pages of copies of family records: 'King Henry VIII was seized in the manor or lordship of Exton and Katherin and of St. Katherine's Court sometime belonging to the late dissolved priory of Bath. Henry VIII granted it to his servant John Mawlt (sic) taylor and his bastard daughter Etheldred alias Dingley. John Mawlte died, Ethledred married John Harrington, of London, esquire, father of the John Harrington party to these present. 1554–55 Second and third King Phillipp and Queen Marie, John Harrington and Etheldred held the property and had a daughter Esther. By 1558–59, Etheldred was dead and John Harrington had married Isobell [Isabella], daughter of Sir John Markham, knight. After the death of John and Isobel, the property descended to the son and heir, John Harrington.'

—————

The date of Etheldreda's death is not known, but on 9 October 1555, a licence was issued which read, 'The like, for 40 marks, to John Harrington, esquire, and Audrey his wife to grant the manors of Watchyngfeld ... Andressy alias Nyland, Batcombe, Kelmeston, Eston alias Bathe Eston, Kateryne alias Katerynes Court ... and Forde, 10 Somerset: to Thomas Harryngton gentleman, and Thomas Thurgood and the heirs of Thomas Harryngton.' A further licence from Harryngton and Thurgood granted Audrey the right of residence for one further month, 'with remainder to John Harryngton and his heirs.'[39] These properties were either those that came directly to Etheldreda, or those left to her by John Malte. Even if she died without surviving heirs, they would revert to her husband as they had had a child, and therefore there had been heirs of Etheldreda's body. However, the manoeuvre may indicate that Etheldreda, and possibly Esther, was ill and believed to be dying. If the properties had stayed in John's hands, and he had got into further trouble, he would have lost everything. As it was, he had effectively sold all the lands to his own kinsman, Thomas Harrington, and Thomas Thurgood. When Etheldreda died, there were no lands to be seized by the Crown or by other possible heirs. As it happened, Esther did not die, but by this strategy John Harrington was able to buy the lands back, when this could be safely done.

231

The second licence that granted Audrey the right to live in the house for a further month could indicate that she had returned to St Catherine's Court as a last hope of restoring her to good health or in anticipation of her death. On 28 November 1555, just over a month later, a further licence was issued, but this time in one name only, 'The like, for 31 6s 8d to John Harryngton of Batheston alias Batheneston, co. Somerset, esquire, to grant his rectory of Batheston ... to the Dean and Chapter of the cathedral church of Christ, Oxford, of the foundation of Henry VIII, and their successors.'[40] This grant was John's in his own right, so Etheldreda's name does not necessarily need to appear. What is noticeable is that after the October licences, Etheldreda's name does not appear again.

It looks as if Etheldreda died at St Catherine's Court, and was buried in the church next door. Her death was probably expected, and her illness may have been longstanding. Unfortunately, the church records for the period have been lost.

On 29 June 1559, there is a 'grant for life, for his service, to John Harrington, the Queen's servant, of the office of Receiver General of the Revenues' of lands in Nottinghamshire and Derbyshire. He later swapped these counties for Dorset and Somerset. There is no mention of a wife, so Harrington was still single at this time.[41] It was several years before John could marry his love, Isabella Markham. In fact, when Sir John Markham died in 1559, his will, dated 1 April, left his daughter, 'Isabella Markham ... £300 for her preferment to her marriage.'[42] Sir John Markham had good reason to object to John Harrington as a son-in-law. For one thing, he had spent quite some time in the Tower, which Sir John knew only too well. All in all, John Harrington did not present the best his daughter could achieve in a husband. Even the accession of Elizabeth as queen on 17 November 1558 had not persuaded Sir John to let Elizabeth I's two friends marry; in fact, he could wonder why so close a friend to the Queen did not achieve a much more brilliant match. The conclusion is that John and Isabella were in love, and finally married in 1559. In

1564 Harrington wrote one of his poems, a treatise on wifely duties, for Isabella.

John and Isabella had their first son, christened in the parish of Allhallows Church in 1560 on 4 August, 'John the sunne of John Harrington'.[43] On 12 March 1563 there was a grant of land at Lenton, Nottinghamshire, to John Harrington and 'Isabel his wife, gentlewoman of the Privy Chamber', in favour of their son.[44] Little John Harrington became one of the 102 godchildren of the Queen. In 1602 Sir John wrote to his wife, 'The goodness of our sovereign lady to me, even (I will say) before born; her affection to my mother who waited in Privy Chamber, her bettering the state of my father's fortune ... have rooted such love, such dutiful remembrance of her princely virtues.'[45]

What of Esther? She is rarely mentioned; in 1568 an estate at Watchfield, Berkshire was the property of John Harrington and 'Hesterus [Hester] Harrington', showing that she was alive in that year.[46] However, one particularly interesting thing happened. On 3 May 1569, a Pardon of Marriage for William Brouncker, son and heir of Henry Brouncker ('aged 20 and more at his said father's death') was made, 'at the suit of John Harrington, the Queen's servant, for £200, which Harrington is bound by five bonds to pay in the Court of Wards.'[47] Harrington had purchased the wardship of William Brouncker for £200, which was valid for less than a year.

The wardship carried an annuity of 40 marks, but this would be paid only once. A valuable ward would be a baby or young child, since the purchaser could expect a series of lucrative annual payments, as well as taking money from the estate of the child for expenses to cover their upbringing. Then, when the child was of a suitable age, a marriage could be arranged; if the child was particularly wealthy, obviously they would be married to a member of the purchaser's own family. Harrington could expect none of the financial rewards; what he purchased was the right to arrange William's marriage, providing it took place between 3 May 1569 and 11 February 1570. He could have been buying a well-to-do husband for his daughter, since he had no intention of letting her take the lands her mother had brought to the marriage, which he had bought outright, and would eventually leave to his son by Isabella.

The licence to enter upon his lands was issued for William Brouncker, son of Henry, on 11 February 1570, as William had now attained the age of 21. Two months later, on 1 April 1570, William Brouncker was issued a licence to alienate lands in Wiltshire, for 55s 8d. He is referred to as 'William Brouncker of Erlestoke, Co. Wilts.'[48] On 1 February 1578, there was issued a pardon of alienation of lands acquired by 'W. Bruncker, Michael Garneley and William Marten ... and the heirs of Bruncker' at Inglesham in Wiltshire and Burwardescott, Berkshire. The trio paid £20 to the Queen's agent.

The Brounckers had been at Erlestoke for only a short time. The estate had belonged to the Earl of Warwick, and had passed through several generations until it was held by the Countess of Salisbury. The Crown seized the lands from the Countess and in 1540, a 21-year lease was sold to Robert Brouncker and his son Henry. In 1544 Henry Brouncker was MP for Devizes, and bought an estate at Melksham. When he died after a fall from a horse, it was Henry's son, William, who ended up as the ward of John Harrington.[49] When William died, his widow was Martha, daughter of Walter Mildmay of Apethorpe, Chancellor of the Exchequer, although there is a stone slab in the church of St James for William Brouncker, his wife Catherine Moore and four children (the arms on the slab are those of Brouncker and Moore). If he did marry Esther, she was his first wife and must have died shortly after their marriage took place.

In 1582, John Harrington died at the Prebendary House, the family London lodging, near the Bishop's Palace. He seems to have retained hold of this, his father's house, and it may well have been his residence when he was in London, attending the Queen. He was buried at St Gregory's Parish Church.[50] The son of John and Isabella, Sir John Harrington, was one of the Queen's godsons. The

Queen visited his house at Kelston on one of her progresses to Oxford, and local rumour says that John had to sell another of his houses, St Catherine's Court, to pay for the privilege. Whatever the reason, in 1591, the year of the progress visit, Sir John leased a separate house called the Hermitage to Thomas Salmon, and the manor and St Catherine's Court to 'John Blanchard of Marshfield, gentleman'.

Sir John Harrington was a colourful character. Like his father, he was a famous poet and writer. He got into trouble with the Queen when he wrote a set of humorous verses called 'The Triumph of Ajax' (or A-jakes); 'jakes' was a slang expression for human faeces, and the piece was a vulgar condemnation of the way people defecated. The Queen was not amused, and John was temporarily banished. The production of these verses seems to have stimulated John Harrington to do something about the problem he had made fun of; he was the inventor of the first design for a flush toilet.

He capped a series of impudent escapades by joining the Earl of Essex on his ill-fated expedition to Ireland in 1599. Whilst there, and contrary to instructions from the Queen, Essex knighted his friends, John Harrington among them. When Essex returned, several of his associates were arrested, including Harrington, who was given the equivalent of a slap on the wrist, where Essex and others were imprisoned in the Tower or under house arrest. After a suitable period, Sir John had his knighthood confirmed by Elizabeth herself, and resumed his visits to court.

Sir John went to see 'my royal godmother' shortly before her death. He found her ill, and to amuse her, showed her some of his latest verses. The Queen, however, was too far gone; 'I am past my relish for such matters', she told John. He was one of the last people to speak to Elizabeth before her death.[51]

THE FAMILY OF JANE SEYMOUR

John Seymour (1425–?) = Elizabeth Coker (1436–?)

John Seymour (1450–91)

=

Elizabeth Darrell

Sir John Seymour (1474–1536) = Margaret/Margery, daughter of Sir Henry Wentworth

Elizabeth (1513–63)
=
1) Sir Anthony Oughtred
2) Baron Gregory Cromwell
3) John Paulet, Marquis of Winchester

Henry (c.1514–68)   Dorothy   Anthony   Margery

◆ Jane (1509–37)
=
Henry VIII, King of England

Edward VI

Thomas (1508–49),
Baron Seymour of Sudeley
=
Catherine Parr

Mary

Edward (1506–52),
Duke of Somerset
=
Anne Stanhope

John (1510)

Edward Seymour (1539–?),
Earl of Hertford
=
1) Catherine Grey
2) Frances Howard

Anne (1540–88)
=
John Dudley,
Earl of Warwick

Jane (1541–?)

Mary (1552–?)
=
1) Andrew Rogers
2) Henry Peyton
3) Francis Cosbie

Elizabeth (1552–1601)
=
Richard Knightley

Lord Henry Seymour (c.1552–?)
=
1) Jane Dudley
2) Joan Percy

John (1552)

◆ mistress of Henry VIII
+ illegitimate child of Henry VIII
= married

10

The Question of Mary or Madge and the Quiet Queen

—◦◦◦—

When Henry married Anne Boleyn, he was passionately in love with her. At a banquet on 1 December 1534, Anne was talking to the French Ambassador, when she suddenly burst out laughing. The Frenchman was annoyed and asked, 'How now, Madam, are you amusing yourself at my expense?' Anne then explained that Henry had gone to bring another guest for her to entertain, and an important one, but on the way he had met a lady and the errand had gone completely out of his head. Now she was his wife and about to give birth to his child, Anne could find his interest in other women amusing. Henry and Anne were two proud and passionate individuals, always fighting and reconciling.[1]

In the summer of 1533 Anne awaited the birth of the longed-for prince. Chapuys wrote that Henry and Anne had an argument when she showed herself jealous of his affair(s), 'and not without legitimate cause.' Henry had been unfaithful to Catherine of Aragon when she was pregnant, and he seems to have behaved in the same way with Anne. When she learned that Henry was having an affair, Anne let him know that she was hurt and angry. According to Chapuys, the King replied, 'that she must shut her eyes and endure as those who were better than herself had done, and that she ought to know that he could at any time lower her as much as he had raised her up.'[2] When she demanded that the other woman be sent away, he told her, 'she ought to be satisfied with what he had done for her; for, were he to begin again, he would certainly not do as much.'[3]

This might refer to Joanna Dingley, Mary Perrot or Jane Stukeley. It may, indeed, be another lady altogether. Henry seems to have fallen into the habit of enjoying brief and light affairs during his wives' pregnancies. The answer was simple for Anne: ignore the meaningless dalliance – and produce a living prince.

Casual affairs aside, Anne was triumphant, but at her moment of greatness, she failed in the one thing that she most needed to succeed at. The longed-for child, whose conception had caused such havoc in England, was a girl. Anne had a difficult pregnancy, but an easy labour and birth. Elizabeth (named after Henry's mother) was born at 3 a.m. on Sunday 7 September 1533. Chapuys wrote, 'The King's mistress was delivered of a girl, to the great disappointment and sorrow of the King, of the Lady herself, and of others of her party, and to the great shame and confusion of physicians, astrologers, wizards and witches, all of whom affirmed it would be a boy.'4 Yet, Henry ordered *Te Deums* (a Catholic ceremony of thanksgiving to God) and a magnificent christening.

After Anne Boleyn became queen, she saw a change in Henry's attitude towards her. He had given up so much to make her his wife, and the birth of another daughter made all the national upheaval seem for nothing. What Henry would put up with in an adored and unattainable mistress, could not be countenanced in a wife. What had been pure love was now entangled with loyalty and duty. In fact, Anne Boleyn was rapidly becoming a liability in so many ways. She had produced a daughter when the birth of a legitimate, living son was so desperately needed. Her temperament was sometimes abrasive. Marriage to Anne had also prevented Henry from making a valuable foreign alliance by taking a French, Spanish or German princess as his wife. Anne and her faction had also given their support to aspects of the Reformation far more radical than Henry liked. He was less speedy to abandon the religion of his upbringing; he was, after all, older than Anne, and more set in his ways. He recognised that he had given up a lot for her, and all he had to show for it was another daughter. Anne needed to get pregnant again quickly, and to have a son.

The people of England felt cheated as well. They had had an unpopular nobody foisted on them for the main purpose of providing an heir to the throne. Amongst the learned men of England, the Abbot of Whitby commented, 'the king's grace was ruled by one common stewed whore, Anne Bullan, [sic] who made all the spirituality to be beggared and the temporality also.'[5]

Anne had the political support of her immediate faction – her father, brother, relatives and friends – but she had powerful enemies in the nobles who found themselves denied access to the King by the Boleyn faction. The nobility who resented Anne's meteoric rise to power was always on the lookout to place some other lady in Henry's orbit to distract him from his new wife.

MARGARET SHELTON

Margaret (also known as 'Madge') was Anne Boleyn's cousin, the daughter of Sir Thomas Boleyn's sister, Anne, who was married to Sir John Shelton. The Sheltons had a large family: Margaret, John, Anne, Mary, Ralph, Thomas, Elizabeth, Emma and Gabrielle.

After she became queen, Anne initially seems to have favoured the Sheltons, appointing Lady Shelton to the post of governess to the young Princess Elizabeth. This job carried an additional duty; Lady Shelton was to be as spiteful as possible to Princess Mary, to put her in her place. Mary had also been ordered to attend her new half-sister as a lady-in-waiting, and the Queen is supposed to have advised Lady Shelton to box Mary's ears 'for a cursed bastard'.

In February 1534, Chapuys wrote to the Emperor that Mary was living in poverty with hardly any clothes. She had also been refused permission to attend Catholic Mass. He reported that she was 'kept close at hand' and was forbidden to do anything without the permission of Lady Shelton. Norfolk and Rochford, he wrote, spoke to Lady Shelton about being less pleasant to Princess Mary, and that she had replied that even if Mary were the bastard of some poor gentleman, she deserved respect and kindness because of her 'goodness and virtues'. That apart, Mary was threatened with beatings and Lady Shelton told her that if she remained stubborn and refused to take the oath relating to the Act of Succession, she would be beheaded for treason.

The baby Elizabeth, 'My Lady Princess', was given her own household at Hatfield, Hertfordshire, and Lady Shelton and Alice Clere, another of Anne's aunts, were to run it. Margaret Bryan (related to the Norfolks and thus to Anne's mother) was appointed 'Lady Mistress', directly responsible for the baby's personal wellbeing. Mary was forced to join the household and told to call the baby 'Princess'. Mary replied that she would call her 'sister' as she called Richmond, 'brother', but she would not call Anne Boleyn's child 'Princess' as she was Henry's only lawfully born daughter. Mary was forced to sit at the common table to eat and had to give precedence to the baby. She furthermore was not allowed to leave the house to attend Mass. When the King visited, Mary was also kept out of his sight.[6] Lady Shelton told Mary that if she had been the King she would have thrown her out of the house for her stubbornness and disobedience to her father's wishes. However, Henry had no real intention of harming his eldest daughter. After his affair in 1534 with Joanna Dingley he softened towards Mary, and Lady Shelton's behaviour reflected this. Early in 1535 Mary fell ill and Lady Shelton took some pains to care for her. Chapuys wrote to Lady Shelton and sent her gifts, complimenting her on her actions but hinting that, should Mary die, she would have to answer for her previous treatment of the young Princess.

Anne Boleyn's attitude to Mary can best be explained by her feelings of insecurity over Catherine of Aragon, and her feelings of inferiority when she compared her own daughter's position in the world with Mary's. Anne was loathed by the people, whereas Catherine was remembered with love, respect and admiration. No matter how many of Catherine's jewels Anne wore, and no matter how much she pretended it didn't matter, Anne

Boleyn was 'the goggle-eyed whore' not the true queen to many of the ordinary people of England.

Since the King's infatuation with Anne was no longer an all-consuming passion, some of the courtiers decided to introduce him to other ladies who might catch his fancy. With Anne's example to look to, noble ladies now realised that, far from just accepting a place as a mistress as Bessie Blount had done, they might aspire to actually be queen. Members of the Boleyn faction introduced Margaret Shelton to Henry, who made her his mistress for a time. Presumably they did so to weaken the authority of Anne – they may even have hoped that Margaret could replace her as queen. Margaret may have had a gentler disposition than Anne, one that could be better managed so that the Boleyns and their supporters could hold on to power. This may also have been a safety net; if Henry were to discard Anne in favour of Margaret, his new queen would still represent the Boleyn–Howard interests and they could continue to enjoy the wealth and power that they wielded. It has even been suggested that Anne herself chose her cousin to engage the King's affections to prevent someone else from a rival faction taking the position.

It is not known when Margaret Shelton was born, although it is likely to have been after 1505. This would have made her close in age to Anne Boleyn, perhaps even a little younger. Since she caught the King's eye, it can be assumed that Margaret was a beauty (an ambassador wrote that the lovely Christina of Denmark looked a little like Margaret Shelton). She was certainly the kind of lady whom Henry found attractive – possibly fair, and quite possibly quieter and more subservient than her forceful cousin. The difference in temperament may account for the briefness of the affair and explain why the King eventually returned to Anne. He still found her wit, learning and beauty exhilarating.

Anne undoubtedly knew about the affair and may have known that her own family was behind it. She now knew enough to keep quiet and not annoy the King, but she could certainly do her best to punish Margaret. According to one of Anne's chaplains, William Latimer, Anne severely reprimanded Margaret Shelton for jotting 'idle poesies' in her prayer book.[7] This was, of course, rank hypocrisy as Henry's Book of Hours had romantic margin notes by both him and Anne, written during their courtship. However, while Anne the lover might write her beloved a note in a prayer book, Anne the queen would not countenance such behaviour in one of her ladies.

Margaret Shelton's name was also linked with Henry Norris, later also accused of being one of Anne Boleyn's lovers. As a young man, Henry Norris had come to Court as a gentleman of the King's chamber. He was friendly with the King and received lavish awards of posts, including Keeper of the King's Privy Purse. Norris was one of Anne's circle and was involved in the plot against Cardinal Wolsey; he was present on 25 October 1529 when Wolsey was forced to resign as Chancellor. In that same year, he became Groom of the Stole, a post once held by Sir William Compton. There was talk of Norris's marriage to Margaret Shelton but any attraction between the two came to nothing – rumours of an affair with Anne led to his arrest. Although he pleaded his innocence, Norris was subsequently found guilty and executed.

In 1535 Anne accused Francis Weston of spending too much time flirting with Margaret Shelton, and not only ignoring his own wife, but also keeping Margaret away from Henry Norris. Weston countered by saying that Norris was more interested in Anne herself than in Margaret. He continued that he loved a lady much more than either his wife or Margaret Shelton. When Anne asked who it was, Weston replied: 'It is yourself', at which Anne 'defied' him, denying such a love. This kind of flirting was part of a romantic chivalric game that Anne had herself introduced to Court. Her old mentor, Margaret of Austria, had been highly adept at such things, but Anne seems to have been far less successful. While such behaviour might work for a single, widowed princess of high rank and impeccable reputation, it did not work for a flirtatious, lowborn queen with a jealous husband.[8]

As for Margaret Shelton, she always seemed to be in competition with her cousin. In 1535, she was the object of the attention of Henry Norris, Francis Weston and Henry VIII, all also supposedly in love with Anne. It was in that year that Chapuys wrote to his master that the King was enamoured of the daughter of Sir John Shelton, 'first cousin of the concubine [Anne Boleyn], daughter of the new governess of the princess [Mary]' and most scholars agree that it was Margaret who was Henry's mistress. She was certainly part of the circle that surrounded the King, but another Shelton, her younger sister, Mary, could also have been the mistress.

Some research argues that the name 'Marg' (Margaret) should be read as 'Mary', as the Tudor 'g' and 'y' were similar, and therefore Henry's mistress was Mary, not Margaret Shelton. Another piece of evidence presented is that there is a Holbein sketch entitled 'Mary Lady Heveningham' (Mary Shelton's married name); however, it is not definitely Mary.[9] A lot of the Holbein sketches were attributed years later and are therefore not credible. The argument that a portrait exists of Mary and not Margaret, which shows that Mary was more important, fails to take into account the number of sketches that have not survived and the number of unattributed sketches held in collections, any of which could be Margaret.

Margaret eventually married Sir Thomas Wodehouse, son of Sir Roger Wodehouse and Lady Elizabeth Ratcliff. Margaret provided her husband with a good number of children: Roger, John, Thomas, Elizabeth, Mary, Anne, Loy and Henry. Margaret's husband and son Thomas, both died at the Battle of Musselborough in Scotland on 10 September 1547. Margaret's eldest son, Sir Roger Wodehouse, acted as host to Elizabeth I on one of her progresses at their house, Kimberley Tower in Norfolk. The family owned a valance that had been made for Henry VIII and Anne Boleyn, with the initials 'H' and 'A' entwined and they placed this relic of Elizabeth I's parents at her disposal, along with other household furnishings. Margaret survived her husband by many years. The Wodehouse line carried on, and one of Margaret's

243
◎

direct descendents was P. G. Wodehouse, the author of the Jeeves and Wooster, and Blandings novels.

—◦◦◦—

Before Anne Boleyn's fall from grace, in early September 1535 Henry and Anne stayed at Wolf Hall, Savernake, near Marlborough. This was the home of Sir John Seymour and his family. Sir John's wife had been born Margaret Wentworth, a distant connection of the Tudor family. One of Seymour's daughters, Jane (born in 1509, eldest of his eight children), had been a lady-in-waiting to Catherine of Aragon. Jane left her service when her staff was reduced in 1533, but now she served Queen Anne. On New Year's Day 1534, Jane was one of the Queen's ladies who received a gift from the King. Henry, therefore, knew her quite well.

Between 1534 and 1535, Henry seems to have become attracted to Jane Seymour. She is described as being 'full of goodness ... not a woman of great wit, but she may have good understanding.'[10] She may well have reminded Henry of his mother. It is also tempting to see her pale goodness as an antidote to Anne's dark liveliness, and that Henry just wanted some peace. In early 1536 the Bishop of Tarbes, also the French Ambassador, noted that Henry seemed interested in Jane. On 10 February 1536 Chapuys also commented on Henry's behaviour: '... towards a damsel of the Court, named Mistress Seymour, to whom he has latterly made very valuable presents.'[11] Anne was about five months pregnant at this time.

Jane's family and its supporters were on hand to coach her. Anne Boleyn had shown what was at stake and what could be achieved if a woman was ambitious enough. Henry had set a precedent in divorce that meant that an English lady of nobility, who might previously have aspired only to be a mistress, could now become queen. The people of England disliked Anne; only the King's love and the support of Anne's own faction kept her in her position as queen.

Jane was also an adherent to the New Religion, as were her brothers, Edward and Thomas. She was, however, less extreme than Anne Boleyn. Indeed, she does not appear to have had very strong views about anything.

The needs of the Crown overcame any scruples the King might have had about damaging the Roman Catholic Church. In 1535 the movement to separate the English Church from the Papacy in Rome continued. Henry's ministers and advisers began inspecting religious houses around the country, looking for corruption, false relics, loose morals – anything that made them unsuitable to continue. Starting with the smaller houses, monasteries were disolved and destroyed with the whole matter culminating in 1540 with the closure of the last great religious house, Waltham Abbey in Essex. The reason for the dissolution was principally twofold – to destroy the Papacy's powerbase in England and so that the Crown could appropriate all the lands, buildings, goods and precious artefacts that the Church held.

In that same year, Anne Boleyn became pregnant a second time, but lost the child early on. However, she fell pregnant again late in 1535, and waited in hope for a longed-for son to be born. In January 1536 Catherine of Aragon died, and Anne's case became desperate. If Henry were to rid himself of Anne, he would once again be able to join the European political marriage arena.

On 29 January 1536 Anne miscarried. The lost baby was clearly a boy. Several tales are associated with this event: Henry had been injured at a joust at Greenwich, when his horse fell on him and the King was knocked unconscious. Chapuys reported that Anne blamed Norfolk for her miscarriage, saying that he had burst in on her with news of Henry's injuries. Also according to Chapuys, Henry told his friends that he saw the hand of God again, that witchcraft had been used to persuade him to marry Anne. Henry is supposed to have said, 'I see that God will not give me male children.'[12] Anne is also rumoured to have told Henry that his affair with Jane had precipitated the miscarriage. George Wyatt, Nicholas

Sander and Jane Dormer all reported the latter version, and Sander stated that Anne said, 'See, how well I must be since the day I caught that abandoned woman Jane sitting on your knees.' Dormer claimed 'there was often much scratching and bye-blows between the Queen and her maid.'[14] It was even said that Anne cut her hand when she ripped a necklace that Henry had given her from Jane's neck.[13]

Henry began making serious overtures to Jane Seymour. He had decided in his own mind that the marriage with Anne was over; it was up to his Privy Council to come up with a sustainable reason. He was busy looking for another wife, and Jane Seymour was the lady he had chosen. She was the opposite of Anne, fair where Anne was dark, shy where Anne was outspoken, gentle where Anne was acerbic, meek where Anne was opinionated.

According to a Spanish account, '... the lady Mistress Semel [Seymour] ... besought the king ... to consider carefully that she was a gentlewoman, born of good and honorable parents and with an unsullied reputation. She had no greater treasure in the world than her honour which she would rather die a thousand times than tarnish, and if he wanted to give her money she begged that he would do so once God had sent her a good match.'[14] Henry then said that he would only see Jane in the company of her family. He took Cromwell's rooms at Greenwich and installed Edward Seymour and his wife there; the apartment connected with the King's. A faction grew supporting Jane and pushing her to work against Anne. The group included Lord Montagu, the Earl of Exeter; Sir Nicholas Carew, Sir Thomas Elyot and Jane's own brothers.

Chapuys reported to the Spanish King on the wooing of Jane by the King, 'To cover the affection he has for the said Seymour he has lodged her seven miles away in the house of a grand esquire, and says publicly that he has no desire in the world to marry again, unless he is constrained by his subjects to do so.'[15] Jane moved to Sir Nicholas Carew's house at Beddington, near Croydon, supposedly for propriety, but probably more so that Henry would have to make an effort to see her, riding or going by boat to

Carew's, and thereby taking his mind off Anne and making Jane the focus of his attention. It also made it almost impossible for any members of the Boleyn faction to get to Henry, surrounded as he now was by the Seymours and their supporters.

Cromwell moved the final plot against Anne, because he believed she was the major block to his plans of an Imperial alliance, which was impossible while Anne remained queen. Anne and her supporters were pro-French, and the Emperor also hated her. On 24 April, Henry gave his approval for a routine assize court, to discuss all and any treasonable activities in Middlesex and Kent. This was a cloak for a secret Commission to look into how Henry could divorce Anne. The King saw, once again, the hand of God in his failure to have a living son. Henry's ministers eventually came up with the reason of Anne's multiple adultery – with Henry Norris, Frances Weston, William Brereton and Mark Smeaton as named partners – and Anne was also accused of having an incestuous relationship with her brother George. The Commission also suggested that Anne had poisoned Catherine of Aragon, and planned to do the same to Henry's children, Princess Mary and the Duke of Richmond.

The very fact that Anne had miscarried a son may have given weight to the belief, expressed by his courtiers, that the King had been the victim of witchcraft and that Anne Boleyn had cast a love spell on him. This explained why the King had abandoned the saintly Catherine of Aragon and married an unworthy woman, and still failed to have a living son. If Anne had had sex with other men while she was married to the King this was treason, a crime punishable by death. Anne's familiarity with the young men of the Court only gave colour to the story.

The inclusion of Anne's brother amongst her supposed lovers originated, in part, from their close relationship. Even George Boleyn's wife was supposed to be jealous of Anne, a sister who held so great a place in his affection. George was also famous as a womaniser, and so the jump from women in general to his sister in particular was made. It also supported the charge of witchcraft – a witch would be prepared to ignore the sacred laws of God and man, such as incest.

It was George's wife, Jane Parker, who raised the old story of the 'poisoning' of the Duke of Richmond, while he had been in France with the Earl of Surrey in July 1533. Jane Parker said that George, under orders from Anne, had tried to poison Richmond, a rival to the throne for any child she might bear. It was added that Richmond remained in France until he heard that Anne had had a daughter and not a son.

Mark Smeaton was arrested for questioning on 30 April. Henry and Anne also had a public quarrel on the same day. Alexander Ales, a Scottish clergyman, was visiting London and was present at Greenwich. He later wrote to Elizabeth I in 1559 of his recollection of that day:

248

'Never shall I forget the sorrow which I felt when I saw the most serene Queen, your most religious mother, carrying you, still a little baby, in her arms and entreating the most serene King your father, in Greenwich Palace, from the open window of which he was looking into the courtyard, when she brought you to him. I did not perfectly understand what had been going on, but the faces and gestures of the speakers plainly showed that the King was angry, although he could conceal his anger wonderfully well ...'

What seems to have happened earlier in the day was that Norris had gone to the Queen's almoner to take an oath that Anne was 'a good woman'. This was the result of a flirtatious exchange either that morning or the previous day that had got out of hand. Anne had been teasing Norris, asking why he was taking so long to sort out his marriage to Margaret Shelton. Norris was non-committal and Anne erupted. She accused him of being too fond of her, 'you look for dead men's shoes; for if ought came to the King but good, you would look to have me.' Norris denied this (to wish for the King's death was treason), but Anne kept on and a quarrel ensued. In the end, they realised what had been said, and tried to minimise the damage.[16]

On May Day Henry and Anne were at Greenwich, but that evening Henry travelled with a handful of servants to Westminster. The following day, Anne was arrested and charged with adultery. She was moved to the Tower of London that afternoon. Cromwell's first batch of arrests were Henry Norris, Mark Smeaton and George Boleyn. Two days later, Sir Francis Weston and William Brereton were also taken into custody. On 5 May, it was the turn of Sir Richard Page and Thomas Wyatt. The Queen was accused of adultery with the first five, affairs that started directly after Elizabeth's birth. She was said to have promised marriage to one of them after Henry was dead and also to have said that she had never loved the King. On 17 May all five were executed; Page and Wyatt were released.

Another of the detainees was Sir Francis Bryan, Anne Boleyn's cousin, who had been the King's Cupbearer in 1516 and Master of Toyles (driven deer provided for hunting) in Greenwich Park in 1518. When Anne was queen, but was falling out of favour, Bryan set up an argument with George Boleyn so that he could distance himself – just in time it seems. Cromwell, however, disliked Bryan enough to have him arrested, but he was freed almost immediately.

Mark Smeaton was 'one of the prettiest monochord players and deftest dancers in the land'.[17] He was also the only one of the accused who was not a 'gentleman'. Smeaton eventually admitted, after torture, that he had slept with the Queen three times, claiming that she had seduced him.

The Wyatts and Boleyns were neighbours – Sir Thomas Boleyn at Hever and Sir Henry Wyatt at Allington Castle, near Maidstone, about 20 miles apart. Thomas Wyatt wrote a poem that encapsulated his relationship with Anne, stating that he had been one of her many admirers, but not the foremost; that he lost interest or withdrew since he saw no hope of winning her and that once she was Henry's mistress, she had become 'off limits' to all men.

Anne had several fits of hysterics, recorded by Sir William Kingston, the Constable of the Tower. One of Anne's ladies, Mistress Cofyn, who, along with Jane Parker shared the Queen's bed, was also Kingston's spy, and reported all Anne's conversations to him.[18] The charges against Anne were very detailed, specifying dates, times and even the locations of her acts of adultery, although many of the dates were quite obviously fabricated. On 20 May, she was allegedly with Weston at Westminster but from 17 May onwards, Anne and Henry were at Richmond together for Whitson. On 20 June, Anne was accused of being with Weston at Greenwich but from 3 to 26 June Anne and Henry were at Hampton Court. On 26 April, she was said to have been with Smeaton at Westminster yet Anne and Henry spent Easter at Greenwich, arriving on 14 April.[19] According to Chapuys, Cromwell confessed that he had himself invented these dates and times.

Almost until the end, Anne believed that Henry would reprieve her, either sending her into exile or to a nunnery. According to Anne, 'The king does this to prove me' – that is, that he was testing her love and faithfulness. Once in the Tower, Anne said, 'I hear say the executioner is very good and expeditious and I have such a little neck', at which she put her hands round her neck and laughed. Kingston wrote, 'I told her it should be no pain, it was so subtle.'[20]

In fact, the King's visits to his latest mistress, while his wife was under arrest and sentence of death for adultery on spurious charges, caused a good deal of public comment. Even Chapuys, who did not like Anne, commented that the situation of her condemnation and Henry's subsequent behaviour had aroused some public sympathy for her. It transpired that many of those people, who had condemned Anne when she displaced Catherine, were not happy with Henry's affair with Jane. Henry wrote to Jane,

'… there is a ballad made lately of great derision against us, which if it go abroad and is seen by you, I pray you to pay no manner of regard to it. I am not at present informed who is the setter forth of this malignant writing; but if he is found, he shall be straitly punished for it'[21]

Two days before Anne's death, on 17 May 1536, Henry had his second marriage declared null and void on the grounds of consanguinity established by his earlier affair with her sister Mary, thereby making his daughter Elizabeth a bastard.

On the morning of her execution Anne said to the Constable of the Tower. 'I hear I shall not die before noon, and I am very sorry therefore, for I thought to be dead by this time and past my pain.' Anne went to the scaffold dressed in a grey damask gown with a crimson underskirt, attended by four of her ladies (one of whom was Margaret Shelton) and a small crowd of onlookers. She took off her ermine-trimmed cloak and white hood and put on a white cap to hold her hair. Blindfolded, she knelt down and arranged her skirts modestly to cover her feet. Anne then gave a scaffold speech:

251

> 'Good Christian people, I have not come here to preach a sermon; I have come here to die, for according to the law and by the law I am judged to die, and therefore I will speak nothing against it. I am come hither to accuse no man, nor to speak of that whereof I am accused and condemned to die, but I pray God save the king and send him long to reign over you, for a gentler nor a more merciful prince was there never, and to me he was ever a good, a gentle and sovereign lord. And if any person will meddle of my cause, I require them to judge the best. And thus I take my leave of the world and of you all, and I heartily desire you all to pray for me.'[22]

Anne was beheaded at 8 a.m. on Friday 19 May. According to a Spanish eye-witness account:

'… the poor lady kept looking about her. The headsman, being still in front of her, said in French, "Madam, do not fear, I will wait till you tell me" …The sword was hidden under a heap of straw, and the man who was to give it to the headsman was told beforehand what to do; so, in order that she should not suspect, the headsman turned to the steps by which they had mounted, and called out, "Bring me the sword". The lady looked towards the steps to watch for the coming of the sword, still with her hand on the coif; and the headsman made a sign with his right hand for them to give him the sword, and then without being noticed by the lady, he struck off her head to the ground. Three of her four ladies carried her body in a sheet; the fourth carried her head in a white cloth. They passed the two new graves outside St Peter ad Vincula; one contained Norris and Weston, the other, Brereton and Smeaton. Inside, her body was put in an elm chest that should have been used to store bow-staves for Ireland, and she was buried in the chancel, near her brother.'[23]

Anne Boleyn was buried in St Peter ad Vincula, the church within the Tower of London, but there is a legend that she was secretly exhumed and reburied in the church at Salle, Norfolk, near her home. Her heart is also said to be buried at All Saints Church, East Horndon, near Billericay, Essex (altar tomb, south transept), or SS Andrew and Patrick Church, Elveden Park, near Thetford, Norfolk (south wall, found and moved to site beneath the organ 1836).[24]

On the day of Anne's execution, Henry went to meet Jane Seymour, whom he had moved to a house in Whitehall after Anne's arrest. The next day, on 20 May, Henry became formally betrothed to Jane, and they were married 10 days later. In the following week, Jane's brothers Edward and Henry Seymour were made Earl of Hertford and a groom of the privy chamber respectively (although Henry Seymour left Court shortly after to live a private life).

This time, the King was not taking any chances. He passed a law stating that he could nominate his successor. If he had Richmond in mind (in lieu of a legitimate son), he was unlucky. Richmond died two weeks after the bill was passed. In 1536, Henry advised his daughter, Mary, once again that her marriage was of the utmost importance. As the eldest of his surviving bastards, Mary was told that she should marry and give Henry a lawful grandson who could then inherit the throne. However, all these plans were set aside when Jane gave birth to a boy, Edward, on 12 October 1537 at Hampton Court. By 24 October the rejoicing was cut short by Jane's death from puerperal fever, a complication in childbirth that was untreatable at that time.

THE FAMILY OF ARTHUR PLANTAGENET, LORD LISLE AND HONOR GREVILLE

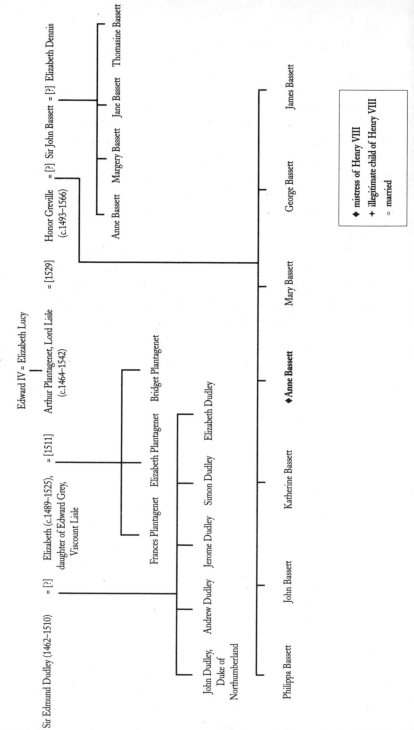

11

The Virgin Queen and the Merry Maidens

———※※※———

Following the death of Jane Seymour, Henry went into extravagant mourning. It was left to Thomas Cromwell to raise the matter of another queen – and the issue of more children – even before Jane Seymour was interred. He approached the King to remarry 'for the good of the realm'.

Henry had time to look for a wife. He had a lawfully born son, as well as two bastard daughters and so he could now make his mark on European diplomacy with a significant marriage. Henry had made two marriages amongst his own subjects, but neither of these had enhanced his international reputation or forged useful links abroad, nor had they generated a substantial dowry.

Henry's ministers approached several courts with a view to entering into a diplomatic marriage. The King of France was making overtures to the Emperor and if they allied, this would leave England out in the cold, vulnerable to French attack. Therefore, a French alliance would seem to be more beneficial. The widowed Marie of Guise, daughter of Claude, duc de Guise of Lorraine, was chosen as a possible prospective bride, but unfortunately, by the time Henry had arranged for Sir Peter Mewtas, courtier and gentleman of the privy chamber, to go to France and report on the lady, Marie was already betrothed to Henry's nephew, James V of Scotland.

If an alliance with France was not possible, what about the Empire? The Emperor's niece, Christina, was the widowed Duchess of Milan, and Sir Thomas Wyatt was instructed to make tentative enquiries as to her availability. At the same time, Sir Philip Hoby was sent to the court of Mary of Hungary, Regent of the Low Countries, where Christina was staying, to report on her physical appearance. The court painter, Hans Holbein, was told to produce her likeness. Holbein's portrait showed her to be exceedingly charming and the King became more cheerful at the prospect of a pretty young wife. A plan was drawn up that Henry would marry Christina, and that his daughter Mary would marry Dom Luis of Portugal, the heir to the throne. Sir John Hutton wrote to Cromwell in December 1537, describing Christina, thus: 'The Duchess of Milan ... is of the age of 16 years, very high of stature for that age ... of goodly personage of body, and competent of beauty, of favour excellent, soft of speech, and very gentle in countenance ... She resembleth much one Mistress Shelton, that some time waited in the court upon Queen Anne.'[1]

Unfortunately there were problems. Henry and Christina stood within the Church's proscribed degrees of consanguinity, and the Pope was hardly likely to give Christina a dispensation to marry a King who had expelled him and his Church from England; Princess Mary was technically a bastard, which also made her a poor match for the heir to the throne of Portugal. The Emperor Charles was quite prepared to ally with England against France, but he had no intention of seeing Christina's Duchy of Milan fall into English hands, or of supporting Henry in the teeth of opposition from the Papacy.

Francis I put forward the names of more French princesses to Henry. Possible candidates were Louise and Renée of Guise, Marie of Vendôme and Anne of Lorraine. Philip Hoby and Hans Holbein had their work cut out providing reports and painting portraits of these ladies. Eventually, to speed up matters, Henry even suggested to the King of France that a number of eligible princesses should be assembled at Calais so he could come and inspect them before making a choice. As can be imagined, Francis I vetoed the idea, adding that French ladies were not commonly displayed like brood mares for sale.

The delays proved costly when Henry's negotiations fell through entirely. In June 1538 Francis I and Charles V met at Nice and signed a 10-year treaty; neither made any mention of England, leaving her friendless and vulnerable. Henry now realised that a new alliance had to be found, and quickly. Cromwell believed that an alliance with the German states would be most valuable to England as a balance against the French and Spanish–Imperial powers. To this end, he settled upon the second daughter of the Duke of Cleves, 24-year-old Anne, since Sybilla, the eldest, was already married. In the previous year it had been suggested that Princess Mary should marry William, then heir to the Duke of Cleves, Anne's brother, but it had come to nothing.

The Duchy of Cleves, incorporating the states of Mark-Jülich-Berg, was of considerable importance amongst the German states, lying as it did on the lower Rhine. Duke William wanted the alliance as badly as Henry: the English King needed a confederate against a French–Imperial alliance, and Duke William wanted a powerful ally in his dispute with Charles V for control of Guelderland, which William claimed through his mother. The Cleves family also had the advantage that, like Henry himself, they had never fully espoused the new Protestant religion, but, like him, saw themselves as Catholics who did not consider it appropriate to be ruled by a corrupt Papacy.

257

The King, ever the romantic, sent Holbein to paint Anne of Cleves' portrait and requested the usual diplomatic report on her appearance. Christopher Mont reported to Cromwell, and he assured Henry that Anne's elder sister, Sybilla, was considered to be a beauty, but Anne 'excelleth as far the Duchess [Sybilla] as the golden sun excelleth the silver moon.' Similarly, Holbein's portrait miniature of Anne of Cleves, enclosed in a carved ivory box shaped like a rose, is romantically supposed to have persuaded Henry that here was a chance to mix politics with personal delight. In the event, the portrait was later agreed to have been hopelessly flattering.

Anne of Cleves possessed none of the characteristics that would have made her acceptable to Henry. She spoke only Low German, and she could only dance slow, formal German steps. Her one skill was in needlework, on which ladylike practice she spent most of her time, and much was made of her modesty (when the King's representative tried to see the lady, she was so wrapped and draped that he could hardly make out her features at all). Nicholas Wotton reported that she had no musical accomplishments, 'for they take it here in Germany for a rebuke and an occasion of lightness that great ladies should be learned or have any knowledge of music ...'[2] It would be more correct to say that she had been brought up by her mother to be formal and worthy, adequately educated and without any sparkle. It would be hard to find a personality that would appeal less to Henry VIII.

In 1539 Henry married Anne of Cleves by proxy, a union that was to last a bare six months. Henry recognised that this marriage was purely political and that if his bride pleased him, he would have to look on that as a heaven-sent bonus.

Anne travelled slowly from Cleves to Calais, where Lord Lisle, the governor, received her. Lady Lisle wrote to her daughter, one of the queen's ladies-in-waiting, that Anne seemed kind, and suggested that she would be an easy mistress to serve. In a letter dated 22 December 1539, Anne Bassett wrote to her mother: 'I humbly thank your ladyship of the news you write me of her Grace [Anne of Cleves], that she is so good and gentle to serve and please. It shall be no little rejoicement to us, her Grace's servants here [London], that shall attend daily upon her ...'

While in Calais Anne attempted to master English card games and began learning about English court manners. She was going to try her best to be a good queen to Henry and to England. The King had to wait to meet his queen, however, as bad weather delayed the sailing beyond Christmas, and it was not until late December that Anne finally set sail. When she arrived in England on 27 December 1539, Anne was met at Dover by a retinue of nobles led by Henry's dearest confidante, Charles Brandon, whose young wife, Katherine d'Eresby, was to be one of her ladies. They travelled to Rochester in Kent for New Year's Day.

On New Year's Day, King Henry played one of those masquerades that he loved and which had been so successful 30 years before:

> 'On new Years Day in the afternoon the King's Grace with five of his Privy Chamber, being disguised with mottled cloaks with hoods so that they should not be recognised, came secretly to Rochester, and so were up unto the chamber where the said Lady Anne was looking out of a window ... and suddenly he embraced and kissed her, and showed her a token which the King had sent her for a New Year's gift, and she being abashed and not knowing who it was thanked him, and so he spoke with her ... and when the King saw that she took so little notice of his coming he went into another chamber and took off his cloak and came in again in a coat of purple velvet. And when the Lords and knights saw his face they did him reverence, and then her Grace, seeing the Lords doing their duties, humbled herself lowly to the King's Majesty ...'

259

Henry had never played his game of disguised, romantic stranger with so little success. Anne did not know that she was supposed to be intrigued and entranced by this handsome and powerful gentleman whose obvious nobility should have been clear. Instead she may well have been embarrassed by personal contact with someone she took for an impertinent noble. Nobody in the Court of Cleves had ever behaved in such a way and Anne must have been puzzled and possibly a little frightened. It was only when Henry reappeared in his own character that she was able to respond, but the damage had been done. He could have accepted awe, excitement, even a little frisson of desire or fear, but he would never accept the indifference of a bride who barely looked at him.

When Henry left Anne at Rochester Abbey on New Year's Day, he was not impressed. Travelling back to Greenwich by water, he told Sir Anthony Browne, 'I see nothing in this woman as men report of her and I marvel that wise men would make such reports as they have done.' That evening, Cromwell, who had praised her, asked Henry how he liked his bride; the King replied, 'Nothing so well as she is spoken of. If I had known as much before as I know now, she should never have come into the realm.'

Charles de Marillac, the French Ambassador, wrote to Francis I that Anne was, 'tall and thin, of middling beauty, with determined and resolute countenance.' To the Constable, Anne de Montmorency, he wrote she was, 'not as young as was at first thought, nor so handsome as people affirmed.' Lady Browne, who was a member of Anne's household, wrote that she was so unsuitable that the King was never likely to love her.[3]

They were married in great splendour on Twelfth Night (6 January 1540) in her rooms at Greenwich. Henry sulked throughout, and Anne found herself married to a man who barely spoke to her. Henry told anyone who would listen that he had been badly treated, and that he was only going through with the marriage for the sake of England, '… if it were not to satisfy the world and my realm, I would not do that I must do this day for none earthly thing.' The wedding night turned into a disaster, with the King maintaining he found the Queen completely unattractive, and the Queen displaying all the enthusiasm of a totally innocent virgin – he didn't want to and she didn't know how.

The next day the King told Cromwell she was, 'nothing fair, and had very ill smells about her.'[4] Whereas Henry's description of her as a 'Flanders mare' may be apocryphal, she turned out to be a tall and anxious woman, with a pockmarked face and a big nose, who talked with a heavy German accent. Henry certainly did remark that, having felt her naked breasts, he did not believe she was a virgin. He also later claimed that he could not bring himself to consummate the marriage. Henry's choice tended to fall on vivacious beauties, not sturdy German hausfraus. For four nights, the ill-matched couple shared a bed, but, according to Henry, only to sleep. At the end of this time, he said, 'I liked her not well before, but now I like her much worse.'[5] Still, for the sake of the Cleves alliance, the marriage continued.

When, some weeks later, her ladies quizzed Anne on whether or not she might be pregnant, she said, no. Lady Edgecombe asked her, 'How is it possible for Your Grace to know that and lie every night with the King?' Lady Rochford went a little further, 'By Our Lady, Madam, I think your Grace is a maid still.' Anna told them that at night, when they were alone in bed together, 'he kisses me and taketh my by the hand and biddeth me, "Goodnight, sweetheart", and in the morning kisses me and biddeth me, "Farewell, darling".' Lady Rochford told her, 'Madam, there must be more than this, or it will be long ere we have a Duke of York, which all this realm much desireth'. Anne seemed puzzled, 'Nay, is not this enough? I am contented with this, for I know no more.'[6]

On 4 February Henry and Anne came by barge from Greenwich to Westminster; they were greeted by a 1,000-gun salute from the Tower. She now joined her new household of 126 people, a few German, but mostly English. Henry had insisted that all her ladies should be 'fair', that is, good looking. All the noble families wished to place their relatives in service with the queen.

Cromwell could see the way the wind was blowing. Almost immediately he began making enquiries about a precontract between Anne and the Duke of Lorraine; if valid, it would mean that the marriage with Henry might be illegal and could be dissolved. Unfortunately this supposed contract had already been examined, and it had been accepted by all parties as being irrelevant. At this stage Cromwell seemed to be managing things quite well. In May 1540 he was made Earl of Essex and Lord Great Chamberlain. He had matters in hand to end the Cleves marriage and even when

261

William of Cleves backed out of marrying Princess Mary, and looked for a French wife, this was not seen as a major problem; he would still make a good ally against the Emperor. Religious divisions and quarrels were to seal Cromwell's fate. These problems, caused by radical Protestants, were largely due to Henry's policy over many years, done with his agreement and approval, but Cromwell was blamed for everything that now went wrong. He was arrested on 10 June, charged with treason (maladministration and abuse of power), found guilty, and executed on 28 July.

For Henry, the only bright spot in the whole marriage fiasco was that he met and fell in love with one of Anne's ladies-in-waiting, the 19-year-old Catherine Howard, which provided another reason for ending the German marriage. Burdened with a dull, sexually unattractive wife with whom he was not sleeping, it is not surprising that his eye roved over the lovely ladies who surrounded her.

On May Day, Anne attended the official Court celebrations. She had been improving her English and people seemed to like her. It was to be her last formal appearance; from this time on, she was marginalised. On 25 June she was at Richmond, where the King's Commissioners came to her and advised that Henry planned to divorce her on the grounds that he had been coerced into marriage by Cromwell and that the marriage had never been consummated. Henry gave his word that he had not had sex with Anne, and this was sufficient for a divorce, since one of the principle reasons for marriage was the sanctioned production of children. All Anne had to do was agree that she remained a virgin.

Where Catherine of Aragon or Anne Boleyn might have hotly denied this and fought for their position, Anne apparently took the whole thing quietly and calmly. She wrote to Henry saying that she would be bound by whatever he decided, and signed the letter, not 'Queen', but 'Daughter of Cleves'. Henry's delight at such a helpful wife manifested itself in a more than generous separation gift of estates valued at £3,000; the only condition of divorce was that Anne would have to remain in England as Henry's subject. Anne had no objections; she seems to have liked England, liked her freedom, and made some good friends.

It is perhaps ironic that Anne understood Henry the best of any of his wives. Her letter of submission to him, written on 11 July 1540 from Richmond, struck all the right notes. She started by pointing out that the whole question had been raised by the King's Council and the Clergy, and Henry was not to blame. She recognised her love for him (and implied his love for her), but acknowledged that there were greater forces at work: '... this case must needs be most hard and sorrowful unto me, for the great love which I bear to your most noble person, yet having more regard to God and his truth than to any worldly affection ...' They would be divorced because it is the right thing to do, and Anne would remain his devoted friend and sister.[7] With Anne so compliant and agreeable, the alliance with Cleves could be maintained. Duke William had no cause to say that his sister had been ill treated; in fact, she had done very well. She was even given precedence over all English ladies, save the king's wife (when he had one) and Henry's daughters, Mary and Elizabeth. Anne was to be the king's 'good sister'. Thus William was able to keep England as a friend and supporter against the Emperor, and Henry was able to keep a hand in European politics.

Two years later, during the investigation into the misbehaviour of Catherine Howard, rumours began to fly that Henry VIII was considering taking back his fourth wife. Chapuys wrote to Charles V that Henry had been out hunting and might have visited Anne. Her brother, the Duke of Cleves, had sent letters to his ambassador, Dr Heinrich Olisleger, broaching the subject of Henry remarrying Anne. At such a sensitive time, on 5 December 1541, the Privy Council recorded that a lady named Frances Lilgrave had 'slandered the lady Anne of Cleves, and therein, the King ...'[8] Lilgrave had been sent to the Tower along with Richard Tavernor, a Clerk of the Signet, to whom she had told her tale and who had reported it to the Council.

263

This refers to an incident that had taken place several months before when a baby had been born to one of Anne's servants. Rumours were circulated that the child was Anne's and, worse still, that the father was Henry himself. According to Chapuys, the King's assertion that he and Anne had never had sex was false; she and the King had been having sexual relations, the result being that that summer Anne had retired to the country to give birth.[9] The King certainly visited Anne and it was not impossible that he went to bed with her. Well-dressed, contented and relaxed, speaking English, no longer under pressure to impress, Anne may at last have shown Henry the slender, serene, intelligent girl in the miniature with whom he had fallen in love. This would have been disastrous. The King could not have a child by a divorced wife whom he insisted that he had never slept with, especially as he had just married Catherine Howard, who might yet become pregnant. In any event, Anne of Cleves always maintained that the child was that of her servant.

Some years later, in 1546, Stephen Vaughan, the King's Factor in Antwerp, wrote to colleagues in the English Court that there were rumours in Holland that Henry was planning to divorce Catherine Parr and marry again: 'a merchant … had dined with certain friends, one of whom offered to lay a wager with him that the King's Majesty would have another wife …'. Vaughan went on that there were rumours circulating that the next queen was to be Anne of Cleves, that she and the King were lovers, and that she had already had two sons by him.[10]

Anne ended her days in England, rich in lands and houses, and popular with her Tudor family. She got on well with Catherine Howard, formally visiting her at Court during her brief reign, and was a favourite 'aunt' to the Tudor children, Edward, Mary and Elizabeth. She didn't have such a good relationship with Catherine Parr, and tried unsuccessfully to have her annulment overturned once Henry was dead so that Anne, not Catherine Parr, would be Queen Dowager.

Anne of Cleves died on 16 July 1557, and was buried in Westminster Abbey. She had never remarried, although there wasn't a reason why she should not. Perhaps, once having tasted freedom, she never wanted to give it up again. Perhaps the farce with Henry had put her off the very thought of marriage.

ANNE BASSETT

Back in 1540, living in comfort at her house at Hever, Anne of Cleves may have congratulated herself on a lucky escape, when the tragedy of her successor unfolded. However, Catherine Howard had not been the only woman who tempted Henry before and during his marriage to Anne of Cleves. There was another possible British candidate for queen – Anne Bassett, stepdaughter of Lord Lisle, and servant to Jane Seymour before her death.

Arthur Plantagenet, Lord Lisle, was a remarkable man, in that he, and his sister Elizabeth, Lady Lumley, managed to live under the Tudors at all. He was the only surviving bastard son of Edward IV by Elizabeth Lucy, a widow and daughter of Thomas Wayte, a gentleman from Hampshire. When Richard III reported that his brother's marriage to Elizabeth Woodville had been illegal and their children were therefore bastards, it was a precontract with Elizabeth Lucy that he used as evidence. A precontract was almost as valid as a marriage, and the two children tended to lend support to the claim by Richard that his brother, the King, had made some kind of promise of marriage to the lady.

Perhaps Arthur Plantagenet's survival was due, in part, to the fact that he had no son who could raise a claim to the English throne. Arthur had three daughters by his first wife and no children by his second. However, he did accumulate a large family of stepchildren from both marriages. His first wife, Elizabeth Grey, was the widow of Edmund Dudley by who she had three sons. His second wife, Honor Grenville, was the widow and second wife of Sir John Bassett and had three sons and four daughters by him; Honor also cared for four daughters of Sir John Bassett by his first wife, Elizabeth Dennys.

265

Lord and Lady Lisle made an interesting couple. Henry VIII said of Lisle that he had 'the gentlest heart living'[11] and he was universally loved as a kind and gentle person. Arthur's second wife, Honor Grenville, on the other hand, was a less lovable person; she ran up huge bills with tradesmen like the king's tailor, 'Mr Skut'. She was domineering and ruthless, especially where her Bassett children were concerned; Honor and Lisle had no children.

The Lisles had settled in Calais in 1533 when Lord Lisle was given the post of governor, and unusually Lady Lisle took Frances Plantagenet, Lisle's daughter, and the four Bassett girls – Philippa, Katherine, Mary and Anne – with her, rather than leaving them with noble families in England to be educated, as happened with Elizabeth and Bridget Plantagenet. Anne Bassett was about 12 years old at that time.

Once in France, Lady Lisle placed Anne and Mary Bassett with noble French families, while the three remaining daughters stayed with their parents. Anne went to the household of one of her father's dearest friends, the soldier Thybault de Rouaud and his wife, Jeanne de Saveuzes, who lived at Pont de Remy, near Abbeville in northern France. The Rouauds were a fine old Poitou family, and Jeanne was related by blood and marriage to the finest families in Artois and Picardy. Anne Bassett's sister Mary went to the household of Thybault de Rouaud's sister, Anne, who had married Nicholas de Montmorency, siegneur de Bours. Mary, we learn from de Bours, was considered the beauty of the two, although Anne must have been almost as lovely. Anne de Bours wrote to Lady Lisle on 9 August 1534: 'I find her of such an excellent disposition that I love her [Mary] as if she were my daughter, and she is beloved of all them that see her.' De Rouaud wrote a year later, 'My wife and I have been very sorry that Mistress Anne hath been taken with a certain sickness [possibly smallpox], but thanks be to God she is now wholly recovered from it … As for Mistress Marie, who is with my sister, she is merry, and is indeed the fairest maiden in the world to look upon.'

One of the principle purposes of placing the girls in French households was for them to learn to speak, read and write French; in a letter of March 1536, Mary records, 'I have given the schoolmaster who taught me to read and write ten sols ...' She wrote to her sister Philippa, who was still living in the Lisle's household in Calais, 'I enjoy myself so much here in this country that I should be right well content if that I would often see my lady my mother, never to return to England.'[12] Anne Boleyn had established the fashion for French manners, and the presence on the throne of France of the handsome Francis I maintained France as a leader in fashion. The Lisles were not going to have their beautiful daughters be disadvantaged by not following the fashion of the day.

Letters also advised of Mary's musical talent; she was receiving instruction on the lute, virginals and spinet. She was also working at her needlework, playing cards and hunting with hawks. One can assume that Anne had similar tuition. There are also many references in letters relating to both girls, to clothing and jewels, so that they should be well dressed as the daughters of so illustrious an English noble and his lady.

In September 1536, Anne Bassett returned to Calais to be reunited with her family, and plans were afoot for her future. Mary stayed with the de Bours for the time being. Like her sisters, Anne Bassett would have a reasonable dowry (100 marks) and was of a good family, so she might expect to make an advantageous marriage. Coupled with this, she was a beautiful and talented girl whose stepfather's contacts at Court meant that she might expect to move in more exalted circles than other girls from the same background.

The early months of the year saw the fall and execution of Anne Boleyn in May, followed rapidly by the marriage of Henry to Jane Seymour. In 1537 Lady Lisle learned that two Arundel nieces had found places at Court and she set about bribing her noble friends and relatives to find similar places for her daughters, Katherine and Anne. Initially some of these friends seemed to doubt that Anne was old enough, being only 16, and Katherine was the daughter most likely to find a place. In order to get the girls into the Court, Lady Lisle was making plans to place Katherine in the household of the Duchess of Suffolk, and Anne with the Countess of Rutland. Once at Court, if only as part of a lesser household, it would be easier for them to be considered when the next vacancy occurred in the queen's circle of ladies. In the meanwhile, Lady Lisle sent gifts to a variety of contacts, primary amongst whom were the Dowager Countesses of Sussex (Elizabeth Stafford) and Rutland (Anne St Leger), and Lady Anne Seymour, the wife of Edward Seymour, Queen Jane's brother. Through them, she sent presents of game birds to the Queen. A letter from Sir John Russell to Lord Lisle, dated 20 May 1537, sent from Hampton Court, explains the nature of the gift: 'My lord, the King commanded me to write to you for some fat quails, for the Queen is very desirous to eat some but here be none to be gotten. Wherefore, my lord, I pray you in anywise that ye will send some with as much speed as may be possible; but they must be very fat.'

The quail, which were found in abundance in the area around Calais, were set before the King and Queen by the end of May, and were much remarked upon and enjoyed. Jane Seymour eventually agreed to meet the Bassett girls and take one into her household, as John Hussee wrote to lady Lisle on 17 July 1537: '... the Queen ... chanced, eating of the quails, to comment of your ladyship and of your daughters ... her Grace made grant to have one of your daughters; and the matter is thus concluded that your ladyship shall send them both over [from Calais], for her Grace will first see them and know their manners, fashions and conditions, and take which of them shall like her Grace best ...'[13]

In fact it was several months before Anne and Katherine went to London. Lady Lisle believed she was pregnant; both she and her husband hoped for a son and heir. Unfortunately the 'pregnancy' dragged on well beyond the customary nine months, and by August it became obvious that her symptoms were the result of illness. It was not until September that the girls arrived, and John Hussee was able to write to Lady Lisle on 17 September 1537, 'Your ladyship shall understand that Mrs Anne your daughter is sworn the Queen's maid on Saturday last past, and furnisheth the room of a yeoman-usher ... Mrs Katherine doth remain with the Countess of Rutland till she know further of your pleasure.'

Henry VIII was not oblivious to the charms of Anne Bassett. He had already mentioned her preferment to the Queen, although this was before she came to London with her sister Katherine from Calais, and he merely supported the Queen in taking one of the Bassett girls into her household, as his cousin Lisle's stepdaughter. However, Peter Mewtas wrote a letter to Lord Lisle on 9 October, indicating that Anne had made quite an impression on Henry, 'Sir, the King's Grace, not two days past, talked of you and your children, amongst which I advertised him of your daughter that last came out of France. Howbeit his Grace thought Mistress Anne Bassett to be the fairest, but I said how that your youngest [Mary] was far fairer.'[14]

On 12 October, Jane Seymour gave birth to Edward, the Prince of Wales, but five weeks after Anne Bassett joined the Queen's household, Jane was dead. Anne had attended the Prince's christening, and now she performed her last office for the late Queen at Jane's funeral. At the age of 16, Anne was once again out of a post. She went into the house of her cousin, Lady Sussex, while her sister Katherine was still with the Countess of Rutland. However, all was not lost. Presumably Anne had made a significant impression on Henry and he appears to have wanted to keep her in the queen's household until he could marry again. John Hussee, the family's London servant, wrote to Lady Lisle, 'The King's Grace is good Lord to Mistress Anne, and hath made her grant to have her place whensoever the time shall come.'[15]

Anne Bassett joined the circle of beautiful, clever, talented young people around the King. Even though they presently had no queen to serve, the ladies of the queen's privy chamber paid a visit to Portsmouth in August 1539 and wrote a round robin letter to Henry concerning his 'Greate Shippe' (the *Harry Grace a Dieu*) which they had visited. The signatories were 'Maybell Sowthampton', 'Margaret Tayleboise', 'Margaret Howarde', 'Alys Browne', 'Anne Knevytt', 'Jane Denny', 'Jane Meows [Mewtas]', 'Elisabeth Tyrwhyt', 'Elsabeth Harvy' and 'Anne Basset'. The ladies laid on their praise of the King and the Prince of Wales with a liberal hand, and of the ships that they had seen:

> '... which things so goodly to behold that in our lives we have not seen (excepting your royal person and my lord the Prince your son) a more pleasant sight; we beseech your Majesty to accept in good part, advertising the same that there rest now but only two sorrows; the one for lack of your royal presence that ye might have seen your said ships now at this time when we might have waited on you here; the other that we think long till it may eftsoons like you to have us with you, which we all most heartily beseech our Lord God may be shortly ...'

Anne continued to be singled out by Henry for appreciation. He made her a present of a horse and riding saddle. When Anne was indisposed, she wrote to her mother that Henry ordered that she spend time with Jane Denny, a distant relative: '... I am now with my Cousin Denny, at the King's grace's commandment; for whereas Mistress Mewtas doth lie in London there are no walks but a little garden, wherefore it was the King's grace's pleasure that I should be with my Cousin Denny; for where as she lieth there are fair walks and a good open air; for the physician doth say that there is nothing better for my disease than walking ...'[16] Henry was entering upon one of his courtship rituals, giving Anne Bassett the means to ride out and take walks, both circumstances that could lead, quite naturally, to a sudden and 'unexpected' meeting between Henry and the lady away from the public gaze.

As matters progressed with the political marriage to Anne of Cleves, it seemed that Anne Bassett would soon be able to renew her position in the household of the queen of England. As luck would have it, Anne of Cleves spent some time in Calais, travelling to England, and Anne's parents were able to write to her about her new mistress. Unfortunately, Lisle was ordered to stay in Calais, and Honor stayed with him, so Anne never got her wish to see her parents accompany the new Queen to London. Lady Lisle had written to Anne expressing her disappointment on not coming to Court, and Anne had duly relayed the information to the King: 'This shall signify your ladyship that I received your letter ... and according to the contents thereof, I have declared unto the King's Highness all things, as your ladyship willed me to do, so that his Grace took the same in right good part, accepting your good will and towards mind ... For I knowledge myself most bound to his Highness of all creatures: if I should, therefore, in any thing offend his Grace willingly, it were a pity I should live.'[17]

271

Muriel St Clare Byrne, editor of one edition of the *Lisle Letters*, says that Anne was one 'whom the king so fancied at one time that she was tipped for the dangerous honour of being the fifth Queen of Henry VIII.' However, unlike Anne Boleyn or Catherine Howard, Anne Bassett could not or did not try to wrap Henry VIII around her finger. She wrote to her mother on 19 February 1540, thanking her for the preserves she had sent which Henry enjoyed. Lady Lisle had hoped for some gift or 'token' from the King, but Anne could not guarantee that one would be sent. A woman who enjoyed the king's favour might be more forceful in getting her own way. Anne Bassett may have been unsure of how strong the King's affection for her actually was; perhaps she adored Henry to the point of worship (as she says in her letter) and was too shy to press for any favours either for herself or her family. It is more likely that her upbringing under such a domineering mother meant that she was naturally shy and diffident. It may have been this diffidence that reminded Henry of Jane Seymour, so that this, coupled with her beauty, initially attracted him.

Lord Lisle fell from favour during his time as Governor of Calais. The city was a haven for Catholics fleeing England, and Lisle was accused of sympathy with them, of allowing them to stay too long, and of not doing enough to deal with these enemies of the state. Lisle and his Council were away from the changing religious and political scene in London, and he was unable to apply the current rules, as he often did not know what they were. In July 1538 he wrote to Cromwell: 'My lord, herebefore your lordship hath written and hath alleged that papish dregs did remain here with us of Calais. My lord, I dare well say, the King's Highness hath not within his realm no manner of people who favour less the traditions of popes than the King's servants and subjects do here, from the highest degree to the lowest ... therefore I may know the King's pleasure and yours, which shall be obeyed to the last drop of blood in my body.'[18]

He was further seen as a partisan of Reginald, Cardinal Pole, the outspoken enemy of Henry VIII. Pole and Lisle were cousins, as Lisle's father, Edward IV, was the brother of Pole's grandfather, George, Duke of Clarence. Lisle was a close friend of Reginald's mother, the Countess of Salisbury. Despite this, Lisle was aware of a plot hatched by Henry VIII to have Pole kidnapped and brought to England to stand trial for treason, yet did nothing to warn Pole. Pole knew of the plot when he realised he was being watched. However, despite his continued service to the King, Lisle's loyalties in this area were always suspect as far as Henry VIII was concerned. In November 1538 Henry had Margaret, Countess of Salisbury, her two sons, Lord Montague and Geoffrey Pole, who stayed in England, and her cousin Henry Courtney, Marquis of Exeter, (grandson of Katherine, youngest daughter of Edward IV) arrested on suspicion of treasonable plotting with Cardinal Pole. Lisle would have known that he would always be in a suspect position, because of his parentage. Undoubtedly, only his bastardy had saved him from execution as the last of the direct male heirs of the Plantagenets.

In April 1540, Lisle, who was visiting England on the invitation of Henry VIII, was arrested on Cromwell's orders and confined to the Tower of London. Cromwell was desperately trying to save his own career by sacrificing anyone else who could be blamed for any of the religious confusion that the ill-thought-out elements of the Reformation had thrown up. Lord Lisle was effectively 'framed' as being responsible for the religious confusion in Calais, and for supposedly having knowledge of a pathetically inept (and possibly imaginary) plot to surrender Calais to French and Papal forces. In fact, the arrest of Lord Lisle only delayed things. Cromwell was arrested and executed with considerable speed when Henry, in his turn, needed someone to blame for the failures of his own religious policy.

In Calais, Honor Lisle was held under house arrest in the Palace, and her daughters were sent to lodge with various families within the town. The matter of Honor's arrest was complicated by the discovery that her daughter Mary had become secretly betrothed to Gabriel de Montmorency, seigneur de Bours, the son of her French hostess. The French were the enemy, and Mary should have told her parents, who should, in turn, have asked Henry's permission for such a marriage. Honor Lisle ended up staying in the house of Francis Hall, a Calais official (a 'Spear'), while she waited for news of her husband's situation. Records suggest that she had a nervous breakdown.

It became obvious quite quickly, however, that Henry did not hold his cousin to blame for any of the feeble charges against him. For one thing, during a torrent of executions, Lisle was not marked for death immediately, as happened to so many of those whom Henry VIII suspected of treason. Henry was supposed to have remarked that Lisle had fallen, 'more through simplicity and ignorance than through malice.' A further point in his favour was that Anne Bassett maintained her position in the queen's household.

Lord Lisle remained in the Tower for 18 months, but the replacement of his arms in the Garter Knights' chapel at Windsor, removed at the time of his indictment, suggested that he was soon to be released and returned to favour. At the end of January 1542, Henry VIII was dining with his courtiers, when the Imperial Ambassador noted that he was paying much attention to Lord Cobham's sister. He also commented that the King was paying similar attention to 'a daughter that the wife of the former Deputy of Calais had by her first husband.' This suggests that Henry was already thinking about a new queen, and that at least two ladies – young and lovely 16-year-old Elizabeth Cobham and Anne Bassett – had taken his fancy.

ELIZABETH COBHAM

As it turned out, Elizabeth Cobham did not marry Henry VIII, but her married life was almost as complicated as the King's. In 1547 Elizabeth married William Parr, Marquis of Northampton, the brother of Catherine Parr. He had previously been married to Anne Bourchier, only child and heiress of Henry Bourchier, Earl of Essex. Once the marriage was finalised, Anne had almost immediately left William and set up home with 'one Hunt alias Huntly' who was the father of her children. Northampton divorced her in 1547, but he retained the title of Earl of Essex and married Elizabeth Cobham. Unfortunately, it later turned out that the divorce had not been correctly completed, so a bizarre farce unfolded. Firstly, in 1552, an Act of Parliament was passed 'disannulling' the marriage of the Marquis of Northampton and Lady Anne Bourchier, and for 'the confirmation of the marriage between him and Lady Elizabeth, daughter of Sir George Broke, Lord Cobham and for the legitimation of the children that shall be between them'. In order to fully legitimise the marriage of Northampton and Elizabeth Cobham, in 1553 another Act revoked the Act for their marriage. This meant that now a formal divorce could be completed correctly between Northampton and

Anne so that he and Elizabeth could marry again and the whole thing would be legal. Elizabeth died in 1565 from breast cancer. Despite all the efforts to legitimise the marriage for the sake of the heirs, she and her husband were childless. Northampton married again, this time to Helena von Suavenburgh, who survived him.

...AND ANNE BASSETT, AGAIN

With Catherine Howard arrested and awaiting trial and death, her household was disbanded. Anne Bassett, however, was retained at Court. Some of the Queen's attendants returned to their families, while, 'One maid of honour, Anne Basset, daughter of Lady Lisle, who had originally come from Calais to serve Anne of Cleves, was now specially favoured.'[19] It may be that because Henry liked her (and even briefly considered her as his next wife) that he was reluctant to execute her father; she may have used her influence to ask the King to be lenient. In fact, there is little evidence that Henry really believed Lord Lisle was guilty of anything serious, and so he had no reason to be hard on Anne, or her stepfather.

275

On the death of Catherine Howard, Henry signed Lisle's pardon and ordered his release. Tragically, Lisle died in the Tower the next day, supposedly 'through too much rejoicing' on being advised of his imminent release. Francis Sandford recorded the event in his *Genealogical History of the Kings of England*, published in 1707: '... receiving so great a pressure of Joy, his [Lisle] Heart was over-charged therewith, and the Night following ... he yielded up the Ghost ... this King's Mercy was as fatal as his Judgements.'

With Lord Lisle's death, Henry sent word to Honor Lisle that she was now at liberty, and in March she returned to England. She lived another 24 years, dying in 1566 at Tehidy, a house belonging to her grandson, Arthur, son of John and Frances Bassett. The house was also home to her son George Bassett, his wife Jacqueta Coffin, and their children, so her declining years were spent surrounded by her children and grandchildren.

Lord Lisle's three daughters all married. The eldest, Frances, married first her stepbrother, John Bassett, and then Thomas Monk of Potheridge. By this union she was the great-grandmother of General Monk who played a key role in the Restoration of Charles II. Elizabeth married Sir Francis Jobson and produced four sons. Bridget married William Carden, and was widowed within 10 years. Thus the blood of the last Yorkist king continued.

Anne Bassett, thanks to the support of Henry VIII, remained a lady-in-waiting. She served Jane Seymour, Anne of Cleves, Catherine Howard and Catherine Parr. When Edward VI came to the throne, Catherine Parr continued to maintain a household, and Anne Bassett received an annuity for her post, a sum paid to her even though she did not actually attend the Queen Dowager. When Catherine Parr died, Anne retired from Court. She was not to appear again until she became a lady of the privy chamber for Mary I.

In 1554, Anne Bassett finally met her match. She married Walter Hungerford, the son of Baron Hungerford, a supporter of Thomas Cromwell, who had died on the scaffold in 1540. When they married, and with the addition of a gift of 5,000 Marks from Mary I, the title of baron that had been lost when his father was executed was restored to Walter along with family lands in Wiltshire, Somerset and Cornwall. The reestablished Baron Hungerford was 21 years old, and his Baroness was 33 when they married in Mary I's private chapel at Richmond Palace.

Baron Hungerford was known as 'The Knight of Farley'. His portrait, mounted and costumed for the hunt, has an inscription that states that at the commencement of the reign of Elizabeth I he was a 'champion huntsman' and, if the image does not lie, something of a dandy. The marriage ceremony between Sir Walter and Anne Bassett was a cheery affair, according to a letter written by Robert Swyfte to the Earl of Shrewsbury from London, dated 11 June 1554: 'On Thursday last was married at Richmond, Basset the Queen's maid, to Mr Hungerfurthe, son and heir of Lord

Hungerfurthe, at which day the Queen showed herself very pleased, commanding all mirth and pastime.'[20]

Happiness was to be short-lived for Anne Bassett. The date of her death is not known, but within four years Hungerford was free to remarry and we must assume that Anne died during this period. There are no children recorded for the marriage.

Hungerford's second marriage took place in July 1558, and as the new Lady Hungerford, Anne Dormer, was one of the queen's ladies, Mary I made a grant to return more of the Hungerford lands. Anne was the sister of one of the Queen's favourites, Jane Dormer, who had captivated and married Don Gomez Suarez, the Spanish Duke of Feria.

Several letters survive from Anne to her sister, 'ye Right Honourable the Duches of Ferya her grase'. The marriage did not go well and the Hungerfords parted company in 1569. Baron Hungerford refused to pay his wife any alimony and took her children away from her. She was obliged to fight for an allowance and, after his death, for her widow's jointure and her children's inheritance: '... the aforesaid Anne (Lady Hungerford), before claim to dower, viz on the 22nd of September 1597, disagreed to her jointure, and prosecuted her writ to recover her rightful dower against Sir Edward Hungerford [Sir Walter's brother and heir], who was commanded to restore to her "the reasonable dower which fell to her of the freehold of Farley, Wellow, Telford, Rowley, and Wittenham". So Lady Hungerford finally defeated the machinations of her late husband and his instigators, and spent the remainder of her life in comfortable circumstances. She died, at Louvaine, in 1603.' At least Anne had something to leave to her daughters, but the bulk of the estate still went to Sir Edward. Four years later, Edward too was dead, childless; the estates and title went to yet another Edward Hungerford, son of Lucy Hungerford, one of the despised daughters of that Sir Walter who married Anne Bassett.[21]

THE FAMILY OF CATHERINE PARR

Sir William Parr = Elizabeth, daughter of Henry Fitzhugh, Lord Fitzhugh

Sir William Parr (?–1547)
=
1) Mary, daughter of Sir William Salisbury
2) Elizabeth Wylde

Sir Thomas Parr (c.1484–?)
=
Maud (1495–1529), daughter of Sir Thomas Green

Anne (c.1514–52)
=
William Herbert, Earl of Pembroke

Issue

Catherine Parr (1512–48)
=
1) Edward Borough (?–1533), Baron Borough
2) John Neville (?–1543), Baron Latimer
3) **Henry VIII** (1491–1547)
4) Sir Thomas Seymour (1508–49), Baron Sudeley

Mary Seymour

William Parr (c.1512–71)
Marquis of Northampton
=
1) Anne, daughter of Henry Bourchier, Earl of Essex
2) Elizabeth, daughter of George Brooke, Baron Cobham
3) Helena von Snakenburg

◆	mistress of Henry VIII
+	illegitimate child of Henry VIII
=	married

THE FAMILY OF KATHERINE D'ERESBY

William Willoughby (1482–1526), Baron Willoughby d'Eresby = Maria (c.1490–1539), daughter of Martin de Salinas

Katherine d'Eresby (1519–80) = 1) Charles Brandon, Duke of Suffolk   2) Richard Bertie (1516–82)

Henry Brandon (1535–51), Duke of Suffolk

Charles Brandon (1537–51), Duke of Suffolk

Susan Bertie (1554–c.96)
=
1) Reginald Grey, Earl of Kent
2) Sir John Wingfield

Sir Peregrine Wingfield

Peregrine Bertie (1555–1601), Baron Willoughby d'Eresby
=
Mary, daughter of John de Vere, Earl of Oxford

Sir Robert Bertie, Earl of Lindsey

12

The Foolish Queen, the Last Queen and the Last Love

———≈∿∿≈———

Henry's marriage to Catherine Howard was remarkably brief. Less than two years after the ceremony, in July 1540, Catherine was executed in the Tower. It turned out that Henry was not the only man who had found Catherine attractive, although he appears to have been one of the few she did not sleep with immediately. Catherine's relatives saw to it that she kept the King at arm's length and held out for the ultimate goal of marriage.

Catherine's early life had been one of neglect and she suffered from lack of direction. One of the 10 children of Joyce Culpepper and Lord Edmund Howard, a younger brother of the Duke of Norfolk, Catherine spent her childhood in the house of her grandmother, the Dowager Duchess of Norfolk. Catherine's mother had died when she was four years old and her father was a man of very little substance, emotional or financial. A letter from Lord Edmund Howard, demonstrates his sense of frivolity, as such an important letter reads:

> 'Madame, so it is I have this night after midnight taken your medicine, for the which I heartily thank you, for it hath done me much good, and hath caused the [gall]stone to break, so that now I void much gravel. But for all that, your said medicine hath done me little honesty, for it made me piss my bed this night, for the which my wife hath sore beaten me, and saying it is children's parts to bepiss the bed. Ye have made me such a pisser that I dare not this day go abroad, wherefore I beseech you to make mine excuse to my

Lord and Master Treasurer, for that I shall not be with you this day at dinner. Madame, it is showed me that a wing or a leg of stork, if I eat thereof, will make me that I shall never piss more in bed, and though my body be simple yet my tongue shall be ever good, and especially when it speaketh of women; and sithence such a medicine will do such a great cure God send me a piece thereof.

All yours, Edmund Howard.'[1]

According to Muriel St Clair Byrne, Edmund was 'always in debt and the despair of his family'. His friends, however, seem to have come to his rescue and he was for a time, under Lord Lisle, Comptroller of Calais. This would have given Edmund an income; professional staff would have taken care of the day-to-day running of the Comptroller's office. His daughter, Catherine, was to show a similar frivolous attitude to life.

Placed as a lady-in-waiting in the house of her grandmother, Catherine Howard's first lover was Henry Mannox, her music teacher; Catherine was 14. About a year later, in 1537, she fell in love with Francis Dereham, a gentleman in the Dowager's household. They may have considered marriage, since Dereham's rank was that of a gentleman and Catherine, despite her Norfolk relatives, was from a poor but large family. Certainly, Dereham gave Catherine a series of lover's gifts; they called each other husband and wife, and appeared before the other household members in this guise. There were no repercussions, however; Catherine is supposed to have said, 'a woman might meddle with a man and yet conceive no child unless she would herself.'[2] In any event, Catherine's family managed to get her a place at court with Anne of Cleves and, once there, she caught the eye of the King.

Catherine is never described as beautiful. She was described as small and fairly pretty. What Catherine had was youth and vivacity, and she was a neglected child suddenly presented with a fairytale place at court. It must have reminded Henry of his own youth

280

when he fell in love with Bessie Blount. Catherine, this joyful, loving, sparkling, sexy girl was just what Henry imagined he wanted. As to the rest, he could persuade himself that she was chaste and loving, both of which assumptions were, in this case, cruelly false. Catherine's contrast with his wife, Anne of Cleves, must have been almost overwhelming.

The Howards set about advising Catherine on how to behave and told her to promise all, but to give nothing until the King married her. Either they did not know about her past, or presumed that she would be discreet. Henry, meanwhile, dazzled Catherine with a stream of rich gifts – which must have seemed like a dream come true to the Howards' poor relation.

The annulment of Henry's marriage to Anne of Cleves was granted on 9 July, and his marriage to Catherine took place on 28 July 1540, at the palace at Oatlands. Henry was besotted with her. Ralph Morice, Cranmer's secretary, wrote, 'The king's affection was so marvelously set upon that gentlewoman, as it was never known that he had the like to any woman.' The French Ambassador Marillac wrote to Montmorency in September 1540: 'The King is so amorous of Catherine Howard that he cannot treat her well enough and caresses her more than he did the others.'[3]

Once she was married, Catherine proved herself to be a good bedfellow, but a poor companion. She was badly educated and relied on the King's infatuation to keep him interested in her. Within a few months of the marriage, Henry became ill; his leg became so bad that it was believed that he might die. He did not want to be with Catherine while he was sick, possibly as it brought home to him how much older he was than his wife. At any event, when they resumed their life as husband and wife, the careless delight of the courtship and honeymoon had gone.

Catherine was given an enormous budget (£4,600 a year), and a household which was filled with her family and supporters. After a very short time, both Mannox and Dereham very unwisely joined her household; Dereham became her Usher of the Chamber and

Private Secretary. They were joined by Joan Bulmer, who had shared a dormitory with Catherine in her childhood, and knew about Mannox and Dereham.

Catherine also gave places in her household as chamberers (chamber maids) to Alice Restwold, Katherine Tylney and Margaret Morton, all from the Duchess's household. The more noble Ladies of the Chamber were rightly annoyed to see that these girls were apparently held in greater esteem than they were. It was inevitable in the Tudor Court, riven with intrigue, that her secret relationships with Mannox and Dereham became known to enemies of Catherine and the Howard faction.

Once she was queen, Catherine seems to have had an affair with Thomas Culpepper, the King's body servant. They had known each other while she lived with the Dowager Duchess, as he was Catherine's distant cousin. Seeing Henry VIII ailing and realising that his cousin might soon be Queen Dowager, Culpepper tried to secure her affections. Even if they were not lovers physically, they were looking forward to a time when they would be free to marry. Later, Catherine tried to claim that she had been pestered by Culpepper, but had not responded, but a letter she wrote to him suggests otherwise:

'Master Culpepper,
I heartily recommend me unto you, praying you to send me word how that you do. It was showed me that you was sick, the which thing troubled me very much till such time that I hear from you praying you to send me word how that you do, for I never longed so much for a thing as I do to see you and to speak with you, the which I trust shall be shortly now. That which doth comfortly me very much when I think of it, and when I think again that you shall depart from me again it makes my heart die to think what fortune I have that I cannot be always in your company. It my trust is always in you that you will be as you have promised me,

and in that hope I trust upon still, praying you that you will come when my Lady Rochford is here for then I shall be best at leisure to be at your commandment ... and thus I take my leave of you, trusting to see you shortly again and I would you was with me now that you might see what pain I take in writing to you.

Yours as long as life endures, Katheryn.'[4]

Rather than using her secretary, Catherine wrote this letter with her own hand. She made it clear that she longed for Culpepper's presence and could trust only one of her servants to act as a messenger between them, although Lady Rochford, one of her ladies-in-waiting, also seemed to be privy to what was going on. It is hardly the letter of a devoted wife, a queen – or even a sensible woman.

The matter came to a head when Mary Hall, another lady who had shared a dormitory with Catherine, told her brother, John Lascelles, about Catherine's previous sexual activities. Lascelles promptly told Cranmer, who, rather tentatively, told Henry. The King would not believe the story, but ordered a discreet enquiry. Lascelles and Mary Hall were interviewed, as were Mannox and Dereham, who admitted their relationships with her before her marriage. Indeed, when he learned that Catherine had had these affairs, at first, Henry was prepared to forgive her, but too many people had a vested interest in removing the Howards and the Queen from power. Catherine's uncle and aunt, Lord William and Lady Margaret Howard, were arrested, as was Catherine's sister-in-law, her aunt, Lady Bridgwater, and her grandmother, the Dowager Duchess of Norfolk. Anne Boleyn's widowed sister-in-law, Lady Rochford, who was now one of Catherine's ladies, was also arrested and questioned; she had a breakdown and apparently went mad.

Catherine Howard was to be formally arrested – leading to one of the most poignant stories to come out of the whole affair. Catherine was staying at Hampton Court with Henry. Due to the investigation they had been separated, but Catherine knew that Henry would be hearing Mass in the chapel. She ran from her room along a gallery towards the chapel door, in order to find Henry and put her side of the story to him. She believed, with some justification, that if she were to explain to him and persuade him that it was all quite innocent or someone else's fault, Henry would still be prepared to forgive her – even to take her back. In the event, the guards stopped her, and Catherine's screams as she was dragged back along the passage are said to haunt the gallery even today.

Once the full story came out, nothing could save Catherine. The French Ambassador reported of Henry that, 'He has changed his love for the Queen into hatred, and taken such grief at being deceived that of late it was thought he had gone mad, for he called for a sword to slay her he had loved so much … [he regrets his] ill-luck in meeting with such ill-conditioned wives.'

All those involved were questioned again, under the severest conditions, until a case had been constructed. Even after torture, however, Culpepper and Dereham both denied having any relations with Catherine after her marriage. Mannox admitted he had been familiar with Catherine, and Dereham admitted that they had had sex while she was living at Lambeth with the Duchess. Catherine herself finally agreed that they had slept together, 'in such sort as a man doth use his wife many and sundry times'. However, this had all happened before she came to Court, when she possessed, 'the ignorance and frailness of young women …'. As Catherine wrote to Henry, 'I was so desirous to be taken unto your Grace's favour, and so blinded with the desire for worldly glory that I could not, nor had grace, to consider how great a fault it was to conceal my former faults from your Majesty, considering that I intended ever during my life to be faithful and true unto your Majesty after.'[5]

It was Culpepper who destroyed any hope Catherine had of forgiveness. He denied that they had had sexual relations, but said that they had both desired it ('he intended and meant to do ill with the Queen and in likewise the Queen so minded to do with him.'[6])

284

The condemnation of Dereham and Culpepper seemed to be for their intentions, rather than any specific acts – that they spent time with Catherine and by admiring her they were intending to commit adultery, even if they did not actually do it. This was treason and they were condemned to death.

It was bad enough that Catherine had had lovers before Henry married her, and was not a virgin when she went to her marriage bed but it was treason if she had had sex with anyone other then Henry after their marriage. Culpepper, Dereham and Mannox all claimed nothing had happened after the wedding, but Lady Rochford, Catherine's confidante, gave additional evidence pointing to a sexual relationship, even though she could offer no proof. Amongst other things, Culpepper had visited Catherine's private rooms when the King was away. Catherine was doomed. Henry would forgive a lot, but never adultery. In the end, all three men were found guilty of treason and executed. On 10 December 1541, Culpepper was beheaded at Tyburn, and Dereham was hung, drawn and quartered. Their heads were set up on Tower Bridge.

When Catherine Howard had first been accused, in November 1541, she had retired to Syon House, near Richmond, once a Brigittine nunnery and now a private house. She was moved to the Tower for her execution in February 1542. Catherine was allowed only four ladies-in-waiting and two chamberers. She was loaded on to a barge to go to the Tower. She struggled and had to be dragged on board. When they passed under Tower Bridge, the heads of Culpepper and Dereham were already on display.

On the evening on 12 February 1542, Catherine was told that she would die the next day. She asked that the block be brought into her room so she could practise kneeling and placing her head, so she would not disgrace herself the next day. She spent some time practising until she felt sure she could accomplish her death with dignity. She was executed at 7 a.m. on 13 February. She seemed calm, but had to be helped up the steps to the scaffold and gave her final words in a quiet speech. After her death, all her relatives, except Jane Parker, were released; Jane was also executed. Catherine, like her cousin, Anne Boleyn, was buried in St Peter ad Vincula.

The debacle with Catherine Howard seemed to sober Henry in his relationships with women. He had fallen in love with Catherine with the passion of his youth, and he took longer to recover from her treachery. However, in July 1543, Henry made his last marriage, to the lady who had started life as Catherine Parr.

CATHERINE PARR

Catherine Neville, Lady Latimer, at 30, was already a widow. She was born Catherine Parr in 1512, the eldest child of Sir Thomas Parr and Maud Greene, of Kendal Castle, Westmoreland. Sir Thomas died when Catherine was five. Her mother arranged her marriage to Edward Borough or Brough in 1529, but he was in poor health, and died three years later. Catherine then married John Neville, Baron Latimer, a year later when she was 21 and he was around 40; their principal residence was at Snape Castle, near Bedale in Yorkshire. Her role had twice been both wife and companion-nurse to an older man, a role that Henry may well have appreciated.

In 1542 Lord Latimer died after a lengthy illness and Catherine became a wealthy widow. Henry VIII had been quietly courting her for some weeks before her husband's death. Why he chose her is a puzzle. She was not particularly beautiful, sparkling, youthful or, indeed, any of the other things that had attracted him in the past. However, she was a handsome woman, brown-eyed and auburn-haired, and might yet provide him with another child.

Catherine had existing connections with the Court. Her mother, Maud, had been a lady-in-waiting to Catherine of Aragon, and she herself had been one of the young girls educated with the Princess Mary; they already knew each other and were close friends. Her sister, Anne, was married to William Herbert, an esquire of the body, and her brother, William Parr, was Lord

Warden of the Scottish Marches and had been in the household of the Duke of Richmond. Certainly, she had no children of her own, but she had been married to two invalids (her first marriage to Borough may never have been consummated due to the state of his health). She was kind, cheerful, modest and gentle, used to living with older husbands, an experienced nurse; she would not be demanding nor set her expectations too high. She was intelligent, well read and a scholar in the New Religion. It was the latter that made Henry uneasy and which might, had he lived longer, have triggered yet another divorce.

Catherine gathered those of the New Faith around her, including the outspoken young Duchess of Suffolk, Katherine d'Eresby, widow of Charles Brandon, who named her pet spaniel, 'Gardiner', after the Bishop of Winchester as an insult; he was Catholic, she was extreme Protestant. Her forthright wit was rather attractive, to both the Queen and the King.

287

In 1545, Henry gave his permission for Bishop Gardiner to examine Catherine as to her religious belief. In fact, Catherine had been discussing her burgeoning Protestantism with her husband, who felt that sometimes he was being lectured. Gardiner gleefully drew up his charges against the Queen, but a copy of the paper was dropped (probably on purpose) and subsequently found by one of Catherine's servants. She was shown the paper, and promptly threw herself on her husband's mercy.

The story is told by Foxe that Henry was annoyed when Catherine took an interest in religion and made her opinions known to him: 'A good hearing it is when women become such clerks; and nothing much to my comfort in mine old days to be taught by my wife.' Henry told her, 'You have become a doctor, Kate, to instruct us, as we take it, and not to be instructed or directed by us.' Catherine denied this vehemently; she had set up a disputation in order to take his mind off his illness and to learn from his superior arguments. 'And is it even so, sweetheart, and tended your arguments to no worse end? Then perfect friends we are now again, as ever at any time before.' Henry forgave her, and when Sir Thomas Wroithesley came to arrest her, he found Henry and Catherine walking arm in arm, the best of friends. He was sent away with a flea in his ear.[7]

Friends they may have been, but Henry VIII wanted to be in love. Even with the approach of death, there were rumours at the time that Henry was considering divorcing Catherine Parr and marrying Katherine d'Eresby. According to the Imperial Ambassador, Van der Delft, there was talk of a change of queens: 'Some attribute it to the sterility of the present Queen, while others say there will be no change during the present war. Madame Suffolk is much talked about and in great favour …'[8] However, on the night spanning 27 and 28 January 1547, Henry died.

Katherine d'Eresby had come into Charles Brandon's household in 1529, as his ward. She was the only child and very wealthy heiress of the widowed Maria de Salinas, Lady Willoughby d'Eresby and Brandon planned to marry her to his son, Henry, Earl of Lincoln. As the only legitimate son of the Henry VIII's sister, Mary, the child Henry, had he lived, might very well have succeeded Edward VI as king of England, had Mary and Elizabeth been removed from the succession. Henry VIII had excluded the children of his sister Margaret from the succession. Brandon suffered the death of his wife, Mary, on 24 June 1533, and the death of their son the following year. Although Katherine was much younger than he (she had been born in 1520 and was 14 to his 49), Brandon married her later that year, on 7 September.

Katherine's parentage was eminently respectable. Her father was William Willoughby d'Eresby, 8th Baron Willoughby. Her mother Maria de Salinas (Saluces), was one of Catherine of Aragon's maids of honour and her distant relative.

To add to Brandon's two surviving daughters by his first wife, Mary, Katherine gave him two sons, Henry, born in 1535 and Charles, in 1537. Henry was a contemporary of Edward VI, and the two little boys were educated together, sharing the tutor Sir

John Cheke. Perhaps Henry VIII and Charles Brandon hoped their sons would grow up to be as good friends as their fathers.

Charles Brandon, Duke of Suffolk, died on 24 August 1545 at Guildford. He was buried at Windsor, according to the wishes of Henry VIII. In 1551, Brandon's sons Henry and his brother Charles were at St John's College in Cambridge when the sweating sickness broke out. Despite all that was done for them, both boys died on 16 July. Charles was Duke of Suffolk for 30 minutes – the time that he survived Henry. The title of Duke of Suffolk eventually passed to Henry Grey as the husband of the eldest surviving daughter, Frances.

Katherine d'Eresby now caught the King's attention. She possessed all the qualities that he most admired – she was pretty, witty and intelligent. The Dowager Duchess of Suffolk was, as Fuller reported, 'a lady of a sharp wit and sure hand to thrust it home and make it pierce when she pleased'. She must have amused and entertained the King, and to cap it all she was the chosen partner of his dearest friend. Henry made very tentative enquiries about divorcing Catherine Parr and remarrying, but he was already ill and dying, and the plans came to nothing.

In 1548, after Henry VIII's death, Catherine Parr married Thomas Seymour. They had been in love and contemplating marriage before Henry stepped in and broke up their relationship. Catherine now wrote to Thomas Seymour:

> 'I would not have you think that this mine honest good will toward you to proceed from any sudden motion of passion; for, as truly as God is God, my mind was fully bent, the other time I was at liberty, to marry you before any man I know. Howbeit, God withstood my will therein most vehemently for a time ...'[9]

With Seymour, at last Catherine Parr was able to start a family. She gave birth to a daughter, Mary. A letter, from the Duke of

Somerset to his brother Thomas, congratulating the Queen Dowager on having been delivered of 'so pretty a daughter', is dated 1 September.[10] The baby was born on 30 August 1548, and Catherine died on 7 September, of the puerperal fever that had also killed Jane Seymour.

On 17 January 1549 Thomas Seymour was arrested, imprisoned and tried. He was executed in March. The 'pretty daughter', Mary, first went to the Duchess of Somerset, Seymour's sister-in-law, who didn't want her and was happy to hand her over to Katherine d'Eresby's household. Catherine Parr and Katherine d'Eresby had been close friends, since both were fervent supporters of the Reformation and the New Religion. It was only natural that she should take an interest in her friend's only child. It was also said that Catherine Parr had requested her friend to take her daughter in a dying wish. Katherine d'Eresby may even have contemplated a marriage between the infant heiress and her second son, then about 11 years old.

In a letter from her house at Grimsthorpe, dated 24 July 1549, to William Cecil Katherine wrote that if she was to maintain the Dowager's child as befitted her rank, she needed an annual pension for this purpose. She described the child's 'miserable furniture' (household equipment) that did not befit her rank. She added that she would have placed the responsibility and expense of the child on the Marquis of Northampton, Catherine Parr's brother, except that he was 'ill able to bear it'. In fact, not only was he in financial difficulties, he was physically ill, and died shortly after his sister.[11] The Duke of Somerset had been supposed to send money for his niece, but he too was in difficulties and no funds were forthcoming from him either. As a result of Katherine's letters to Cecil, the Council decided to restore Thomas Seymour's lands and property to his daughter, thereby providing her with revenue suitable to the only daughter of the Queen Dowager.

Mary Seymour then vanishes from the records. The historian, Agnes Strickland, suggests that she married Sir Edward Bushel and had a daughter, and that her descendants were amongst the members of the Lawson family in Westmoreland and Cumberland. However, this is by no means proved, and tends to rely on anecdotal evidence from the family.

Katherine d'Eresby wrote frequently to Cecil, a fellow Protestant intellectual, on a variety of topics. On 9 May 1550 she asked his opinion about a marriage between her son, Henry Brandon, and Anne Seymour, the daughter of the Duke of Somerset. She wanted the children to have a free choice about the match. On 8 September, Katherine wrote, thanking him for his letter and news. She had received a letter from the Duchess of Somerset and had answered it. All this planning came to nothing, however. A further letter from Grimsthorpe, dated September 1551, was one of resignation. She thanked Cecil for his friendship during her 'last sharp and bitter trial' – the death of her sons in Cambridge.[12]

Katherine did not remain a widow. In 1552, she married Richard Bertie, a like-minded extreme Protestant. He had read Law at Oxford and taken service with Katherine as her Gentleman Usher and Master of Horse. They were safe under the reign of the Protestant Edward VI, but when Mary I, a fervent Catholic, came to the throne the Berties felt it expedient to spend some time abroad. It is almost certain that Mary, as happened with other people whom she was fond of, ordered that an official 'blind eye' be turned to the flight of the Berties. The journey of the couple and their adventures abroad were so exciting and unusual that they led to a ballad by Thomas Deloney, a play by Thomas Dive, and a book by Richard Bertie himself.

This enforced exile meant that when Katherine gave birth to her son, Peregrine Bertie, it was at Lower Wesel, Cleves. Legend said that she went into labour in the church porch, and it was there that Peregrine was born. Richard later reported in his book about their travels in Europe that this was an exaggeration. Peregrine had been born in the local hotel where his parents were staying. When

291

the family eventually returned to England in 1559, following Elizabeth I's ascension to the throne, Peregrine Bertie had to be naturalised. The family returned to Katherine's house at Grimsthorpe, which became their principal residence again. Here Katherine also gave birth to a daughter, Susan, who married firstly Reginald Grey, Earl of Kent, and later, Sir John Wingfield.

Perhaps it was her love of children that made Katherine so amenable to taking on other people's offspring. She had cared for Catherine Parr's daughter, and in 1568 she also took responsibility for the sons of Catherine, her stepgranddaughter and Jane Grey's sister. In 1560, Catherine Grey had carried out a secret marriage with Edward Seymour, Earl of Hertford, heir to the executed Duke of Somerset, and had two sons. It was a most foolish move. Apart from anything else, the 1536 Act of Succession to the Crown made it illegal for any member of the Royal Family to marry without the permission of the Monarch. This automatically made the marriage null and void, and any children would be illegitimate. Elizabeth I was furious about the marriage and both Catherine and Edward Seymour were sent to the Tower, where Catherine gave birth to their son, Edward, on 24 September 1560 and their second son, Thomas in 1561.

Catherine Grey was now the mother of two sons who might have stood in the succession to the English throne, but she could not prove the marriage. The boys were unwanted by the Greys or the Seymours, and so ended up in the care of Katherine d'Eresby. The eldest son, Edward, tried throughout his life to claim all his father's titles, but without success. His son, William Seymour, would eventually be given the title of Duke of Somerset, after a disastrous marriage with Arabella Stuart, James VI of Scotland's cousin and rival claimant to the English throne. Arabella spent most of her life in prison after this marriage and an abortive attempt to flee the country to rally foreign support for her claim. They got engaged when William was 15 years old and Arabella was 35.

Katherine d'Eresby finally died on 19 September 1580. On 23 September Peregrine Bertie wrote to Sir Francis Walsingham from Willoughby House. He put forward his claim to the titles of the baronies of Willoughby and d'Eresby, which rightly came to him now through his deceased mother. He asked Walsingham to put in a good word for him with the Queen.[13] He challenged for and won the extinct title of Lord Willoughby de Eresby, which had last been bestowed on his mother's father.

Peregrine Bertie married Mary, the daughter of John de Vere, the 16th Earl of Oxford. In 1582, his eldest son, Robert, was born; he would go on to have another four sons (Peregrine, Henry, Vere and Roger) and one daughter, named Katherine. He became one of Elizabeth I's military commanders; however, like many of her servants, he was rarely paid. By 1590 he had virtually retired, ill and sadly short of money. He set out to visit various European spa cities in the hope of finding relief from his illness. He only returned to England in 1596. Peregrine Bertie finally died on 25 June 1600, and was buried at Spilsby, Lincolnshire.

293

THE FAMILY OF HENRY VIII

Henry VIII (1491-1547)

1) Catherine of Aragon =

Mary I, Queen of England

◆ **Elizabeth Blount**

+ Henry Fitzroy, Duke of Richmond

◆ **Mary Boleyn**

+ Henry Carey

2) Anne Boleyn =

Elizabeth I, Queen of England

◆ **Jane Pollard**

+ Thomas Stukeley

◆ **Mary Berkeley**

+ Sir John Perrot

◆ **Joanna Dingley**

+ Etheldreda Malte

3) Jane Seymour =

Edward VI, King of England

4) Anna of Cleves =

5) Catherine Howard =

6) Catherine Parr =

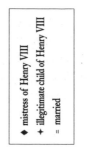

◆ mistress of Henry VIII

+ illegitimate child of Henry VIII

= married

According to Rumour ...

There are a number of stories and rumours of other mistresses and other illegitimate children belonging to Henry VIII. The very nature of Henry made him a focus for such stories; of ladies who were said to have become his mistress, such as Elizabeth Bryan and Mistress Parker; ladies who he may have loved, such as Elizabeth Brooke and Elizabeth Amadas, and children he may have fathered, including Sir Henry Lee and Richard Edwardes. Even if the events relating to these people are unsupported by historical references, they cannot merely be denied or ignored as they are part of the story of this most fascinating man. Thus, no history of Henry VIII would be complete without them.

ELIZABETH BRYAN

Elizabeth, the daughter of Sir Thomas Bryan and Margaret Bourchier, was born c.1500 into a family who existed in the heart of the Court. Her parents both held court positions and her mother would go on to hold the post of Lady Governess to Henry VIII's children, Princess Mary, Henry Fitzroy, Princess Elizabeth and Prince Edward.

It was said that she was still a child, aged about 12, when she caught Henry's attention. She performed in the masques that the King so enjoyed and Henry gave her a diamond necklace and a fur coat; he also presented her mother with a gift of £500. It is even suggested that, at age 12, Elizabeth gave birth to Henry's child. Whatever her relationship with the King, in December 1514, she married Sir Nicholas Carew when he was 19 and she was 14. Henry attended their wedding and gave a gift of land worth 50 marks, a considerable sum, to the young couple. It was also

295

reported that the King gave the new Lady Carew gifts of 'innumerable jewels'.

In all likelihood Henry never took Elizabeth Bryan as his mistress. His own grandmother had been married at 12 and was a mother at 13; despite two more marriages, Margaret had had no more children. Henry VII had delayed sending his daughter Margaret to Scotland to her husband because he feared the damage that might be done to her if she had sexual relations too soon. Henry VIII would have known all this and his preferred partners were grown women, capable of enjoying sex and also of joining in with all his other interests. A 12-year-old child would not fit into this picture, except as a delightful diversion.

Henry had affection for the whole Bryan family; Margaret Bourchier's paternal great-grandmother had been Anne Plantagenet, so Elizabeth's mother was actually a distant cousin to the King. She went on to become one of Henry's most trusted family servants, caring for his children. Elizabeth's brother, Sir Francis Bryan, despite a reputation as a libertine, was also a close friend to the King.

Elizabeth and Nicholas Carew had four daughters, Elizabeth, Mary, Anne and Isabel, and a son, Sir Francis Carew. Her granddaughter, Elizabeth Throckmorton, married Sir Walter Raleigh. In 1520 at the Field of the Cloth of Gold, 'Mistress Carew' attended as one of the Queen's gentlewomen. Sir Nicholas became involved in the various plots within the Court, jostling for power. He was very deeply involved in the plotting against Anne Boleyn. Finally, he was accused of treason – of speaking against the King, and was beheaded on Tower Hill on 3 March 1539. Elizabeth died in 1546.

ELIZABETH BROOKE, LADY WYATT

In 1521 the 18-year-old Elizabeth, daughter of Thomas Brooke, Baron Cobham, married Thomas Wyatt, the poet. Their son, also named Thomas, was the leader of Wyatt's Rebellion in 1554, the unsuccessful uprising that sought to remove Mary I from the throne and replace her with Elizabeth I.

Elizabeth Brooke's marriage to Wyatt was not successful and after the birth of their son in 1521 the couple's relationship deteriorated. Wyatt later admitted to his son, 'the fault is both in your mother and me', adding, 'but chiefly in her.'[1] He may have been referring to the fact that in 1522 Anne Boleyn came to Court and Wyatt became one of her admirers; whether Elizabeth already had a lover or whether she took one in response to her husband's activities, is debatable. In 1524, possibly at the start of Henry's affair with Anne Boleyn, Wyatt was sent abroad as an ambassador, a post he held, on and off, until his death. Elizabeth is reputed to have set up house with her lover although there is no record of his identity.

In 1536 Wyatt had been arrested on suspicion of having been one of the 'lovers' of Anne Boleyn, but had been released. In 1540 he was arrested again on charges of treason and this time it was Catherine Howard who interceded with Henry VIII for his release. The reconciliation with his wife was one of the conditions of his release. Back with Elizabeth and restored to his post as Ambassador, in 1542 Wyatt became ill, dying on 11 October. After Catherine Howard was condemned to death, Henry VIII dined with various ladies and showed especial affection for two of them, fuelling rumours that he was already searching for a new wife. One was Anne Bassett, and the other, presumably with the knowledge that Wyatt was terminally ill, was Elizabeth Brooke. If the King showed her such attention, presumably her reputation was not that bad. Perhaps Wyatt's remarks to his son were more in self-justification than truth.

SIR HENRY LEE

Another rumoured illegitimate son of Henry VIII's was Sir Henry Lee. John Aubrey, in his *Brief Lives*, wrote of Sir Henry Lee (1530–1610): 'Old Sir Harry Lee [was] knight of the Garter and was supposed brother of Queen Elizabeth. He ordered that all his family should be christened Harry's.'

He also recorded that 'He [Sir Henry] was never married' and that he kept a mistress, Mrs Anne Vavasour. His tomb monument showed Sir Henry at rest with Anne kneeling at his feet. Aubrey quoted the following verses:

> 'Here lies good old knight Sir Harry
> Who loved well, but would not marry.
> While he lived, and had his feeling,
> She did lie and he was kneeling.
> Now he's dead and cannot feel
> He doth lie and she doth kneel.'

Aubrey, barely holding back a snigger, says that Sir Henry, 'kept women to read to him when he was abed. One of these readers was Parson Jones's wife of Wotton. I have heard her daughter (who had no more wit) glory what a brave reader her mother was and how Sir Harry's worship much delighted to hear her.'[2]

Certainly Sir Henry Lee (1533–1611) lies buried in St Peter's Chapel in Quarendon; the chapel was largely rebuilt by Sir Henry, but fell into disrepair and is a virtual ruin. His effigy was portrayed in gilded armour. Anne Vavasour is also buried in the chapel with her own effigy, although the verse on her tomb is slightly less vulgar than the one quoted by Aubrey:

> 'Under this stone entombed lies a fair and worthy dame,
> Daughter to Henry Vavasour, Ann Vavasour her name:
> She living with Sir Henry Lee for love, long time did dwell;
> Death could not part them, but here they rest within one cell.'[3]

It is not only the verse that Aubrey seems to have got wrong. Sir Henry Lee was indeed married, to the daughter of Lord Paget. She died in 1584 and is buried with her own family at Aylesbury.

Sir Henry Lee was the son of Sir Anthony Lee and Margaret, the daughter of Henry Wyatt, Privy Councillor to Henry VIII. There was certainly no contemporary suggestion that Sir Henry Lee was Henry VIII's son. He was born c.1533, and as a child he was sent to the household of his uncle, Sir Thomas Wyatt, the poet.

Lee was Elizabeth I's Champion from 1570 to 1590 (when he was 57 and his 'golden locks time hath turned to silver'), and Master of the Royal Armouries from 1580. He organised the Accession Day tourneys, held each year on 17 November. He assembled the contestants and at the beginning of each of his bouts he threw down a gauntlet in Elizabeth's defence as the Queen's champion, dressed in elaborate costume and with a laudatory speech, some of which he certainly penned himself.

After his wife's death Sir Henry, aged almost 60, set up house with Mistress Anne Vavasour, one of the gentlewomen of the queen's bedchamber since 1580. When she moved in with Sir Harry, she was indeed known as his 'reading lady', an anachronistic term that gave a polite face to their true relationship. In 1581, Anne Vavasour, daughter of Henry Vavasour and Margaret Knyvett, had enjoyed a liaison with Edward de Vere, Earl of Oxford, (he was married to Lord Burghley's daughter) that resulted in her giving birth to his son, later known as Sir Edward Vere. Elizabeth I was not amused. Sir Francis Walsingham wrote to the Earl of Huntingdon: 'One Tuesday at night Anne Vavysor was brought to bed of a son in the maidens' chamber. The E of Oxford is avowed to be the father, who hath withdrawn himself with the intent, as it is thought, to pass the seas. The ports are laid for him and therefore if he had any such determination it is not likely that he will escape. The gentlewoman the selfsame night she was delivered was conveyed out of the house and the next day committed to the Tower.'[4]

Oxford's action led to a state of warfare existing between Oxford's supporters and the Vavasour and Knyvett families for

299

some years. The boy, however, seems to have been close to his mother. Young Edward may well have accompanied his mother to Sir Henry Lee's house, where she eventually gave birth to his half-brother, Thomas Vavasour (also known as Thomas Freeman), Sir Henry's son. Sadly Thomas could not claim his father's estate; this passed to a cousin, another Sir Henry Lee. The irony was that Anne gave both Oxford and Sir Henry a son, yet both men died without legitimate male heirs.

Not unsurprisingly, Elizabeth I seems to have disapproved of their relationship at first, but in 1592 Elizabeth visited Ditchley where Sir Henry and Anne Vavasour acted as her hosts. The visit was so successful that Sir Henry commissioned a portrait of the Queen, known as the Ditchley Portrait, painted by Marcus Gheeraerts. The Queen is shown standing on a map of England, her foot on Oxfordshire and her heel on Ditchley. Behind her are shown a storm over her left shoulder and a sunny day over her right, symbolising her power and her glory.

RICHARD EDWARDES

When David Dean Edwards of Baltimore wrote his family history, *The Edwards Legacy* (1992), he found one of his ancestors to be of particular interest. Richard Edwardes was born in March 1525, to William Edwardes and his wife Agnes. At least, the boy was born to Agnes, whose maiden name is variously given as Blewitt, Bewitt and Beupine. According to family legend, Henry VIII was Richard's father.

The child grew up at North Petherton in Somerset where there was a Royal hunting park and a hunting lodge that Henry VIII used to use. It was surmised that it was here that the King set eyes on the lovely Agnes and had an affair with her. When she was pregnant, Henry may have arranged for her marriage to a suitable gentleman. However, she may have already been the wife of William Edwardes, the father of her other two sons, William and Henry. Richard grew up in the Edwardes family and, again from family history, he may have spent part of his childhood as one of the choirboys to the Chapel Royal where he would have received an early education in music. Alternatively, he may have been brought up by his mother's family in Scotland.

At the age of 15, Richard was sent to Corpus Christi college, Oxford University. The Edwardes family was poor, but on two occasions money was made available for the education of family members. In the year after Richard was born, money was found to send his uncle Edward Edwardes to Oxford and, again, in 1540 funds became available to send Richard. Family history recorded that Henry VIII rewarded the Edwardes family on the child's birth and then sponsored Richard, paying for his tuition. One of Richard's poems recorded the 'poore estate' of his family.

At Oxford Richard studied music with George Etheridge, one of the country's most distinguished musicians. In 1544 Richard became a Fellow and received his BA; two years later he took his MA and was ordained as a priest in the Church of England. In 1550 Richard was elected Theologian at Christ Church College. Around this time he was given the living of St Helen's in Worcester, as there is a record of his resigning from the position of Rector dated to July 1555.

By 1558 Richard was associated with the Chapel Royal as he was one of the gentlemen given seven yards of black cloth to provide his mourning for Mary I. Shortly afterwards he received four yards of scarlet for the coronation of Elizabeth I. In May 1560 he received a patent as a Gentleman of the Chapel Royal, Deputy Master of the Children and a year later, when the Master died, Richard took over his position. This was an important role and meant that Richard would have been in regular attendance on the Queen. He was also expected to write words and music for the boys to sing and plays suitable for them to perform.

In April 1560 Richard married Margaret Babb, at North Petherton. The following November his first son, William, was born, but his wife did not survive. In 1562 Richard married again,

301

with an infant son to provide for. His second wife, Helene Griffith, had four more children; Marie, Gwyn, Elizabeth and John.

Richard Edwardes is credited with the writing of several plays for his young charges. *Damon and Pithias* (first published, posthumously, in 1571), whose title page reads, 'The excellent Comedy of two the most faithfullest Friends, Damon and Pithias, Newly imprinted, as the same was showed before the Queen's Majesty, by the Children of her Grace's Chapel, except the Prologue that is somewhat altered ... Made by Master Edwardes, then being Master of the Children, 1571.'

He also wrote a play called *Misogomus*, and a comedy called *Palamon and Arcite*, which was performed before Elizabeth I at Oxford in 1566. Unfortunately, one reason that the performance is remembered is that at some time during the play the stage collapsed: five people were injured and three killed. In true thespian traditions, the show went on. As the play concluded, the Queen made a speech, thanking Richard and all those involved. The following day he waited beside her on the steps outside St Mary's Church where they stood 'exchanging witticisms'.

In the 1560s Richard was also assembling a collection of contemporary poems from poets like Lord Vaux, the Earl of Oxford and others, to be published as *The Paradyse of Dainty Devises*. It remained incomplete at his death, and was printed some time later under his name, including 10 of his own verses.

In 1567 Richard died, at the relatively young age of 42, at Edwards Hall near Cardiff. Bruce Edwards wrote in his family history that the house had been the Edwardes family home since the 11th century. [5]

LADY ELEANOR LUKE

This particular lady appeared as a character in the recent television series, *The Tudors*, from US network Showtime, starring Jonathan Rhys Meyers. The Lady is fictional, but she is already appearing on internet pages as one of the King's mistresses. One wonders how long it will be before she is assigned dates of birth and death, a family and a history![6]

MISTRESS PARKER

'Mistress Parker' is sometimes referred to as one of the mistresses of King Henry VIII (particularly on web pages devoted to him) at around 1520, after his relationship with Bessie Blount and before Mary Boleyn. According to writer and historian Beverley Murphy, Bessie Blount was not in attendance at the Field of the Cloth of Gold, possibly indicating that her affair with the King was over by then. Hubert S. Burke cites an Arabella Parker, 'the wife of a city merchant' as Bessie's successor. Although there was a Mistress Parker in the revels of March 1522, this was probably Margery Parker, who had been part of Princess Mary's household since 1516.[7] The major work of Hubert S. Burke was his *Historical Portraits of the Tudor Dynasty and the Reformation Period*, Vols. I–IV, John Hodges, London, 1879–83. Burke appears to be the only source for information on this 'Arabella Parker'.

303

Another candidate is Jane Parker, daughter of Sir William Parker, born c. 1505 and so about 15 years of age in 1520. She appeared in the masque of the Chateau Vert (the Green Castle) in 1522 and would make her mark on the Tudor Court when she married George Boleyn, Viscount Rochford. She was a witness for the prosecution at the trials of both Anne Boleyn and Catherine Howard. In 1520, however, she was still a child and so is unlikely to have been Henry VIII's lover.

Another possible 'Mistress Parker' was Jane's mother, Alice St John, born c.1484, who had married their father, Henry Parker, Baron Morley; in 1520 the lady would have been in her mid-30s.

ELIZABETH AMADAS

In 1532, a lady called Elizabeth Amadas was arrested on charges of treason. She had called Anne Boleyn a harlot and said that she should be burned. The diatribe, including a rant that the King had set a precedent for the men of England by putting aside his loyal wife for a younger woman of questionable morals, may have been influenced by the fact that her own husband, Robert Amadas, had recently left her. Elizabeth went further and admitted that she was herself 'a witch and a prophetess', and gave details of having been solicited to enjoy a romantic liaison with Henry VIII. According to Elizabeth, the couple had used Sir William Compton's house in Thames Street for their rendezvous and Compton and Master Dauncey (Sir Thomas More's son-in-law and a Knight of the Body to the King) had acted as messengers between the couple, although she did not report whether or not the liaison had been consummated.[8]

In spite of these confessions, Elizabeth Amadas was released. Part of this may have been that she was not in her right mind or may have been due to her family and background. Elizabeth was the daughter of the courtier Sir Hugh Brice, the son of Hugh Brice, the Court goldsmith. Her husband, Robert Amadas, was also a goldsmith, an extremely wealthy man with strong connections to the King and Court, Master of the Jewel House and the Mint. He and Elizabeth had a daughter, also called Elizabeth, born in 1508, who married Richard Scrope (they had one child, yet another Elizabeth) and died in 1531, the year before her mother's breakdown. Robert, having abandoned his wife of more than 20 years for another woman, also died that year. The loss of both her only child and her faithless husband may have been seen as mitigating circumstances to her outburst.[9]

Later, in 1532, Elizabeth remarried. Her second husband was Thomas Neville, great-grandson of Ralph Neville, Earl of Westmorland, and Joan Beaufort, the illegitimate daughter of John of Gaunt, third son of Edward III. Elizabeth, born c.1580, would have been around 50, but she was the sole heiress of one wealthy goldsmith (her brother Hugh had died in infancy) and the widow of another. It is to be hoped that Neville was kind to his second wife.

Conclusion

As Prince of Wales and King of England, Henry VIII was perfect and immaculate, incapable of doing wrong or behaving badly. He was a man with a strong sexual appetite who lived at a time and in a society that applauded him if he strayed from the marriage bed. He was handsome, lusty and charming and possessed that ultimate aphrodisiac, wealth and power – and yet he longed for love. He was inspired by the chase, by romantic pursuit of the lady he loved; he could be enormously generous, even humble, to the woman who won his devotion.

The question remains what would have happened if even one of Catherine of Aragon's sons had lived? Henry would have most probably remained married to her. Wolsey would have stayed as Cardinal, never quite achieving his ambition to be Pope, and the Roman Catholic Church would have continued in England. Anne Boleyn might have been a mistress, dearly beloved, but very easy to discard if he tired of her. Henry would have found a husband for Anne and most probably never set his sights on the plain, quiet Jane Seymour. He would have carried on choosing his loves and likes, spending years with the same mistress whilst offering his occasional adoration to a range of charming, married ladies.

Henry Fitzroy, Duke of Richmond, might never have risen to such a high status or, indeed, have ever been acknowledged. As Earl of Richmond he would have been a discreet if loveable ornament to his father's Court. Etheldreda would have been joined by Elizabeth as the bastard daughters of the King; Elizabeth too would have been fostered out to a suitable family and lived a shallow, blameless married life in the shadow of her half-brother Henry IX. Henry Carey would still have served; Thomas Stukeley would still have connived; John Perrot would still have blustered.

History, however, has no room for such imponderables. The three children of Henry VIII are, in fact, the eight children of Henry VIII. A man who longed for a son actually had five; a man who didn't want daughters had three. The tragedy was that so many of them were outside the lawful boundaries of marriage.

Henry VIII was a man who longed for love. His tragedy was that he was looking for a love that could never exist. He had a vision of the perfect woman, an image of his mother, and no woman could measure up to this fantasy. Apart from this was the obsessive need for a male heir. These two, together with the power struggles going on amongst the noble families and foreign diplomats, distorted Henry's natural desire to love and, most of all, to be loved. He often played the game of the disguised stranger. He would appear at a joust or feast, disguised and masked, and revel in the applause. Who is this masked stranger, people would ask? How strong and talented he is! The men would envy him and the women desire him. Eventually someone, perhaps the queen herself, would utter the sentiment, I wish the King were here; only he could equal or excel this stranger! This was the cue to unmask, and to revel in the adulation that followed because he had heard that people loved and admired him for himself and not just because he was the king.

His mistresses gave him this adulation and devotion, whether for hours or years. With them he was the ardent young king again and basked in their love. From Elizabeth Denton to Katherine d'Eresby, each woman's humble reverence touched him and made him happy. As each love faded, a new love would appear ready to take her predecessor's place.

None of his bastards was planned for, and each one has a different mother; no lady had a second child by Henry without a wedding ring. Yet they are all Tudors, and their charm and exceptional natures let King Harry's Bastards make an indelible mark on the history of the Tudor period.

Endnotes

⟨⟨⟨⟩⟩⟩

Introduction

1   Marie Louise Bruce, *The Making of Henry VIII*, Collins, London, 1977, p.75

2   Edward Lord Herbert of Cherbury, *The Life and Raigne of King Henry the Eighth*, Thomas Whitaker, London, 1649, p.175

3   Alison Plowden, *Tudor Women: Queens and Commoners*, Weidenfeld & Nicholson, London, 1979, p.96

4   Alan Haynes, *Sex in Elizabethan England*, Sutton Publishing, Stroud, 1997, p.72

5   William J Tighe, 'The Gentleman Pensioners in Elizabethan Politics and Government', Dissertation, 1984, p.399

Chapter 1

1   G. Milne, Sir Roland de Velville (1474–1535), http://www/gmilne.demon.co.uk/roland.htm

2   Michael K. Jones & Malcolm G. Underwood, *The King's Mother: Lady Margaret Beaufort, Duchess of Richmond and Derby*, CUP, 1992, p.69–70

3   Roger Lockyer & Andrew Thrush, *Henry VII, Seminar Studies in History*, Longman, 1997

4   Christopher Falkus (Ed.), *The Private Lives of the Tudor Monarchs*, Folio Society, London,

1974, p.16]

5   Marie Louise Bruce, *The Making of Henry VIII*, Collins, London, 1977, p.21

6   Ibid., p.72–3

7   Ibid., p.86

8   Thomas Hinde, *Hinde's Courtiers: 900 Years of English Court Life*, Victor Gollancz, London, 1986, p.39

9   Peter Green, *John Skelton*, Longmans Green & Co, 1960, p.12

10 'Holinshed's *Chronicles of England, Scotland and Ireland*, Vol. III, London 1808, p.527

11 Marvin H. Albert, *The Divorce*, George G. Harrap & Co, London, 1966, p.29–30

12 Marie Louise Bruce, *The Making of Henry VIII*, Collins, London, 1977, p.134

13 Ibid., p.140

14 Neville Williams, *The Life and Times of Henry VII*, Book Club Associates, London, 1973, p.194

15 Neville Williams, *Henry VIII and His Court*, Weidenfeld & Nicholson, London, 1971, p.194

16 *The Reign of Henry VII from Contemporary Sources*, Vol. III, University of London Historical Series, Longmans, 1914

17 Christopher Falkus, *The Private Lives of the Tudor Monarchs*, Folio Society, London, 1974, p.19

18 Marie Louise Bruce, *The Making*

of Henry VIII, Collins, London, 1977, p.198

19 Frederick Chamberlain, *The Private Character of Henry the Eighth*, Bodley Head, London, 1932, p.92

20 *The Reign of Henry VII from Contemporary Sources*, Vol. III, University of London Historical Series, Longmans, 1914

21 Marie Louise Bruce, *The Making of Henry VIII*, Collins, London, 1977, p.201–2

22 S. B. Chrimes, *Henry VII*, Eyre Methuen, London, 1972, p.301

23 Marie Louise Bruce, *The Making of Henry VIII*, Collins, London, 1977, p.166–8

24 Marie Louise Bruce, *The Making of Henry VIII*, Collins, London, 1977, p.196

25 Ibid., p.223

Chapter 2

1 *Letters and Papers Foreign and Domestic: Henry VIII*, Vol. I 1509–1513, HMSO, London, 1920, p.54 & 64

2 John Schofield, *The Building of London from the Conquest to the Great Fire*, British Museum, 1984, p.61 & 104

3 Charles Lethbridge Kingsford (Ed.), *A Survey of London by John Stow, 1603*, Clarendon Press, Oxford, 1908, p.236–7

4 Nicholas Harris Nicholas, (Ed.), *Privy Purse Expenses of Elizabeth of York: Wardrobe Accounts of Edward IV*, William Pickering, London, 1830, p.99

5 Neville Williams, *The Life and Times of Henry VII*, Book Club

Associates, London, 1973, p.124

6 Michael K. Jones & Malcolm G. Underwood, *The King's Mother: Lady Margaret Beaufort, Duchess of Richmond and Derby*, CUP, 1992, p.272

7 T. N. Cooper, University of Sheffield, http://www.midlands history.bham.ack.uk/issues/1994/coopertn

8 J. L. Laynesmith, *The Last Medieval Queens: English Queenship 1445–1603*, p.147

9 John Strype, *A Survey of the Cities of London and Westminster*

Chapter 3

1 *Hall's Chronicle: Containing the History of England, etc*, London 1809, p.507

2 J. J. Scarisbrook, *Henry VIII*, Eyre & Spottiswoode, London 1968, p.12

3 J. S. Brewer, *The Reign of Henry VIII: From his Accession to the Death of Wolsey*, Vol. I, John Murray, London, 1884, p.5

4 Barbara J. Harris, *Edward Stafford Third Duke of Buckingham 1478–1521*, Stamford University Press, California, 1986

5 Alison Weir, *Henry VIII: King and Court*, Jonathan Cape, London, 2001, p.28

6 Barbara J. Harris, *Edward Stafford Third Duke of Buckingham 1478–1521*, Stamford University Press, California, 1986

7 *Letters and Papers Foreign and Domestic: Henry VIII*, Vol. I, HMSO, London, 1920, p.474

8   Neville Williams, *Henry VIII and his Court*, Weidenfeld & Nicolson, London, 1971, p.47

9   Holinshed's *Chronicles of England, Scotland and Ireland*, Vol. III, London, 1808, p.558

10 Charles Cruickshank, *Henry VIII and the Invasion of France*, Alan Sutton Publishing Limited, 1994, p.29–30

11 Ibid., p.110

12 Ibid., p.120

13 Ibid.

14 Alan B. Hinds (Ed.), *Calendar of State Papers and Manuscripts Existing in the Archives and Collections of Milan*, Vol. I 1385–1618, HMSO, London, 1912, p.394–403

15 *Letters and Papers Foreign and Domestic: Henry VIII*, Vol. I Pt.II, HMSO, London, 1920, p.3163

16 http://genealogy.euweb.cz//French/neufchtl2

17 *Privy Purse Expenses of Elizabeth of York*, p.23

18 British Museum MSS 7100

19 Neville Williams, *Henry VIII and his Court*, Weidenfeld & Nicolson, London, 1971, p.66

20 Maria Perry, *Sisters to the King*, Andre Deutsch, London, 1998, p.85–6

21 Alison Plowden, *The House of Tudor*, Sutton Publishing, Stroud, 1998, p.71

22 M. le Dr. Hoefer (Ed.), *Nouvelle Biographie Générale*, Vol. IV, Firmin Didot Freres, Paris, 1862, p.810

Chapter 4

1   Alison Plowden, *The House of Tudor*, Sutton Publishing, Stroud, 1998, p.97

2   *Letters and Papers, Foreign and Domestic*, Vol. IV, Introduction – E. Hall, 'Chronicle Containing the History of England', H Ellis (Ed.), 1809

3   P. Mordant, *The History and Antiquities of the County of Essex*, Vol. I, 1763; Vol. II, 1768

4   Patent Rolls, 18 Feb, year 20 Henry VIII

5   *Letters and Papers, Foreign and Domestic*, Vol. IV, Introduction

6   Beverley A. Murphy, *Bastard Prince: Henry VIII's Lost Son*, Sutton Publishing, Stroud, 2001, p.52

7   Letters Patent, 11 August 1525

8   John Gough Nichols, Inventory of the Wardrobe, Plate, etc of Henry Fitzroy, Duke of Richmond & Somerset, *The Camden Miscellany*, Vol. III, Camden Society, 1854, p.xxii–xxvii

9. Ibid.

10 C. R. N. Routh, *Who's Who in Tudor England*, Shepheard-Walwyn, 1964, p.54

11 J. S. Brewer, *The Reign of Henry VIII: From his accession to the Death of Wolsey*, Vol. II, John Murray, London, 1884, p.105

12 John Gough Nichols, Inventory of the Wardrobe, Plate, etc of Henry Fitzroy, Duke of Richmond & Somerset, *The Camden Miscellany*, Vol. III, Camden Society, 1854, p.xci

13 Ibid.

14 Ibid., p.xc

15 Douglas Brooks-Davies (Ed.),

Silver Poets of the Sixteenth Century, Everyman, 1997, p.112

16 John Martin Robinson, *The Dukes of Norfolk: A Quincentennial History*, OUP, 1982

17 *The Chronicles of Calais*, The Camden Society, p.41

18 Holinshed's *Chronicles of England, Scotland and Ireland*, Vol. III, London 1808, p.776

19 John Gough Nichols, Inventory of the Wardrobe, Plate, etc of Henry Fitzroy, Duke of Richmond & Somerset, *The Camden Miscellany*, Vol. III, Camden Society, 1854, p.xcv

20 'Mary Duchess of Richmond', *The Gentleman's Magazine*, May 1845

21 John Gough Nichols, Inventory of the Wardrobe, Plate, etc of Henry Fitzroy, Duke of Richmond & Somerset, *The Camden Miscellany*, Vol. III, Camden Society, 1854, p.xcvii–iii

22 Ibid., p. xvciii

23 Ibid.

24 E. W. Ives, *Anne Boleyn*, Basil Blackwell, 1986, p.409

25 Carolly Erikson, *Bloody Mary: The Life of Mary Tudor*, Robson Books, 1978

26 Heather Hobden, 'Roger Parsons' Lincolnshire World: Elizabeth Blount', http://homepages.enter-prise.net/rogerp/blount

27 Alison Plowden, *The Young Elizabeth*, Sutton Publishing, Stroud, 1999, p.61

28 John Gough Nichols, Inventory of the Wardrobe, Plate, etc of Henry Fitzroy, Duke of

Richmond & Somerset, *The Camden Miscellany*, Vol. III, Camden Society, 1854, p.xcv

29 Neville Williams, *Thomas Howard Fourth Duke of Norfolk*, Barnie & Rockcliff, London, 1964, p.14–6

30 Ibid., p.16

31 Muriel St Clare Byrne, *The Letters of King Henry VIII*, Cassell, London, 1936, p.422

Chapter 5

1 Carolly Erickson, *Bloody Mary: The Life of Mary Tudor*, Robson Books, 1978, p.34

2 E. W. Ives, *Anne Boleyn*, Basil Blackwell, 1986, p.32

3 Ibid., p.34

4 Alison Plowden, *Tudor Women: Queens and Commoners*, Weidenfeld & Nicolson, London, 1979

5 Edward, Lord Herbert of Cherbury, *The Life and Raigne of King Henry the Eighth*, Thomas Whitaker, London, 1649

6 *Letters and Papers Foreign and Domestic*, Vol. III, p.33

7 E. W. Ives, *Anne Boleyn*, Basil Blackwell, 1986, 47

8 J. J. Scarisbrick, *Henry VIII*, Eyre & Spottsiwoode, London, 1968, p.148

9 E. W. Ives, *Anne Boleyn*, Basil Blackwell, 1986, 331

10 *Letters and Papers Foreign and Domestic*, Vol. IV. Introduction

11 Ibid., Introduction

12 Marvin H. Albert, *The Divorce*, George C. Harrap & Co, London 1966, p.92–3

13 J. S. Brewer, *The Reign of Henry*

VIII: From his accession to the Death of Wolsey, Vol. II, John Murray, London, 1884, p.166

14 E. W. Ives, *Anne Boleyn*, Basil Blackwell, 1986, p.334

15 Anne Somerset, *Elizabeth I*, Phoenix, London, 1998, p.463

16 John Guy, *Tudor England*, Oxford University Press, 1988, p.429

17 http://en.wikipedia.org/wiki/ Henry_Carey,_1st_Baron_ Hunsdon

18 http://www.westminster-abbey.org/history-research/ monuments-gravestones

19 Sally Varlow, *Sir Francis Knollys's Latin Dictionary: New evidence for Katherine Carey*, Institute of Historical Research, 2006

Chapter 6

1 *White's Devonshire Directory*, 1850

2 Richard Simpson, *The School of Shakespeare*, Chatto & Windus, London, 1878

3 Birmingham City Council, Leisure and Tourism web page

4 Richard Simpson, *The School of Shakespeare*, Chatto & Windus, London, 1878

5 Ibid.

6 Ibid.

7 Ibid.

8 Patent Roll, Philip & Mary

9 Richard Simpson, *The School of Shakespeare*, Chatto & Windus, London, 1878

10 Ibid.

11 Juan E Tazón, *The Life and Times of Thomas Stukeley c.1525–78*, Ashgate Publishing, Aldershot, 2003, p.52

12 Richard Simpson, *The School of Shakespeare*, Chatto & Windus, London, 1878

13 Ibid.

14 Ibid.

15 Ibid.

16 Ibid.

17 Ibid.

18 Ibid.

19 Hans Claude Hamilton (Ed.), *Calendar of State Papers: Ireland, Henry VIII–Elizabeth I 1509–1573*, HMRO 1860, p.263

20 Richard Simpson, *The School of Shakespeare*, Chatto & Windus, London, 1878

21 Hans Claude Hamilton (Ed.), *Calendar of State Papers: Ireland, Henry VIII– Elizabeth I 1509–1573*, HMRO 1860, p.263

22 Richard Simpson, *The School of Shakespeare*, Chatto & Windus, London, 1878

23 Ibid.

24 Charles Edelman, *The Stukeley Plays*, Manchester University Press, 2005

25 Hans Claude Hamilton (Ed.), *Calendar of State Papers: Ireland, Henry VIII–Elizabeth I 1509–1573*, HMRO 1860, p.292

26 Ibid., p.408

27 Richard Simpson, *The School of Shakespeare*, Chatto & Windus, London, 1878

28 Ibid.

29 Ibid.

30 *Calendar of State Papers: Ireland, 1509–73*, p.446

31 Richard Simpson, *The School of Shakespeare*, Chatto & Windus, London, 1878

32 Ibid.

33　Hans Claude Hamilton (Ed.),
　　Calendar of State Papers: Ireland,
　　Elizabeth I 1574–85, HMRO,
　　1974, p.20

34　Richard Simpson, *The School of*
　　Shakespeare, Chatto & Windus,
　　London, 1878

35　Ibid.

36　Ibid.

37　http://en.wikipedia.org/The_
　　Battle_of_Alcazar

38　George Peele, *The Battle of*
　　Alcazar, fought in Barbarie,
　　between Sebastian King of
　　Portugal, Abdelmelec King of
　　Marocco, with the death of Captain
　　Stukeley

Chapter 7

1　J. C. Smith & E. de Selincourt,
　　The Poetical Works of Edmund
　　Spenser, OUP, 1912, p.lii

2　*Dictionary of Welsh Biography,*
　　Hon. Soc. of Cymrodorion, 1959

3　Hester Chapman, *The Last Tudor*
　　King: A Study of Edward VI,
　　Jonathan Cape, London, 1958,
　　p.179–80

4　Ibid., p.178–9

5　*Calendar of State Papers: Ireland,*
　　1509–1573, p.500

6　Ibid., p.501

7　W. L. Richards, 'Great Men of
　　Pembroke (4)', *West Wales*
　　Guardian, 22 April 1983

8　Hans Claude Hamilton (Ed.),
　　Calendar of State Papers: Ireland,
　　Elizabeth I 1574–85, PRO,
　　London 1974, p.3

9　*Dictionary of Welsh Biography to*
　　1940, Hon. Soc. of
　　Cymrodorion, 1959

10　Hans Claude Hamilton (Ed.),

　　Calendar of State Papers: Ireland,
　　Elizabeth I 1574–85, PRO,
　　London 1974, p.516

11　Ibid., p.516

12　Ibid., p.524

13　Ibid.

14　Ibid.

15　Ibid.

16　Ibid.

17　Hans Claude Hamilton (Ed.),
　　Calendar of State Papers: Ireland,
　　Elizabeth I 1586–88, PRO,
　　London 1974, p.20

18　Ibid., p.30

19　Ibid., p.44

20　Ibid., p.138

21　Ibid., p.210–3

22　Ibid., p.227

23　Ibid., p.255

24　Ibid.

25　Ibid.

26　Ibid.

27　Ibid.

28　Hans Claude Hamilton (Ed.),
　　Calendar of State Papers: Ireland,
　　Elizabeth 1588–92, HMRO
　　1974, p.12–3

29　Ibid., p.78

30　Ibid., p.116

31　Ibid., p.227–8

32　Ibid., p.330

33　Ibid., p.298

34　Ibid., p.305

35　Ibid., p.336

36　Ibid., p.350–4

37　Ibid., p.355

38　Ibid., p.383

39　Ibid., p.384

40　Ibid., p.451

41　Ibid., p.439

42　http://members.ozemail.com.
　　au/~tPerrot/sirjohn

43　Hans Claude Hamilton (Ed.),

Calendar of State Papers: Ireland,
Elizabeth 1588–92, HMRO
1974, p.446

Chapter 8

1 Alison Plowden, *The Young*
   Elizabeth, Sutton Publishing,
   Stroud, 1999, p.23–4
2 E .W. Ives, *Anne Boleyn,* Basil
   Blackwell, 1986
3 Ibid.
4 Ibid.
5 Herbert Beerbohm-Tree, *Henry*
   VIII and his Court, Cassell & Co,
   London, 1910
6 E. W. Ives, *Anne Boleyn,* Basil
   Blackwell, 1986
7 *Letters and Papers, Foreign and*
   Domestic, Henry VIII, Vol. III,
   Pt.I, 1519–21
8 E. W. Ives, *Anne Boleyn,* Basil
   Blackwell, 1986
9 Ibid.
10 Emrys Jones (Ed.), *The New*
   Oxford Book of Sixteenth Century
   Verse, OUP, 1992, p.76
11 Robert Lacey, *The Life and Times*
   of Henry VIII, Book Club
   Associates, London, 1972
12 E. W. Ives, *Anne Boleyn,* Basil
   Blackwell, 1986
13 Ibid.
14 Alison Plowden, *Tudor Women:*
   Queens and Commoners,
   Weidenfeld & Nicolson,
   London, 1979
15 Ibid.
16 Anne Crawford (Ed.), *Letters of*
   the Queens of England
   1100–1547, Alan Sutton, Stroud,
   1994, p.190
17 Christopher Falkus, *The Private*
   Lives of the Tudor Monarchs, Folio

Society, London, 1974, p.24–5
18 E. W. Ives, *Anne Boleyn,* Basil
   Blackwell, 1986
19 Ibid., p.153
20 Anne Crawford (Ed.), *Letters of*
   the Queens of England
   1100–1547, Alan Sutton, Stroud,
   1994, p.188
21 E. W. Ives, *Anne Boleyn,* Basil
   Blackwell, 1986, p.161–3
22 Garrett Mattingly, *Catherine of*
   Aragon, Quality Paperback
   Books, USA, 1941
23 Ibid., p.280
24 Ibid., p.283
25 Ibid., p.312
26 Ibid.
27 Ibid., p.334
28 E. W. Ives, *Anne Boleyn,* Basil
   Blackwell, 1986, p.184
29 Alison Plowden, *Tudor Women:*
   Queens and Commoners,
   Weidenfeld & Nicolson,
   London, 1979
30 E. W. Ives, *Anne Boleyn,* Basil
   Blackwell, 1986, p.197–9
31 Garrett Mattingly, *Catherine of*
   Aragon, Quality Paperback
   Books, USA, 1941
32 E. W. Ives, *Anne Boleyn,* Basil
   Blackwell, 1986, p.219–21
33 Mattingly, Garrett, *Catherine of*
   Aragon, Quality Paperback
   Books, USA, 1941
34 Ibid.
35 Ibid., p.425

Chapter 9

1 Ian Grimble, *The Harrington*
   Family, Jonathan Cape, London,
   1957, p.13
2 *Letters and Papers, Foreign and*
   Domestic, Henry VIII, Vol. IV, Pt.

II, 1526–8, p.1570

3 *Letters and Papers, Foreign and Domestic, Henry VIII*, Vol. I, Pt.II

4 *Letters and Papers, Foreign and Domestic, Henry VIII*, Vol. V, 1531–2, p.713

5 *Letters and Papers, Foreign and Domestic, Henry VIII 1545*, Vol. XX, Pt.II

6 *Letters and Papers, Foreign and Domestic, Henry VIII 1546–7*, Vol. XXI, Pt.II

7 John Timbs, *Curiosities of London*, 1855

8 Bentley, James, *A Calendar of Saints*, Orbis, London, 1986

9 Ruth Hughey, *John Harrington: Tudor Gentleman*, Ohio State University Press, 1971, p.17

10 Rev. John Collinson, *The History and Antiquities of the County of Somerset*, 1791

11 *Letters and Papers, Foreign and Domestic, Henry VIII*, Vol.X, 1536, p.383

12 *Calendar of State Papers – Domestic, Edward VI, 1547–1580*, PRO, London, 1856, p.212

13 *Letters and Papers, Foreign and Domestic, Henry VIII 1546–7*, Vol.XXI, Pt.II

14 *Letters and Papers, Foreign and Domestic, Henry VIII*, various

15 *Letters and Papers, Foreign and Domestic, Henry VIII 1546–7*, Vol.XXI, Pt.II

16 pers. comm. Mr W. C. Fallows

17 Ida M. Roper FLS, *The Monumental Effigies of Gloucestershire and Bristol*, Henry Osborne, Gloucester, 1931, p.254–7

18 *Letters and Papers, Foreign and Domestic, Henry VIII*, Vol. VII, 1534, p.xxxii

19 Ibid., p.462

20 Ibid., p.484–5

21 Ibid., p.491

22 Ibid., p.1534

23 Geoffrey Strutt, *A Short History of St Catherine's Court*

24 *Letters and Papers, Foreign and Domestic, Henry VIII*, Vol.XIII, ii, p.283

25 Ian Grimble, *The Harrington Family*, Jonathan Cape, London, 1957, p.87

26 Rev. Henry Harrington (Ed.), *Sir John Harrington, Nugae Antiquae*, J Dodsley, London, 1779, p.83

27 Margaret Irwin, *Elizabeth, Captive Princess*, Reprint Society, London, 1948

28 Ian Grimble, *The Harrington Family*, Jonathan Cape, London, 1957, p.90

29 Ruth Hughey, *John Harrington: Tudor Gentleman*, Ohio State University Press, 1971, p.19

30 Hester Chapman, *Lady Jane Grey*, Pan, London, 1962

31 Hester Chapman, *Lady Jane Grey*, Pan, 1962

32 Ruth Hughey, *John Harrington: Tudor Gentleman*, Ohio State University Press, 1971, p.19

33 Letter, J.B.N., *The Gentleman's Magazine*, January 1824, p.40

34 Ruth Hughey, *John Harrington: Tudor Gentleman*, Ohio State University Press, 1971, p.35

35 J A Muller, *The Letters of Stephen Gardiner*

36 Rev. Henry Harrington (Ed.), *Sir John Harrington, Nugae Antiquae*, J Dodsley, London, 1779, p.73

37 Ibid., p.52

38 Ibid., p.52–3

39 *Calendar of the Patent Rolls, Philip and Mary*, Vol. III, 1555–7, HMSO, 1938, p.95–6

40 Ibid., p.93

41 *Calendar of Patent Rolls, Elizabeth I*, Vol. I, 1558–60. HMSO, 1938, p.90

42 Ruth Hughey, *John Harrington: Tudor Gentleman*, Ohio State University Press, 1971, p.37

43 B. Jupp & R. Hovenden (Eds.), 'Registers of Christenings, etc of the Parish of Allhallows, London Wall'

44 *Calendar of Patent Rolls, Elizabeth I*, Vol. II, 1560–3, HMSO, 1938, p.510

45 C. Falkus, *The Private Lives of the Tudor Monarchs*, Folio Society, London, 1974

46 William Page & P. H. Ditchfield (Eds.), *A History of the County of Berkshire*, Vol. IV, 1924, p.536

47 *Patent Rolls, Elizabeth I*, Vol. IV, p.350

48 Ibid., p.119 & 140

49 R. B. Pugh (Ed), *A History of Wiltshire*, Vol. VII, The Victoria History of the Counties of England, OUP, 1953, p.82–6

50 B Jupp & R. Hovenden (Eds.), 'Registers of Christenings, etc of the Parish of Allhallows, London Wall'

51 Christopher Falkus, *The Private Lives of the Tudor Monarchs*, Folio Society, London, 1974, p.123

Chapter 10

1 E. W. Ives, *Anne Boleyn*, Basil Blackwell, 1986, p.245

2 Alison Plowden, *The Young Elizabeth*, Sutton Publishing, Stroud, 1999, p.38

3 Alison Plowden, *Tudor Women: Queens and Commoners*, Weidenfeld & Nicolson, London, 1979

4 Alison Plowden, *The Young Elizabeth*, Sutton Publishing, Stroud, 1999, p.23–4

5 E. W. Ives, *Anne Boleyn*, Basil Blackwell, 1986, p.250

6 Alison Plowden, *The Young Elizabeth*, Sutton Publishing, Stroud, 1999, p.49

7 E. W. Ives, *Anne Boleyn*, Basil Blackwell, 1986, p.321

8 Ibid., p.366

9 Paul G. Remley, 'Mary Shelton', in Peter C. Herman (Ed.), *Rethinking the Henrician Era*, University of Illinois Press, 1994

10 Anthony Martinssen, *Queen Katherine Parr*, Secker & Warburg, London, 1973, p.69–70

11 Frederick Chamberlin, *The Private Character of Henry the Eighth*, Bodley Head, London, 1932, p.166

12 Alison Plowden, *The Young Elizabeth*, Sutton Publishing, Stroud, 1999, p.49

13 Christopher Hibbert, 'Tower of London', Reader's Digest Association Limited, London & Newsweek, New York, 1971, p.55

14 E. W. Ives, *Anne Boleyn*, Basil Blackwell, 1986, p.338

15 *Letters and Papers Foreign and Domestic*

16 E. W. Ives, *Anne Boleyn*, Basil Blackwell, 1986, p.343

17 Christopher Hibbert, 'Tower of

London', Reader's Digest
Association Limited, London &
Newsweek, New York, 1971,
p.54–5

18 Ibid., p.57

19 Muriel St Clare Byrne, *The Lisle
Letters*, University of Chicago
Press, 1983, p.160

20 Christopher Hibbert, 'Tower of
London', Reader's Digest
Association Limited, London &
Newsweek, New York, 1971, p.58

21 Hester Chapman, *The Last Tudor
King: A Study of Edward VI*,
Jonathan Cape, London, 1958,
p.20

22 E. W. Ives, *Anne Boleyn*, Basil
Blackwell, 1986, p.410

23 Alison Plowden, *The Young
Elizabeth*, Sutton Publishing,
Stroud, 1999, p.56

24 Douglas Greenwood, *Who's
Buried Where in England*,
Constable, London, 1982, p.65

Chapter 11

1 Derek Wilson, *Hans Holbein:
Portrait of an Unknown Man*,
Weidenfeld & Nicolson,
London, 1996, p.253

2 Alison Plowden, *The Young
Elizabeth*, Sutton Publishing,
Stroud, 1999, p.71

3 Neville Williams, *Henry VIII and
his Court*, Book Club Associates,
London, 1971

4 Hester W Chapman, *The Last
Tudor King*, Jonathan Cape, 1961

5 Elsie Thornton-Cook, *Her
Majesty: The Romance of the
Queens of England 1066–1910*,
Ayer Publishing, 1970, p.170

6 Alison Plowden, *Tudor Women:*

Queens and Commoners,
Weidenfeld & Nicolson,
London, 1979, p.88

7 Anne Crawford, *Letters of the
Queens of England 1100–1547*,
Alan Sutton, Stroud, 1994, p.203

8 *Letters and Papers, Foreign and
Domestic, Henry VIII*, Vol. XVI,
1540–1

9 Ibid.,

10 Anthony Martinssen, *Queen
Katherine Parr*, Secker &
Warburg, London, 1973, p.207

11 Muriel St Clare Byrne (Ed.), *The
Lisle Letters*, University of
Chicago, 1983

12 Ibid.

13 Ibid.

14 Ibid.

15 Ibid.

16 Ibid.

17 Ibid.

18 Ibid., p.304

19 Neville Williams, *Henry VIII and
his Court*, Book Club Associates,
London, 1971

20 William John Hardy, 'Sir Walter
Hungerford of Farley', *The
Antiquary*, p.238–43

21 Ibid., p.242–3

Chapter 12

1 Muriel St Clare Byrne (Ed.), *The
Lisle Letters*, Penguin/ University
of Chicago, 1983, p.68–9

2 Alison Plowden, *Tudor Women:
Queens and Commoners*,
Weidenfeld & Nicholson,
London, 1979, p.96

3 Neville Williams, *Henry VIII and
his Court*, Book Club Associates,
London, 1971

4 Anne Crawford (Ed.), *Letters of*

the Queens of England
1100–1547, Alan Sutton, Stroud,
1994, p.210

5   Alison Plowden, *Tudor Women:
Queens and Commoners*,
Weidenfeld & Nicolson,
London, 1979

6   Lacey Baldwin Smith, *A Tudor
Tragedy: The Life and Times of
Catherine Howard*, Jonathan
Cape, London, 1961, p.168

7   Neville Williams, *Henry VIII and
his Court*, Book Club Associates,
London, 1971

8   Anthony Martinssen, *Queen
Katherine Parr*, Secker &
Warburg, London, 1973, p.207

9   Alison Plowden, *Tudor Women:
Queens and Commoners*,
Weidenfeld & Nicolson,
London, 1979

10 *Calendar of State Papers –
Domestic: Edward VI 1547–1580*,
PRO, London, 1856, p.11

11 Ibid., p.21

12 Ibid., p.37–9

13 *Calendar of State Papers –
Domestic: 1547–1580*, PRO,
London, 1856, p.677

Chapter 13

1   Jonathan S Gibson, 'Sir Thomas
Wyatt', in *The Literary
Encyclopedia*, 2007, http://www.
litencyc.com/php/speople

2   Richard Barber (Ed.), *Brief Lives
by John Aubrey*, The Folio Society,
1975, p.193–4

3   'Magna Britannia', 1806,
http://met.open.ac.uk/GENU-
KI/big/eng/BKM/Quarrendon

4   Gwynneth Bowen, 'Sir Edward
Vere and His Mother, Anne

Vavasour', in *Shakespearean
Authorship Review*, 1966

5   Further information on Richard
Edwardes may be found in: *Bruce
Montgomery Edwards, The
Edwards Family of Northampton*

6   Tudorhistory.org Questions and
Answers Blog, and
uk.answers.yahoo.com

7   Beverley A. Murphy, *Bastard
Prince: Henry VIII's Lost Son*,
Sutton Publishing Ltd, Stroud,
2001, p.31

8   http://en.wikipedia.org/wiki
/Elizabeth_Amadas

9   http://www.mebib.com/Robert
_Amadas

Acknowledgements

———⟨ᴥ⟩———

The production of this book has been a labour of love and would never have seen the light of day if it hadn't been for a legion of family and friends who offered their support when I needed it. It would require a small book in itself to thank all the staff at the museums, art galleries, collections and libraries who responded with such invaluable assistance and unfailing good humour to the barrage of requests for information and clarification over the last few years, but sincere thanks to you all. I am also very pleased to acknowledge the unwavering encouragement and astonishing expertise of the editors of New Holland, particularly Julia Shone and Aruna Vasudevan.

318

List of Illustrations

Plate 1:
Henry VIII (1491–1547) by Joos van Cleve (c.1485–1541). *Burghley House Collection, Lincolnshire, UK/ The Bridgeman Art Library.*

Plate 2:
Elizabeth of York (1465–1503), c.1502 by British School. Possibly first recorded in the Royal Collection during the reign of Henry VIII. *The Royal Collection © 2009, Her Majesty Queen Elizabeth II.*

Plate 3:
Henry VII (1457–1509), (oil on panel) by English School, (16th century). *Society of Antiquaries of London, UK/ The Bridgeman Art Library.*

Plate 4:
Portrait of a woman, possibly Catherine of Aragon (1485–1536), c.1503/4 (oil on panel) by Michiel Sittow (1469–1525). *Kunsthistorisches Museum, Vienna, Austria/ The Bridgeman Art Library.*

Plate 5:
Portrait of Mary Bullen (Mary Boleyn, 1499–1543), by Hans Holbein the Younger (1497/8–1543), (attr. to). *Hever Castle Ltd, Kent, UK/ The Bridgeman Art Library.*

Plate 6:
Anne Boleyn (1501–36), 1534 (oil on panel) by English School, (16th century). *Hever Castle, Kent, UK/ The Bridgeman Art Library.*

Plate 7:
Jane Seymour (1509–37) Queen Consort of England; third wife
of Henry VIII (1491–1547), 1536 (oil on panel); by Hans
Holbein the Younger (1497/8–1543). *Kunsthistorisches Museum,
Vienna, Austria/ The Bridgeman Art Library.*

Plate 8:
Portrait of a Lady, thought to be Catherine Howard (1522–42),
(oil on panel) by Hans Holbein the Younger (1497/8–1543),
(follower of). *Private Collection/ © Philip Mould Ltd, London/ The
Bridgeman Art Library.*

Plate 9:
Katherine d'Eresby, Duchess of Suffolk (1520–80), c.1534–36 by
Hans Holbein the Younger (1497/8–1543). *The Royal Collection
© 2009, Her Majesty Queen Elizabeth II.*

Plate 10:
Henry Fitzroy, Duke of Richmond and Somerset (1519–36),
c.1534 by Lucas Horenbout (1490/95–1544). *The Royal Collection
© 2009, Her Majesty Queen Elizabeth II.*

Plate 11:
Thomas Stukeley (c.1530–78), drawing of the Battle of the Three
Kings, by Miguel Leitão de Andrada (1553–1630).

Plate 12:
John Perrot (1527–92). *By courtesy of the Haverfordwest Town
Museum.*

Plate 13:
Henry Carey (c.1524–96) stipple engraving by R. Cooper,
probably early 19th century. *National Portrait Gallery, London.*

Index

321
◎

325